Overcoming the Educational Resource Equity Gap

Overcoming the Educational Resource Equity Gap

A Close Look at Distributing a School's Financial and Human Resources

Edited by

Stephen V. Coffin

ROWMAN & LITTLEFIELD
Lanham • Boulder • New York • London

Published by Rowman & Littlefield
An imprint of The Rowman & Littlefield Publishing Group, Inc.
4501 Forbes Boulevard, Suite 200, Lanham, Maryland 20706
www.rowman.com

86-90 Paul Street, London EC2A 4NE, United Kingdom

Copyright © 2023 by Stephen V. Coffin

All rights reserved. No part of this book may be reproduced in any form or by any electronic or mechanical means, including information storage and retrieval systems, without written permission from the publisher, except by a reviewer who may quote passages in a review.

British Library Cataloguing in Publication Information Available

Library of Congress Cataloging-in-Publication Data

Names: Coffin, Stephen, 1954- editor.
Title: Overcoming the educational resource equity gap : a close look at distributing a school's financial and human resources / edited by Stephen V. Coffin.
Description: Lanham, Maryland : Rowman & Littlefield, 2023. | Includes bibliographical references. | Summary: "Our nation's K-12 traditional public schools (TPSs) and districts (TPSDs) must develop new business, operating, and educational models to survive, to provide universal quality education, and to achieve resource equity as well as equal educational opportunity"— Provided by publisher.
Identifiers: LCCN 2022040191 (print) | LCCN 2022040192 (ebook) | ISBN 9781475862454 (cloth) | ISBN 9781475862461 (paperback) | ISBN 9781475862478 (epub)
Subjects: LCSH: School-based management—United States. | School budgets—United States. | School personnel management—United States. Classification: LCC LB2806.35 .O84 2023 (print) | LCC LB2806.35 (ebook) | DDC 371.200973—dc23/eng/20221005
LC record available at https://lccn.loc.gov/2022040191
LC ebook record available at https://lccn.loc.gov/2022040192

Contents

Foreword — vii
   Charles J. Russo

PART I: OVERVIEW — 1

Chapter 1: Mission — 3
   Stephen V. Coffin

Chapter 2: Value Proposition — 7
   Stephen V. Coffin

PART II: CONSTITUTIONAL REQUIREMENTS — 11

2Chapter 3: Lest There Be Any Doubt: Constitutional Sovereignty as the Basis for Education Reform in Kentucky — 13
   William E. Thro

Chapter 4: State School Funding Formula-based Inequities — 27
   Stephen V. Coffin

PART III: INEQUITIES IN HUMAN RESOURCES — 53

Chapter 5: Teachers: Adopting a Culturally Grounded Asset-Based Mindset — 55
   Corinne Brion

Chapter 6: Culturally Proficient Professional Development — 65
   Corinne Brion

Chapter 7: Special Education — 79
   Keith Dewey and Stephen V. Coffin

Chapter 8: Resource Inequities among Deaf and Hard-of-Hearing
Students   89
Thomas Barger

PART IV: INEQUITIES IN CRUCIAL SERVICES   109

Chapter 9: State Preschool Education   111
Karin A. Garver

Chapter 10: School-based Healthcare Services   129
Camille A. Clare and Tanya O. Rogo

Chapter 11: Consumer Education for Attaining Life Goals   157
Luke Greeley

PART V: INNOVATION   173

Chapter 12: Combatting Diseconomies of Scale   175
Stephen V. Coffin

Chapter 13: Gaining Public Support for Public Funding of Public
Education   181
Stephen V. Coffin

Chapter 14: Achieving Economies of Scale and Building Fiscal
Capacity in Large School Districts   203
Stephen V. Coffin

Chapter 15: K-12 N.A.P.R. Holistic Budgeting Model   219
Stephen V. Coffin

PART VI: CONCLUSION   223

Chapter 16: Rescue Plan   225
Stephen V. Coffin

Chapter 17: Redlining Education   235
Stephen V. Coffin

Chapter 18: Achieving Educational Resource Equity   243
Stephen V. Coffin

Index   251

About the Editor and Contributors   251

Foreword

Charles J. Russo

According to an ancient maxim from the Book of Ecclesiastes in the Hebrew Scriptures, Chapter 9, verse 1, "there is nothing new under the sun." Put another way, regardless of the field of human endeavor, it seems the more things change, the more they stay the same. Turning specifically to the world of education, it is unfortunately true that despite more than five decades of litigation aimed at ensuring equitable funding in K-12 schools and for their students, courts and the legislatures have made little, if any, progress in this important arena.

In order to understand, and appreciate, the importance of school finance, it is helpful to engage in a brief review of its judicial evolution. The field now known as school finance burst into prominence nationally in 1971 as the Supreme Court of California's opinion in *Serrano v. Priest*[1] (*Serrano I*) generated more reaction than any other state court case, then or since, on this contentious topic. *Serrano I* invalidated California's funding scheme, which rendered the quality, or in terms of this volume, the value of the education students received, because it depended largely on the property wealth of the local school districts within which they and their families live rather than the needs of children.

Focusing on the inadequate levels of educational programming for children living in poor districts, *Serrano I* created a firestorm of controversy in rejecting California's system of school finance as invidiously discriminating against them in violation of the Equal Protection Clause of the Fourteenth Amendment of the United States Constitution and perhaps the state constitution. According to the Fourteenth Amendment, "[n]o State shall make or deny to any person within its jurisdiction the equal protection of the laws." In other words, although individuals or groups who "are similarly situated should be treated alike,"[2] the Supreme Court California decided that the state's funding system failed to do so, at least in terms of funding for public schools. In *Serano I* the court concluded that because the wealth of school districts was the basis for substantially different per-pupil expenditures, as reflected by how much more boards of education with high property values but lower tax rates, spent per child than others with high tax rates and lower property valuation, this unacceptable arrangement had to be reformed.

Four years later, in *San Antonio Independent School District v. Rodriguez* (*San Antonio*), its only judgment on the merits of school finance, the Supreme Court essentially repudiated *Serrano I*. In often-quoted language, the High Court observed that "[e]ducation, of course, is not among the rights afforded explicit protection under our Federal Constitution. Nor do we find any basis for saying it is implicitly so protected."[3] The Supreme Court's refusal to apply the Federal Constitution to disputes over school finance means that in the years since *San Antonio*, litigation on this far-reaching topic is all but virtually the exclusive concern of state, rather than federal, courts.

Two years later, in the first of a seeming avalanche of state school finance cases, the Supreme Court of California distinguished the controversy from *San Antonio* by relying on language in its state constitution. More specifically, in *Serrano v. Priest II*[4] (*Serrano II*), acknowledging education as a fundamental right under the equal protection clause of the state, rather than Federal, constitution, the court essentially reaffirmed its initial judgment invalidating California's system of school finance. The court explained that insofar as California's property tax-based system of finance discriminated against students in poor school districts, the state legislature had to develop a more equitable system of funding public education, one not based simply on local property wealth.

In the years since *Serrano II* cases, challenges to the equity of school funding systems have occurred in a majority of states with controversies taking on lives of their own as they proceed through multiple rounds of litigation, often with no clear resolution. This torrent of litigation is almost evenly split as plaintiffs have succeeded in about half of the states where they challenged systems of school funding. In light of this steady stream of litigation seeking equity in school funding, *Overcoming the Educational Resource Equity Gap* should serve as indispensable reading for all interested in remedying inequities in funding.

The need for educational equity in funding is particularly important at present in light of the current weakened condition of the United States economy, which has made fewer resources available for education. Yet, school officials need greater financial resources as they work with increasingly diversified student bodies and seek to meet the needs of children with disabilities, who often require specialized programming because providing for their unique needs can be very costly. At the same time, the pursuit of providing equitable funding has been all the more complicated due to, and greatly exacerbated by, the impact of the COVID-19 pandemic on the economy, schools, families, and just about every aspect of American life.

It is important, then, for educational leaders and parents to understand the divergent sources from which school revenues are derived, how school officials manage and account for these monies, and how dollars are spent to what end or outcome if they are to develop ground-breaking ways to provide full, equitable funding for all schools. Whether in traditional school settings or in districts moving to site-based management or other emerging new forms of public education such as charter schools and online academies, particularly in the wake of COVID-19, the focus in this useful book is on implementing the editor's ground-breaking solution designed to provide full and equitable school funding while cutting the Gordian knot that has prevented this from happening for decades.

A topic which can easily devolve into impenetrable jargon to all but specialists in school finance, *Overcoming the Educational Resource Equity Gap* is a welcomed addition because it is written in easy-to-read, non-technical language, accessible to all. Well aware of the history and development of the field of school finance, the well-researched and written chapters offer hands-on analysis on the key topics in today's world of school finance.

Aware of the need for educators and parents to understand the basics of school finance, *Overcoming the Educational Resource Equity Gap*, is divided into six sections. Following an Overview, the sections address Constitutional Requirements (for school funding), Inequities in Human Resources, Inequities in Crucial Services, Innovation, and a Conclusion. This useful volume provides school leaders and parents with worthwhile food for thought. Editor Stephen V. Coffin, Ph.D., Adjunct Professor of Finance at the University of Dayton, Ohio, and Adjunct Professor of School Finance and Higher Education Economics and Finance at Montclair State University, New Jersey, brings a unique blend of academic and real-world experience to the proverbial table, offering a breath of fresh air for readers as he and the authors demystify the complex interrelated topics of school finance and budgeting.

The book's six sections are further divided into eighteen far-ranging chapters covering such important and timely topics as constitutional foundations for school funding; formula-based inequities; funding issues associated with meeting the needs of students with disabilities; early childhood education; the impact of COVID-19 on schools; the need to provide school-based health care; and devising ways to redress failures in funding in order to provide equitable educational programming for all children. The editor and authors hope that their efforts can help educational leaders and parents to strive to provide equitable funding to enhance excellence in their schools as they improve learning outcomes for all students regardless of where they live or the socioeconomic status of their families.

In sum, *Overcoming the Educational Resource Equity Gap* is a most welcomed addition to the literature on school finance because it provides thought-provoking suggestions, along with hands-on information, for improving the way money gets to, and is spent, in schools, designed to provide excellence in education for all children. One can hope that readers will take to heart the lessons contained in this timely volume by working to ensure high quality and value in schooling for all of their own, and all of the nation's, children.

NOTES

1. 487 P.2d 1241 (Cal. 1971).
2. *Cleburne v. Cleburne Living Ctr.*, 473 U.S. 432, 439 (1985).
3. 411 U.S. 1, 35 (1973).
4. 557 P.2d 929 (Cal. 1976), *cert. denied sub nom. Clowes v. Serrano*, 432 U.S. 907 (1977), opinion supplemented by 569 P.2d 1303 (Cal. 1977).

PART I

Overview

Chapter 1

Mission

Stephen V. Coffin

Our nation's K-12 traditional public schools (TPSs) and districts (TPSDs) must develop new business, operating, and educational models to survive, to provide universal quality education, and to achieve resource equity as well as equal educational opportunity. In addition, public education must adapt amid the major crises that grip our nation including:

- An epic pandemic
- Extremism
- Polarization
- Political gridlock
- Deep social divisions exacerbated by an increasing tendency to live within a "bubble"
- Misinformation and disinformation
- Lack of social justice
- Racism
- Economic inequities
- Redlining's legacy
- Growing distrust of public and private sector institutions as well as leaders

The cumulative adverse impact of these crises erodes our democracy, quality of life, and ability for all Americans to achieve the American Dream as well as portend a possible point of no return from civil war.

This is a clarion call for K-12 as well as K-16 public education to adopt new ways of doing the business of public education as well as to employ a universal resource equity and equal opportunity paradigm to educate, enlighten, and inform our nation so that we can unite, transcend our differences, forge consensus, and avert civil war. The solution for K-12 as well as K-16 public education is to use this book's new ways of doing business and achieving universal resource equity and equal opportunity before our nation passes the point of no return.

Public Education's Historical Context

The United States Constitution grants the states rather than the federal government the authority to govern education. Municipal and county governments as well as school districts are creatures of state because they owe their existence and derive their power from the state government. Therefore, states can increase, decrease, or abolish school districts' powers at any time.

The tradition of local control is not only a time-honored governance system but also rooted in our democratic principles. Local control enables public schools to be held accountable by its stakeholders rather than being controlled remotely by a state or county governmental entity that imposes an agenda that is incongruent with local priorities and needs. Typically, remote governing bodies, such as county or state governments, view local TPSDs through a lens that imposes county or state priorities rather than local requirements.

However, the locus of school district control has shifted gradually from a tradition of home rule or local control to state and county control during the past 50 years (Coffin 2020; 2021). Decision making and control over funding, budgeting, human resources, standards, capital projects, operations, curricula, and assessment that were once the sole province of local boards of education has been superseded increasingly by state and county governments. Increased state and county control reduces public support for the proper funding of public education because it prevents *Homevoters* from being true stakeholders and benefitting from the capitalization of quality local public education in their property values, especially their homes, and communities (Fischel, 1998; 2001).

Centralizing control over a TPSD's financial, material, and human resources at the state or county level causes many unintended consequences. Chief among them is the contradictory challenge of trying to hold local school districts accountable to standards, which are made remotely at the state level, that conflict with local educational requirements, needs, and priorities. Typically, when states impose a one-size-fits-all approach to local school district resource allocation, state as well as county funds are used inefficiently and inequitably (Fischel, 1998; 2001). School systems are more accountable if decision making over financial, material, and human resources is made at the local level.

A school district can improve student and school performance best when the district is empowered to allocate its resources according to its educational plan rather than having to follow one-size-fits-all state or county directives. The local school district would have all the tools it would need to hold schools and students accountable because it could make real time decisions based on specific measurable performance goals for each school and student.

The school district is the most qualified to continually calibrate local performance goals because only the local school district can combine a keen understanding of local educational necessities with the timely and specific assessment of individual school and student achievement. State or county control is too remote, which causes not only inappropriate delays but also decisions that are inconsistent with the district's educational plan (Coffin & Cooper, 2017; 2018).

State or county control over a district's financial, material, and human resources creates barriers for achieving accountability. When a local school district is limited by the state's or county's one-size-fits-all approach, the TPSD is prevented from developing more innovative approaches to accountability. For local school districts to innovate, they must be empowered to use more effective approaches for increasing accountability that are best suited to local needs. Improving accountability, therefore, requires the adaptation of new models for the control structure of local public schools that are free of state and county domination.

In response to state or county dominated local school systems, communities need greater control over their schools so that they can benefit from increased accountability. A school district's control structure affects how all the school system's stakeholders combine to produce a quality, equitable, and equal educational opportunity.

School districts nationwide are searching for the most appropriate control structure that will maximize accountability. As a result, school districts are increasingly adapting local control because it provides the maximum accountability possible according to the schools' unique characteristics, needs, priorities, and preferences. What matters most is that municipalities employ the control structure that fosters the greatest public support for the maximum public funding of their public schools.

REFERENCES

Coffin, S. V. (2020). *State policy determinants of charter school market share* (Doctoral dissertation). Rutgers University, Graduate School of Education, New Brunswick, New Jersey.

Coffin, S. V. (Ed.) (2021). *Higher education's looming collapse: Using new ways of doing business and social justice to avoid bankruptcy.* Rowman & Littlefield.

Coffin, S. V., & Cooper, B. S. (Eds.) (2017). *Sound school finance for educational excellence.* Rowman & Littlefield.

Coffin, S. V., & Cooper, B. S. (Eds.) (2018). *District financial leadership today: Educational excellence tomorrow.* Rowman & Littlefield.

Fischel, W. A. (1998). *School finance litigation and property tax revolts: How undermining local control turns voters away from public education.* Lincoln Institute of Land Policy Working Paper.

Fischel, W. A. (2001). *The homevoter hypothesis: How home values influence local government taxation, school finance, and land-use policies.* Harvard University Press.

Chapter 2

Value Proposition

Stephen V. Coffin

As a graduate student at the Maxwell School of Citizenship and Public Affairs, Syracuse University, the author co-authored a United Nations report: *A Study of the American Educational System*. The report, which was funded by the United Nations, evaluated the American system of K to 12 and higher education. However, despite decades of reform little has changed since that report because a politically polarized Gordian knot prevents universal quality education, equal educational opportunity, and resource equity.

The epic COVID pandemic worsened state school finance formula-based inequities. State school finance formula shortcomings caused funding inadequacy and educational resource allocative inefficiency. These inequities and inefficiencies exacerbated disparities in the provision of quality education among school districts and lessened equal educational opportunities. As a result, school districts face major unbudgeted expenditures to cope with the pandemic amid state aid reductions that drive budgetary exigency. Policymakers, practitioners, and educational leaders can implement the recommendations provided herein to close the educational resource equity gap among schools and districts.

The educational resource equity gap stems from the unequal distribution of financial, material, and human resources among schools that affects schools and districts differently. However, the educational resources equity gap disproportionately affects low-income urban districts especially those with high concentrations of free-and-reduced-price-lunch (FRPL), special needs, and high-per-pupil-cost-to-educate students.

Public education supporters have tried to remedy the disparities among districts by lobbying state governments to provide incremental funds, regulation, and legal challenges to the states' school funding formulae as well as state constitutional protections. Although well-intended, these efforts have failed to solve the problem.

The education industry must shift its K to 12 public education finance model to solve the problem. A politically polarized Gordian knot causes allocative inefficiency that prevents the efficient and equitable allocation of the resources necessary for the provision of universal quality K to 12 public education. States can accomplish this goal by cutting the Gordian knot that prevents access to K to 12 equal educational opportunity and resource equity.

To solve the education industry's challenges, the states must properly, fully, and equitably fund K to 12 public education by eliminating the duplicative and unnecessary layer of county government and repurposing those tax dollars. County government not only duplicates state and local public goods and services but also suffers diseconomies of scale.

Connecticut found that the public goods and services provided by its layer of county government were already provided and more efficiently at either the state or municipal level. In1960, Connecticut proved that county government is duplicative by eliminating it when Connecticut had no state income or sales tax.

For example, ending New Jersey's unnecessary layer of county government would save New Jersey taxpayers about $8 billion annually in duplicative county property taxes. Repurposing the $8 billion annually to fully fund K-12 public education as well as to pay for crucial infrastructure projects, pensions, and healthcare liabilities while providing extensive property tax relief would cut New Jersey's K-16 educational Gordian knot.

The recommendations provided in this book demonstrate how to close the educational resource gap by making the distribution of financial, material, and human resources efficient, effective, and equitable. Policymakers must implement these recommendations to close the educational resource equity gap among schools and districts.

In addition, schools will be better equipped to improve student achievement, especially for those who are disadvantaged, and to close the achievement as well as the opportunity gap. Achieving resource equity will enable the equitable, sustainable, and efficient allocation of the financial, material, and human resources necessary for the provision of quality K to 12 education as well as equal educational opportunity.

The ground-breaking innovation contained in this book is distilling the challenges stemming from the long-term need for educational resource equity in a new way. The innovation assesses the contribution of the book's best practices, strategies, and lessons learned in the context of a more complete and holistic budgeting model. This book provides new ways of performing the business of education constructively and equitably while cutting the Gordian knot that has polarized and prevented sound K to 12 education funding and resource equity.

PART II

Constitutional Requirements

Chapter 3

Lest There Be Any Doubt

Constitutional Sovereignty as the Basis for Education Reform in Kentucky

William E. Thro

> Lest there be any doubt, the result of our decision is that Kentucky's *entire system* of common schools is unconstitutional . . . This decision applies to . . . the whole gamut of the common school system in Kentucky.[1]

With those words, the Supreme Court of Kentucky both transformed education in Kentucky and revolutionized the state judiciary's role in education reform.[2] First, *Rose v. Council for Better Education*[3] launched the "Third Wave" of school finance litigation where the emphasis was on adequacy rather than equity.[4] Second, by invalidating the entire educational system,[5] *Rose* recognized a quality education depends not on money or racial desegregation, but involves the complex interaction of multiple factors.[6] Third, instead of telling the Legislature and Governor how to remedy the constitutional violation,[7] a step that often leads to a constitutional crisis,[8] *Rose* acknowledged legislative and executive officials have "primary responsibility for elucidating, assessing, and solving" the problems of constitutional compliance.[9]

By recognizing the State Constitution limits the Legislature, the need for the judiciary to enforce those limits, and the need for the judiciary to limit themselves by deferring to the elected branches about compliance, the Supreme Court of Kentucky embraced "Constitutional Sovereignty."[10] Constitutional Sovereignty is the notion that sovereignty is vested not in a King or a Parliament, but in a written Constitution. It envisions a government of Constitutions, not People. It distrusts individuals, alliances of individuals, and temporary, but passionate, majorities. Constitutional Sovereignty recognizes the need to limit the government, the need for the judiciary to enforce those limitations, and the need for the judiciary to limit itself. *Rose* illustrates all three aspects. Indeed, the Supreme Court of Kentucky's embrace of Constitutional Sovereignty is why educational reform succeeded in Kentucky. Conversely, the implicit rejection of Constitutional Sovereignty by the high courts of other states is why school reform litigation has failed elsewhere.[11]

This chapter has two parts. Part I explains the concept of Constitutional Sovereignty in some detail. It supplies both an overview of the philosophical and historical basis for Constitutional Sovereignty as well as the implications of the concept. Part II explains how *Rose* embraced Constitutional Sovereignty. It discusses the Court's recognition of limits on legislative discretion, the Court's enforcement of those limits, and the Court's decision to limit its powers by allowing the Legislature and Governor to devise a solution.

THE CONCEPT OF CONSTITUTIONAL SOVEREIGNTY

The Philosophical Basis

The Constitution's Framing Generation "appealed frequently to biblical language and principles in their political discourse"[12] and, like John Calvin,[13] assumed "there is never a moment in human history when that which is human can be trusted blindly as a force for good."[14] Reflecting this awareness of Calvinist theology,[15] they recognized "framing a government" requires enabling "the government to control the governed; and in the next place oblige it to control itself."[16]

Consequently, the United States Constitution embodies an "obsessive distrust of government—*all* government—and [the] elevation of law into the ruling power of the state. Indeed, the idea of law itself as *sovereign* is the key."[17] By making the law or, more precisely, the written Constitution, as sovereign, the American Republic vests ultimate authority not in an absolute monarch or a religious leader or the Party or bureaucratic experts or judges who want to do justice or the political majority of the day or even the People themselves,[18] but in inviolable "self-evident" truths.[19]

Of course, because "governments are formed to secure" the rights of the people and "derive their just powers from the consent of the governed,"[20] the sovereign charter setting up and limiting the government must reflect the consent of the governed. "To be sure, a constitution is a document that protects against future democratic excesses. But when it is adopted, it is adopted by democratic process. That is what legitimatizes it . . . "[21] Thus, "before the

Constitution could take effect, the founders called on the states to convene special conventions of the people's representatives. And they insisted on a supermajority of those conventions to ratify the original Constitution."[22]

The Historical Basis

The concept of "Constitutional Sovereignty" where a written constitution, rather than a monarch, is sovereign began in 1215 among "the reeds of Runnymede" with "the first attack on Right Divine."[23] Magna Carta, forced on King John by a group of English Barons,[24] established explicit written limits on the King's power *and* an explicit written enforcement mechanism for those limits:[25] twenty-five men[26] could declare the King in violation of Magna Carta and could make war against the King.[27] While the 1215 Magna Carta did "invent freedom" for the English-Speaking Peoples,[28] it did not permanently establish Constitutional Sovereignty.[29] Over the space of seventeen months from June 1215 to November 1216, the Pope annulled Magna Carta,[30] war broke out between King John and the Barons,[31] King John died,[32] and Sir William Marshal,[33] as regent for the nine year old Henry III, issued a new version of Magna Carta.[34] Since Marshall's 1216 version of Magna Carta lacked an enforcement mechanism, the "question of how to restrain an out of control king would remain alive for the Middle Ages and beyond . . . "[35] Nevertheless, the 1216 version of Magna Carta "is centrist and is the painstaking work of the political process" and this version is "the foundation of English political history."[36] The barons lost; the 1216 Magna Carta was *not* Constitutional Sovereignty. The original Magna Carta's "chapter 61—the *forma secures*—[was] a short term, misconceived expedient . . . "[37]

The British made a second effort at Constitutional Sovereignty. In 1628, with the Petition of Right,[38] Sir Edward Coke tried "to make Magna Carta fundamental law inviolable by either king or parliament. The attempt failed."[39] The following years "brought civil war, a king's execution, the Cromwellian regime, restoration, and a bloodless revolution."[40] Consequently, the "Crown in Parliament," not the monarch alone, became sovereign.[41] In the United Kingdom, the "Crown in Parliament" can "make or unmake any law whatsoever" and no court can "override or set aside" a parliamentary act.[42]

Yet, "[i]n America, the barons have won; chapter 61 [of the 1215 Magna Carta]" is "a far-sighted anticipation of both the letter and the spirit of the" Constitution.[43] Sir Edward Coke "succeeded in America" because the Constitution is "untouchable, fundamental law, to be interpreted not by Congress, still less by the President, but by Justices of the Supreme Court."[44] Instead of a constitutional design that "was largely a set of unwritten customs [like the United Kingdom, the American] founders deliberately rejected that model when they decided to adopt a written Constitution."[45] That choice reflected the colonial experience with written limitations on government[46] as well as the influence of Coke.[47] Indeed, the Mayflower Compact, although only a single paragraph, represents both government by consent and limitations on governmental power.[48]

Implications of Constitutional Sovereignty

As this account of British and American constitutional history shows, Constitutional Sovereignty requires limiting the government by consent of the governed, empowering the judiciary to enforce those limits, and then limiting judges. Each of these three propositions merits greater discussion in the American context.

Limits on Government

First, by the consent of "We the People," the Constitution "withdraws certain subjects from the vicissitudes of political controversy" and "places them beyond the reach of majorities and officials."[49] Initially, there are "certain specified exceptions to the legislative [and executive] authority" within the constitutional text.[50] Those provisions impose both requirements and prohibitions.[51] Additionally, there is the separation of powers. Rather than combining executive, legislative, and judicial power in a single person or even a parliament dominated by a political majority, the Constitution "protects us from our own best intentions" by preventing the concentration of "power in one location as an expedient solution to the crisis of the day."[52] Finally, instead of an all-powerful national government,[53] the Constitution "split the atom of sovereignty . . . establishing two orders of government [federal and state], each with its own direct relationship, its own privity, its own set of mutual rights and obligations to the people who sustain it and are governed by it."[54]

The Judiciary Must Enforce the Constitutional Limits

Second, since our constitutional actors are imperfect humans, there will be times, "where the will of the legislature, declared in its statutes, stands in opposition to that of the people, declared in the Constitution. . . ."[55] "Whenever a particular statute [or executive action] contravenes the Constitution, it will be the duty of judicial tribunals to adhere" to the Constitution and declare the statutes and executive actions void.[56] If the judiciary determines there has been a constitutional violation, its "remedial powers . . . must be adequate to the task,"[57] but legislative and executive officials have "primary responsibility for elucidating, assessing, and solving" the problems of constitutional compliance.[58]

This power of judicial enforcement goes beyond simply declaring a constitutional actor in violation of the Constitution. In *Cooper v. Aaron*,[59] the Supreme Court of the United States declared its decisions interpreting the Constitution were the supreme law of the land even though the other branches or the states may interpret the Constitution differently.[60] After *Cooper*, constitutional actors must "follow the Court's interpretations, not just in the particular case announcing those interpretations, but in similar cases as well."[61] In America, "the government can and does lose in its own courts and then respect those judgements."[62]

The Judiciary Must Limit Themselves

Third, since judges are not perfect, but flawed humans, there must be meaningful limits on how the judiciary interprets the Constitution. Because of judicial supremacy, courts will be tempted to become "a bevy of Platonic Guardians,"[63] that "substitutes their predictive judgments for those of elected legislatures and expert agencies."[64] Conversely, judges may choose to ignore the Constitution and simply defer to the judgment of legislators, bureaucrats, or university administrators.

To preserve "the rule of law from the dictatorship of a shifting Supreme Court majority, . . . judicial opinions should be grounded in consistently applied principle" that respects Constitutional Sovereignty.[65] As Frederick Douglass observed, if the Constitution is "interpreted, as it ought to be interpreted, the Constitution is a glorious liberty document."[66] Respect for Constitutional Sovereignty requires rejecting "the conviction that the Constitution's meaning *changes* over time and that *judges* should determine what changes should be made based on external policy considerations."[67] This "Living Constitutionalism" approach requires judges to "exercise *Will* instead of *Judgment*" and the "substitution of their pleasure to that of" the People's elected officials.[68] Rather, respect for Constitutional Sovereignty requires accepting "the Constitution's meaning was fixed at its ratification [or the ratification of the amendment] and the judge's job is to discern and apply that meaning to the people's cases and controversies."[69] As Constitutions were "written to be understood by the voters, its words and phrases were used in their normal and ordinary meaning as distinguished from technical meaning,"[70] the judiciary may embrace "an idiomatic meaning," but it must reject "secret or technical meanings that would not have been known to ordinary citizens" at the time the Constitution was adopted.[71]

Chapter 3

HOW THE SUPREME COURT OF KENTUCKY EMBRACED CONSTITUTIONAL SOVEREIGNTY

The Court Recognized the Kentucky Constitution Limits Legislative Discretion

State constitutions are fundamentally different from the National Constitution—the National Constitution is a grant of power and the state constitutions are limitations on power.[72] Thus, the presumptions concerning legislative authority are reversed. Congress may not act unless it can identify a specific enumerated power,[73] but the State Legislature may act unless there is an explicit restriction.[74] Moreover, because state constitutions are often amended or even completely revised,[75] they often are more reflective of the contemporary values of society.[76] Yet, these fundamental differences do not diminish the unique nature of constitutional interpretation.

Significantly, the fifty state constitutions often require government to act in a particular way.[77] These requirements are "duties,"[78] and the judiciary must engage in a process-based review to decide if the government has violated its duty of care.[79] For example, the State Education Clauses limit the Legislature by requiring the Legislature to set up a public school system of a particular quality. In the absence of such a state constitutional provision, state legislatures would have absolute discretion whether to pursue the end of a public school system and to choose the means of achieving that end.[80] The Education Clause limits that discretion—state legislatures may not decline to have a public school system. By limiting legislative discretion, the provision effectively compels the legislature to perform an affirmative act—establishing a public system of a particular quality.[81]

Rose reflects this understanding of the Education Clause. Kentucky's education clause provides, "[t]he General Assembly shall, by appropriate legislation, provide for an efficient system of common schools throughout the state."[82] In describing how these "few simple, but direct words" show "the will of the people with regard to the importance of providing public education in the Commonwealth,"[83] the Court explained:

> Several conclusions readily appear from a reading of this section. First, it is the obligation, the sole obligation, of the General Assembly to provide for a system of common schools in Kentucky. The obligation to so provide is clear and unequivocal and is, in effect, a constitutional mandate. Next, the school system must be provided throughout the entire state, with no area (or its children) being omitted. The creation, implementation and maintenance of the school system must be achieved by appropriate legislation. Finally, the system must be an efficient one.[84]

In resolving the critical issue—the meaning of "efficient"—*Rose* considered "foreign cases, along with our constitutional debates, Kentucky precedents and the opinion of experts in formulating the definition of 'efficient' as it appears in our Constitution."[85]

The Court Recognized Its Duty to Enforce Constitutional Limits

Although the Education Clauses clearly limit the government and although the judiciary has a duty to enforce those limits, some courts have found school finance issues to be non-justiciable.[86] Most recently, the Supreme Court of Florida ruled a state constitutional amendment, imposing the highest possible duty on the State Legislature, was simply "puffery."[87]

Such an approach is fundamentally flawed. "Abdication of responsibility is not part of the constitutional design."[88] A court certainly can decide the meaning of the constitutional text. To the extent the constitutional text requires the legislature to act in a particular way or prohibits it from acting in a particular way, the court may evaluate whether the legislature's actions conform to the Constitution. This is nothing more than comparing the facts to the constitutional rule.

In *Rose*, the Court recognized "[t]o avoid deciding the case because of 'legislative discretion,' 'legislative function,' etc., would be a denigration of our own constitutional duty. To allow the General Assembly (or, in point of fact, the Executive) to decide whether its actions are constitutional is unthinkable."[89] Having recognized the judicial responsibility to enforce the constitutional limits, the Court concluded, "Kentucky's present system of common schools falls short of the mark of the constitutional mandate of 'efficient.' When one juxtaposes the standards of efficiency as derived from our Constitution . . . with the virtually unchallenged evidence in the record, no other decision is possible."[90] Instead of confining its decision to finance statutes, the Court recognized the entire "statutory system as a whole and the interrelationship of the parts therein are hereby declared to be in violation of [the Education Clause]."[91]

The Court Recognized Limits on Judicial Power

Under "a government of [the Constitution], and not of [humans],"[92] the judiciary cannot attempt "to solve every problem or right every wrong in our public life."[93] Americans "should not expect courts to do so, and courts should not try."[94] The Judiciary must limit itself. The "myth of the legal profession's omnicompetence . . . was exploded long ago."[95] These self-imposed limitations on the judiciary take two forms. First, any interpretation of the constitutional text must turn on the original public meaning. Courts "are ill advised to adopt or adhere to constitutional rules that bring [the judiciary] into constant conflict with a coequal branch of Government," but "when conflict is unavoidable," the rule should have a "demonstrable basis in the text of the Constitution and [should] objectively be shown to have been met or failed."[96] Second, since any "ruling of unconstitutionality frustrates the intent of the elected representatives of the people,"[97] the judiciary cannot force the legislative and executive actors to choose a particular course when other courses are equally constitutional.[98]

In *Rose*, the Court recognized both the importance of original public meaning and the need to ensure "responsibility for discharging the State's obligations is returned promptly to the State and its officials when the circumstances warrant."[99]

First, given the explicit language of the Kentucky Constitution's separation of powers provisions,[100] the Court recognized it could not keep jurisdiction.[101] Second, because "the *sole responsibility* [for complying with the requirements of the Education Clause] lies with the General Assembly,"[102] the Court "directed the General Assembly to recreate and redesign a new system" that "will guarantee to all children the opportunity for an adequate education, through a *state* system."[103]

In sum, the Court recognized the Kentucky Constitution's Education Clause limited the discretion of the General Assembly, enforced the requirements of the Education Clause, and limited itself by allowing the Legislature to decide compliance.

CONCLUSION

Unlike virtually every other nation, America is defined not by race, blood, soil, language, faith, or culture, but by "the belief in the principles of equality and freedom this country stands for."[104] As a Nation "conceived in liberty and dedicated to the proposition that all . . . are created equal,"[105] we recognize the Constitution, not the winners of the last election, as sovereign. Because "there is a degree of depravity in mankind which requires a certain degree of circumspection and distrust,"[106] our sovereign Constitution has "well-structured [governmental] systems" designed to "deter . . . the human impulse toward tyranny."[107]

In its revolutionary opinion, the Supreme Court of Kentucky recognized and relied on these principles of Constitutional Sovereignty. First, it recognized the Kentucky Constitution's Education Clause limited legislative discretion. Second, the Court enforced those limits by invalidating the entire educational system. Third, the Court recognized the limits of its own powers by allowing the General Assembly to decide how to follow the constitutional mandate.

NOTES

1. *Rose v. Council for Better Educ., Inc.*, 790 S.W.2d 186, 215 (Ky. 1989).
2. *See* Kentucky Education Reform Act of 1990, ch. 476, 1990 Ky. Acts 1208.
3. 790 S.W.2d 186 (Ky. 1989).
4. *See* William E. Thro, *The Third Wave: The Impact of the Montana, Kentucky, and Texas Decisions on the Future of Public School Finance Reform Litigation*, 19 J.L. & EDUC. 219 (1990).
5. *Rose*, 790 S.W.2d at 215.
6. *See* D. Frank Vinik, *The Contrasting Politics of Remedy: The Alabama and Kentucky School Equity Funding Suits*, 22 J. EDUC. FIN. 60 (1996).
7. Joshua E. Weishart, *Aligning Education Rights and Remedies*, 27 KAN. J.L. & PUB. POL'Y, 346, 347–51 (2018).
8. Jeffrey S. Sutton, 51 IMPERFECT SOLUTIONS: STATES AND THE MAKING OF AMERICAN CONSTITUTIONAL LAW 22–42 (2018).
9. *Brown v. Board of Education*, 349 U.S. 294, 299 (1955).
10. I coined the term and developed the concept in William E. Thro, *Angels Do Not Govern: Constitutional Sovereignty as a Response to Humanity's Sinful Nature*, EMORY UNIVERSITY CANOPY FORUM ON THE INTERACTIONS OF LAW & RELIGION (September 2020) (available at https://canopyforum.org/2020/09/09/angels-do-not-govern/).
11. William E. Thro, *Who, What, Why, & How: Reimagining State Constitutional Analysis in School Finance Litigation*, BRIGHAM YOUNG UNIVERSITY EDUCATION & LAW JOURNAL 30 (2020).
12. Daniel L. Dreisbach, *Does Biblical Literacy Enrich Constitutional Literacy? The Bible's Forgotten Influence on the American Constitutional Tradition*, EMORY UNIVERSITY CANOPY FORUM ON THE INTERACTIONS OF LAW & RELIGION (September 2020) (available at https://canopyforum.org/2020/09/23/does-biblical-literacy-enrich-constitutional-literacy-the-bibles-forgotten-influence-on-the-american-constitutional-tradition/).
13. Calvinist theology is the philosophical basis for many aspects of the American Republic. *See* James H. Smylie, *Madison and Witherspoon: Theological Roots of American Political Thought*, 73 AMERICAN PRESBYTERIANS 155 (1995).
14. Marci Hamilton, *The Calvinist Paradox of Distrust and Hope at the Constitutional Convention*, in CHRISTIAN PERSPECTIVES ON LEGAL THOUGHT 293, 295 (Michael W. McConnell, Robert F. Corchran, Jr., & Angela C. Carmella, eds., 2001).
15. Indeed, the Framing Generation had great awareness of the Reformed Theology. Mark David Hall, ROGER SHERMAN AND THE CREATION OF THE AMERICAN REPUBLIC 12–40 (2013).
16. THE FEDERALIST No. 51 (James Madison).

17. David Starkey, MAGNA CARTA: THE MEDIEVAL ROOTS OF MODERN POLITICS 1308 (2015) (Kindle Edition) (emphasis original).

18. For an overview of the process of obtaining the consent of the governed, see Pauline Maier, RATIFICATION: THE PEOPLE DEBATE THE CONSTITUTION, 1787–88 (2010).

19. DECLARATION OF INDEPENDENCE, ¶ 2.

20. *Id.*

21. As Justice Scalia explained during his confirmation hearings, *Nomination of Judge Antonin Scalia to be Associate Justice of the Supreme Court of the United States*, 99th Cong. 89 (1986) (statement of Antonin Scalia).

22. Neil Gorsuch, A REPUBLIC, IF YOU CAN KEEP IT 119 (2019).

23. Rudyard Kipling, *The Reeds of Runnymede* (1922).

24. Dan Jones, MAGNA CARTA: THE BIRTH OF LIBERTY, 123–31 (2015).

25. MAGNA CARTA, ch. 61.

26. For a list of the "Magna Carta Sureties," *see* https://magnacarta800th.com/schools/biographies/the-25-barons-of-magna-carta/.

27. Starkey, *supra* note 17, at 621–630.

28. Daniel Hannan, INVENTING FREEDOM: HOW THE ENGLISH-SPEAKING PEOPLES MADE THE MODERN WORLD 49–55 (2013).

29. Starkey, *supra* note 17, at 1288.

30. Nicholas Vincent, MAGNA CARTA: A VERY SHORT INTRODUCTION 74–75 (2011).

31. Robert Tombs, THE ENGLISH AND THEIR HISTORY 75 (2016).

32. Jones, *supra* note 24, at 176.

33. *Id.* at 181. "Although he was around seventy years old, Marshal was one of the respected figures in England and the only Earl who remained loyal to the end."

34. *Id.* at 182.

35. *Id.* at 184.

36. Starkey, *supra* note 17, at 1288.

37. *Id.* at 1303.

38. Peter Ackroyd, REBELLION: THE HISTORY OF ENGLAND FROM JAMES I TO THE GLORIOUS REVOLUTION 133–34 (2014).

39. Starkey, *supra* note 17, at 1309.

40. A.E. Dick Howard, THE ROAD FROM RUNNYMEDE: MAGNA CARTA AND CONSTITUTIONALISM IN AMERICA 9 (1968; paperback edition 2015).

41. Martin Loughlin, THE BRITISH CONSTITUTION: A VERY SHORT INTRODUCTION 50 (2013).

42. *Id.* at 32.

43. Starkey, *supra* note 17, at 1303.

44. *Id.* at 1312.

45. Gorsuch, *supra* note 22, at 116.

46. Howard, *supra* note 40, at 14–98 (discussing the influence of Magna Carta in the Colonial Charters, the New England Covenants, the Proprietary Colonies, and Pennsylvania).

47. *Id.* at 118–24, 130–32, 369–70.

48. Peter Wood, 1620: A CRITICAL RESPONSE TO THE 1619 PROJECT 32 (2020).

49. *West Virginia State Bd. of Educ. v. Barnette*, 319 U.S. 624, 638 (1943).
50. THE FEDERALIST NO. 78 (Alexander Hamilton).
51. William E. Thro, *No Clash of Constitutional Values: Respecting Freedom & Equality in Public University Sexual Assault Cases*, 28 REGENT UNIV. L. REV. 197 (2016).
52. *New York v. United States*, 505 U.S. 144, 187 (1992).
53. *McCulloch v. Maryland*, 17 U.S. (4 Wheat.) 316, 405 (1819).
54. *U.S. Term Limits v. Thornton*, 514 U.S. 779, 838 (1995) (Kennedy, J., concurring).
55. THE FEDERALIST NO. 78 (Alexander Hamilton).
56. *Id.*
57. *Whitcomb v. Chavis*, 403 U.S. 124, 161 (1971).
58. *Brown v. Board of Education*, 349 U.S. 294, 299 (1955).
59. *Cooper v. Aaron*, 358 U.S. 1, 18–19 (1958) ("It follows that the interpretation of the Fourteenth Amendment enunciated by this Court in the *Brown* case is the supreme law of the land . . . ").
60. Josh Blackman, *The Irrepressible Myths of Cooper v. Aaron*, 107 GEO. L.J. 1135, 1137 (2019).
61. Stephen Breyer, MAKING OUR DEMOCRACY WORK: A JUDGE'S VIEW 60 (2010).
62. Gorsuch, *supra* note 22, at 237.
63. *Griswold v. Connecticut*, 381 U.S. 479, 526 (1965) (Black, J., dissenting) (quoting Learned Hand, THE BILL OF RIGHTS 70 (1958)).
64. *Lingle v. Chevron*, 544 U.S. 528, 544 (2005).
65. *McCreary County v. ACLU*, 545 U.S. 844, 890–91 (2005) (Scalia, J., dissenting).
66. Frederick Douglass, WHAT TO THE SLAVE IS THE FOURTH OF JULY? (1852).
67. Gorsuch, *supra* note 22, at 110.
68. THE FEDERALIST NO. 78 (Alexander Hamilton) (emphasis original).
69. Gorsuch, *supra* note 22, at 110.
70. *United States v. Sprague*, 282 U.S. 716, 731 (1931). *See also Gibbons v. Ogden*, 22 U.S. (9 Wheat.) 1, 188 (1824).
71. *District of Columbia. v. Heller*, 554 U.S. 570, 576–77 (2008).
72. *Hornbeck v. Somerset County Board of Education*, 458 A.2d 758, 785 (Md. 1983); *Board of Educ. v. Nyquist*, 439 N.E.2d 359, 366 n. 5 (N.Y. 1982).
73. *United States v. Morrison*, 529 U.S. 598, 607 (2000).
74. *Almond v. Rhode Island Lottery Comm'n*, 756 A.2d 186, 196 (R.I. 2000).
75. *See* Robert F. Utter, *Freedom and Diversity in a Federal System: Perspectives on State Constitutions and the Washington Declaration of Rights* in DEVELOPMENTS IN STATE CONSTITUTIONAL LAW 239, 241–42 (Bradley McGraw, ed. 1984).
76. A. E. Dick Howard, *The Renaissance of State Constitutional Law*, 1 EMERGING ISSUES IN STATE CONSTITUTIONAL LAW 1, 14 (1988).
77. Emily Zackin, LOOKING FOR RIGHTS IN ALL THE WRONG PLACES: WHY STATE CONSTITUTIONS CONTAIN AMERICA'S POSITIVE RIGHTS 36–47 (2013). See also Helen Hershkoff, *Positive Rights and State Constitutions: The Limits of Federal Rationality Review*, 112 HARV. L. REV. 1131, 1137 (1999).

78. Scott R. Bauries, *The Education Duty*, 47 WAKE FOREST L. REVIEW 705, 747–48 (2012).

79. Scott R. Bauries, *Perversity as Rationality in Teacher Evaluation*, 72 ARK. L. REV. 325, 358 (2019).

80. *See* Scott R. Bauries, *State Constitutions and Individual Rights: Conceptual Convergence in School Finance Litigation*, 18 GEO. MASON L. REV. 301, 358–59 (2011).

81. Bauries, *Education Duty, supra* note 78, at 759–60.

82. Ky. Const. § 183.

83. *Rose*, 790 S.W.2d at 205.

84. *Id.*

85. *Id.* at 210.

86. *Committee for Educational Rights v. Edgar*, 672 N.E.2d 1178, 1191 (Ill. 1996) ("What constitutes a 'high quality' education and how it may best be provided, cannot be ascertained by any judicially discoverable or manageable standards."). *City of Pawtucket v. Sundlun*, 662 A.2d 40, 58 (R.I. 1995) ("What constitutes an appropriate education or even an 'equal, adequate, and meaningful' one is 'not likely to be divined for all time even by the scholars who now so earnestly debate the issues.'").

87. *Citizens for Strong Sch., Inc. v. Fla. State Bd. of Educ.*, 262 So. 3d 127, 141 (Fla. 2019).

88. *Clinton v. New York*, 524 U.S. 417, 452 (1998) (Kennedy, J., concurring).

89. *Rose*, 790 S.W.2d at 209.

90. *Id.* at 213.

91. *Id.* at 215.

92. *Marbury v. Madison*, 5 U.S. (1 Cranch.) 137, 163 (1803).

93. Amy Coney Barrett, *Opening Statement*, CONFIRMATION HEARING OF JUDGE BARRETT TO BE ASSOCIATE JUSTICE OF THE SUPREME COURT OF THE UNITED STATES (October 12, 2020).

94. *Id.*

95. *People Who Care v. Rockford Bd. of Educ. School District No. 205*, 111 F.3d 528, 536 (7th Cir. 1997).

96. *Lane*, 541 U.S. at 558 (Scalia, J., dissenting).

97. *Regan v. Time, Inc.*, 468 U.S. 641, 652 (1984) (White, J., joined by Rehnquist, C.J. & O'Connor, J., announcing the judgment of the Court).

98. *Missouri v. Jenkins*, 495 U.S. 33, 52 (1990).

99. *See Horne v. Flores*, 557 U.S. 443, 450 (2009).

100. Ky. Const. §§ 27–29.

101. *Rose*, 790 S.W.2d at 214.

102. *Rose*, 790 S.W.2d at 216.

103. *Rose*, 790 S.W.2d at 212.

104. Antonin Scalia, *What Makes an American* in SCALIA SPEAKS: REFLECTIONS ON LAW, FAITH, AND LIFE WELL LIVED 15, 17 (Christopher J. Scalia & Edward Whelan, eds. 2017).
105. Abraham Lincoln, GETTYSBURG ADDRESS (1863).
106. THE FEDERALIST NO. 55 (James Madison).
107. Hamilton, *supra* note 14, at 303.

Chapter 4

State School Funding Formula-based Inequities

Stephen V. Coffin

CREATURES OF THE STATE

Local governments including municipalities and traditional public school districts (TPSDs) are creatures of the state, which means that these governmental entities report to the state and are subject to the state's authority. States increased their power over public education, especially school finance and policy, by more closely regulating TPSDs, attaching more stringent conditions on state aid, and applying more rigorous guidelines to determine local fair share funding (Fusarelli & Cooper, 2009).

State and local funding disparities led to court decisions such as *Serrano v. Priest*, which established financial neutrality as the basis for school funding. Subsequent rulings shifted from financial neutrality to focus on adequacy. Court decisions shifted to adequacy (i.e., Third Wave) from equity based on state constitutions (i.e., Second Wave) and equity based on the U.S. Constitution (i.e., First Wave).

Court rulings required state governments to provide resources to disadvantaged districts to offset inter- and intra-district statewide funding disparities and to ensure that the provision of education adequately met constitutional requirements. States tried various ways to comply with the courts' decisions concerning the states' school funding formulae that required specific remedies to resource disparities among districts. These remedies include but are not limited to:

- New or revised school funding formulae.
- Additional state funding.
- Equalizing revenues.
- Eliminating state aid for affluent traditional public schools (TPSs) or TPSDs.
- County-run or regional public schools without locally controlled TPSs or TPSDs.
- Additional state income or sales taxes earmarked for K-12 education.
- Additional state or regional property taxes earmarked for K-12 education.
- Intra- and inter-district school choice.
- Charter and magnet schools.
- Public, private, Catholic, and other religious school vouchers.
- School attendance based on lotteries.
- Statewide class size reduction initiatives.
- Accountability measures.
- State takeovers.

Typically, when the courts dictated specific state remedies the result is a constitutional crisis and legislative stalemate.

KENTUCKY

The Kentucky Supreme Court's ruling and remedy in *Rose v. Council for Better Education, Inc.* (1989) illustrates the complexity and challenges that face state governments as they comply with court decisions. The Kentucky Supreme Court ruled that the Kentucky General Assembly failed to meet the state constitutional requirements to provide a statewide efficient common public school system.

The Kentucky Supreme Court decided that the state's common public school system was inadequately funded, lacked equal educational opportunity, was inequitable, and failed to provide essential educational resources. The Kentucky Supreme Court's remedy required that the statewide school system provide all students with the following essential resources (Baker et al., 2008, p. 156).

1. Adequate communication skills that enable students to perform in an ever-changing economy and society.
2. Sufficient understanding of economic, social, financial, and governmental systems to support informed citizenship and decision-making.
3. Sufficient knowledge of political and governmental systems for students to understand how these systems affect them.

4. Sufficient understanding of physical, emotional, social, mental health and wellbeing.
5. Sufficient understanding of the arts and music to appreciate all persons' cultural and historical heritage and background.
6. Sufficient academic or vocational training with which to inform the pursuit of employment and careers.
7. Sufficient academic or vocational skills with which to enter and to compete successfully in the job market.

These essential resources are known as the *Rose* capacities (Baker et al., 2008).

The Kentucky Supreme Court's ruling in *Rose v. Council for Better Education, Inc.* (1989) illustrates the necessity for constitutional sovereignty rather than judicial omnicompetence in using the courts to achieve or prompt educational reform. However, constitutional sovereignty requires limitations on government, judicial enforcement of those limitations, and meaningful limitations on the judiciary. The Kentucky's Supreme Court decision reflects these principles.

The Kentucky Supreme Court, unlike other state supreme courts, recognized that the Education Clause limits legislative discretion. Second, in deciding what the Education Clause means, the Kentucky Supreme Court refused to defer to the legislature and, more importantly, recognized that the constitutional mandate went beyond financial concerns. Every other court had focused exclusively on finance. Third, instead of dictating a specific remedy, the Court recognized that the judiciary's role was to announce broad principles (e.g., saying what the law is) and leave the details of complying with the law to the elected branches.

Court decisions concerning the state school funding formulae rely on key provisions of the state's constitution. Typically, state legislatures implementing court decisions that focus on the state school funding formula establish a portfolio of necessary educational inputs (e.g., essential resources) or outcomes (e.g., test scores, student performance, achievement, college matriculation, or level of attainment) that meet the courts' constitutional requirements. New Jersey's "thorough and efficient" (T&E) clause is an example.

NEW JERSEY AND NEW YORK

The New Jersey State Constitution's T&E educational clause provides "for the maintenance of a thorough and efficient system of free public schools for the instruction of all children in the state between the ages of five and eighteen years" (Goertz & Weiss, 2009, p. 10). New Jersey's T&E educational state aid is the amount of state funding necessary to provide an adequate education that meets constitutional requirements. Similarly, the New York State Constitution's education clause, which is known as "the Education Article" (Article 11, section 1), mandates that "the legislature shall provide for the maintenance and support of a system of free common schools wherein all the children can be educated" (Shrader, 2007, p. 84).

Allocative Inefficiency

Ladson-Billings' (2006) education debt concept demonstrates that state school funding formulae must meet or exceed constitutional requirements. To meet or exceed constitutional requirements and achieve targeted or constitutional academic outcomes, schools must have the necessary financial, material, and human inputs or resources (Ladson-Billings, 2006). However, the unequal and inequitable distribution of educational resources stems from shortcomings in state school funding formulae (Ladson-Billings, 2006; Ladson-Billings, 2009).

Educational resource inequities stem from the unequal distribution of resources among schools that disproportionately disenfranchises low-income or tax base-poor districts especially those with high concentrations of high-need high cost-to-educate pupils. For example, Ladson-Billings (2006; 2009) blames faulty state school funding formulae rather than schools and teachers for test score disparities among minority and majority students. States must redesign school funding formulae to close educational resource gaps by allocating resources equitably so that schools have the necessary capacity to improve student achievement and outcomes especially for poor students.

Judiciary's Role

The judiciary greatly expanded its influence over states' school finance practices, policy, and reform by mandating constitutional requirements for state school funding formulae beginning in the 1970's. Several landmark New Jersey and New York court decisions exemplify this shift to requiring specific remedies to resource disparities among schools and districts. These court decisions launched a trend of establishing a portfolio of educational inputs (e.g., essential resources) or outcomes (e.g., test scores, student performance, achievement, college admission, or level of attainment) that are necessary to meet the courts' constitutional mandates.

New Jersey

In 1970, East Orange, Jersey City, Paterson, and Plainfield challenged the constitutionality of the state's school funding system. These TPSDs argued that large tax base assessed value variations across districts resulted in disparate per-pupil expenditures that deprived students in low-property-wealth communities of achieving a thorough and efficient (T&E) education. The large disparities in school funding stemmed from disparities in property tax bases among affluent and poor districts (Coffin & Cooper, 2017). New Jersey's education finance system used a guaranteed tax base formula (GTB) to address these disparities that enabled affluent districts to raise disproportionately more property taxes at correspondingly lower tax rates to fund their schools at higher levels than poor districts.

Robinson v. Cahill

The New Jersey Supreme Court ruled in favor of the plaintiffs in *Robinson v. Cahill* and defined a "thorough and efficient" (T&E) education as one that "Embraces that educational opportunity, which is needed in the contemporary setting to equip a child for his role as a citizen and competitor in the labor market" (*Robinson v. Cahill I*, 1973, p. 295). The Supreme Court ruled that New Jersey's GTB formula failed to equalize school spending across districts (Coffin & Cooper, 2017; Coffin & Cooper, 2018). The inequalities prevented tax-base-poor urban districts from providing at least an adequate education.

The Robinson litigation focused more on the school funding formulae and its resource equalization effects across districts than on the educational components of a thorough and efficient public school system. The New Jersey Supreme Court "accepted the legislature's definition of T&E, the input and process standards included in the state's school finance reform law—the Public School Education Act of 1975 (called Chapter 212)" (Goertz & Weiss, 2009, p. 10). The Supreme Court struck down the state's school funding system in *Robinson v. Cahill* based on the state constitution's education clause.

In *Robinson v. Cahill V*, 1976, the New Jersey Supreme Court shifted the standard from economic disparities to educational content. Goertz and Edwards explain that spending parity would no longer be the main criteria in the Court's determining whether a school funding formula was constitutional, "without sufficient resources, other measures of an adequate education will not satisfy the constitutional mandate" (1999, p. 10). The Supreme Court used the "thorough and efficient system of free public schools" clause to assess the level, content, source, and relationship of financial resources to educational outcomes in *Robinson v. Cahill* (Coffin & Cooper, 2017; Coffin & Cooper, 2018).

Abbott v. Burke

The New Jersey Supreme Court focused on thorough education in terms of financial and educational resources and outcomes in its Abbott v. Burke decisions. In addition, the Court defined school funding's role in a thorough and efficient education and "broadened its definition of a T&E education especially as it applied to disadvantaged students in urban communities" (Goertz & Weiss, 2009, p. 11).

In 1981, five years after the implementation of Chapter 212, the Education Law Center (ELC) challenged the constitutionality of this funding law on behalf of students from four cities (Camden, East Orange, Irvington, and Jersey City). Applying the court's new focus on substantive educational opportunities, the plaintiffs argued in Abbott v. Burke, that New Jersey's education finance system caused not only significant educational expenditure disparities but also vast programmatic differences between poor urban and wealthy suburban school districts. (Goertz & Weiss, 2009, p. 11).

In its Abbott v. Burke decisions, the New Jersey Supreme Court ruled that the unequal distribution of financial, material, and human resources resulted in funding disparities among the Abbott and affluent districts, which prevented the Abbott districts from providing a thorough and efficient education. The Court raised the threshold for a thorough and efficient education in its Abbott rulings. The Court decided in Abbott v. Burke, 1990, the second Abbott case, that spending disparities among the Abbott and affluent districts, especially those with a district factor group (DFG) code of I or J, demonstrated that poor urban districts provided inadequate levels of education. Consequently, the state established the kinds, content, and quality levels of the educational programs, curricula, personnel, and facilities in affluent suburban districts as the adequacy standards for poor urban districts.

The New Jersey Supreme Court ordered the state legislature to equalize spending for the regular education programs among poor urban districts and tax base-rich districts (e.g., DFG I and J TPSDs) as well as to provide additional funds to meet the special educational needs of urban districts. This ruling led to the Quality of Education Act (QEA) that replaced the state's GTB formula with a foundation aid formula. Although the foundation level less the amount raised by a school district at a state equalized tax rate was the minimum spending level, the "maximum foundation budget" (Firestone et al., 1997, p. 27) was defined as the combined amount from all governmental revenue sources (Firestone et al., 1997, p. 28).

CEIFA

The Supreme Court declared QEA unconstitutional in *Abbott v. Burke III*, 1994, because it failed to equalize funding among Abbott and tax-base-rich districts as well as to meet the special needs of urban students (Coffin, 2021; Coffin & Cooper, 2017). The New Jersey State legislature enacted the Comprehensive Educational Improvement and Financing Act of 1996 (CEIFA) that focused more on academic outcomes and established "a set of input standards, such as class size, administrators/teachers per-student, schools per district, and types and amount of classroom supplies, services, and materials, that are considered to be sufficient to achieve the state content standards" in response to the Supreme Court's decision (Goertz & Edwards, 2009, p. 19).

The CEIFA defined an adequate education in terms of academic standards and provided funding based on a hypothetical (e.g., a theoretically successful TPSD) school district's resources required to achieve the standards (Baker et al., 2008). "The CEIFA also provided aid for two supplemental programs designed to address the disadvantages of SNDs: demonstrably effective program aid (DEPA), and early childhood program aid (ECPA)" (Baker et al., 2008, p. 158).

New Jersey froze financial aid at the 2001–02 academic-year levels independent of increases in enrollment, operating costs, and state as well as federal underfunded mandates instead of fully funding CEIFA's school funding formula as required by the Supreme Court (Coffin & Cooper, 2017). Many districts that depended on state aid suffered disproportionately from the state aid cut. During the 2005–06 school year the statewide shortfall totaled $846 million, which translated into per-pupil shortfalls of approximately $1,627 in non-Abbott DFG A and B districts, $758 in DFG C through H districts, $386 DFG I and J districts, and $188 in Abbott districts (Reock, 2007, pp. 1–9). Reock found that "the state aid freeze caused massive under-funding of many school districts throughout the state, especially poor non-Abbott districts, and contributed to the property tax problem in the state" (Sciarra, 2008, p. 4).

The Supreme Court declared CEIFA unconstitutional in *Abbott v. Burke IV*, 1997, because it neither linked educational outcome standards for all districts nor met the state's adequacy goals. The Supreme Court found that the State of New Jersey failed to show that its resource delivery system underlying the foundation amount supported the state's Core Curriculum Content Standards (CCCS):

> In the absence of documentation demonstrating that the CEIFA model provided sufficient resources to educate students in districts with high concentrations of poverty, the Court required an interim remedy: Abbott districts would receive

"parity aid," or an amount equal to the average regular education per-pupil expenditures in the State's wealthiest districts. (New Jersey Department of Education, 2007, p. 4)

In addition, the CEIFA failed to meet the Court's three fundamental constitutionality tests:

The Court established a three-part test of the constitutionality of CEIFA.

First, does the law establish standards for defining a thorough and efficient education? Second, does the State provide adequate resources to ensure the achievement of a T&E education? And, third, does the law meet the special needs of disadvantaged urban students? (Goertz & Edwards, 2009, p. 21).

The CEIFA failed to address the special needs of Abbott districts because its efficient school district or theoretically successful TPSD model was not based on the characteristics and needs of the Abbott districts.

The Supreme Court mandated the state to provide parity aid to remedy the unconstitutional funding and educational disparities as well as to equalize per-pupil expenditures and resources among affluent and Abbott districts (Coffin, 2021; Coffin & Cooper, 2017; Coffin & Cooper, 2018). The Court ordered "whole school reform designs" in *Abbott v. Burke V*, 1998, (Goertz & Edwards, 2009, p. 26). In addition, the Supreme Court ruled in *Abbott XX*, 2009, that the School Finance Reform Act of 2008 (SFRA) was constitutional. Superior Court Judge Doyne, who was appointed as special master by the Supreme Court, found that Governor Christie's school funding reductions "violate the state's mandate to provide children 'a thorough and efficient' education" (Rundquist & Calefati, 2011, p. 1).

NEW YORK

In 1978, several tax-base-poor Long Island, New York City, and other large urban districts challenged the state's school finance formula in *Levittown v. Nyquist* because of the funding disparities among their school districts and the state's tax-base-rich districts (Coffin, 2021; Coffin & Cooper, 2017). The New York State Court of Appeals ruled "that the state's constitution guaranteed all New York children an opportunity for a 'sound basic education'" (Chambers, et al., 2006, p. 3). The Court based its decision on the New York State Constitution's education clause, known as the Education Article, which states that "the legislature shall provide for the maintenance and support of a system of free common schools wherein all the children can be educated" even though the Court found that the constitution did not mandate equal funding (Shrader, 2007, p. 84). Although *Levittown v. Nyquist* found that funding inequities did not violate the state's Education Article, the Court did not define a sound basic education (Chambers, et al., 2006, p. 3).

A task force of the New York State Education Department (NYSED) defined a "sound basic education" in response to the Court's decision (Chambers, et al., 2006, p. 4). A "sound basic education" was defined in terms of learning standards that resulted from a "state sponsored research and public engagement process culminating in 1996 in the issuance of the Regents Learning Standards" (Chambers, et al., 2006, p. 4). These standards established benchmarks for student achievement in seven academic content areas and ultimately the definition of adequacy "as providing to all students a full opportunity to meet the Regents Learning Standards" (Chambers, et al., 2006, p. 3).

Campaign for Fiscal Equity

The Campaign for Fiscal Equity (CFE) focused on standards in its lawsuit challenging the constitutionality of New York State's education funding system in *CFE v. State of New York* (1993) (Coffin, 2021; Coffin & Cooper, 2017). The CFE argued that the state's school finance system failed to provide students with a sufficient opportunity to receive a state constitutionally guaranteed "sound basic education" particularly in New York City (Shrader, 2007, p. 84).

In CFE I (1995), the Court of Appeals ruled that the state has an "obligation to provide 'a sound basic education to all the children of the state,'" including "the basic literacy, calculating, and verbal skills necessary to enable children to eventually function productively as civic participants capable of voting and serving on a jury" but the Court declared that even adequate facilities and teachers fulfill the state's responsibility (Shrader, 2007, pp. 84–85). As a result, the Court of Appeals overturned the Appellate Division's ruling.

In CFE II (2001), the CFE prevailed in trial court and State Supreme Court Justice DeGrasse declared "the school funding formula unconstitutional because it failed to supply New York City school children with a 'sound basic education' as required" and affirmed the essential components of "a sound basic education" (Shrader, 2007, pp. 85–86). Justice DeGrasse required the State of New York to ensure that all public schools provided an equal opportunity for a sound basic education for all its students, to ensure that all the Court's standards were met, and to determine the costs of a sound basic education as well as to serve as the basis for a new school finance formula (Coffin, 2021; Coffin & Cooper, 2017; Shrader, 2007).

In CFE III (2002), the Appellate Division reversed Justice DeGrasse's 2001 decision declaring that "Justice DeGrasse exceeded the 'minimally adequate' standards stipulated in the Court of Appeals' 1995 ruling" (Shrader, 2007, p.

88). However, in CFE IV (2003), the New York Court of Appeals overturned the Appellate Court's decision as it "rejected the state's argument that it had satisfied its duty to provide a 'sound basic' education by providing New York City students with an 8th or 9th-grade education" (Baker, et al., 2008, p. 157) and, therefore, "New York State's current educational funding arrangements were definitively determined to be unconstitutional and required to be altered to ensure that school funding is adequate" (Chambers, et al., 2006, p. 4). As a result, in CFE V (2003), "the New York Court of Appeals commissioned a study to determine the cost of providing an adequate education for New York City" (Baker, et al., 2008, p. 159).

STATE SCHOOL FINANCE FORMULAE PARADIGM SHIFT

New York and New Jersey exemplify the shift in state court decisions to achieving adequacy (i.e., Third Wave) rather than equity based solely on state constitutions (i.e., Second Wave) or equity based on the U.S. Constitution (i.e., First Wave). The conceptual framework undergirding the shift is based on trying to achieve wealth and need equalization among school districts.

This adequacy concept focuses on the provision of an adequate education that equalizes outcomes rather than resources or inputs so that all students will have resource equity and an equal opportunity to receive an education that meets or exceeds state standards. The rationale supporting the adequacy concept is that a district's financial resources should be sufficient and adjusted for cost variations beyond a local school district's control to enable the district to meet or exceed the adequacy standards and to provide an opportunity for all students to meet the state standards.

School Finance Reform Act: Adequacy Budget

In New Jersey, the School Finance Reform Act of 2008 (SFRA) provides the formulaic remedy for achieving adequacy. The formula is based on community characteristics that are applied equally to all school districts and require increased funding targeted primarily to Abbott districts. In this way, the SFRA addresses the inequities resulting from the imbalance of resources among districts (New Jersey Department of Education, 2007, p. 4). To meet this definition of adequacy, New York uses the Regents Learning Standards as the barometer for determining whether a district meets its adequacy requirements according to the state's school finance formula.

The SFRA replaced the CEIFA because the New Jersey State Supreme Court found CEIFA's funding provisions unconstitutional and combined the state's remedies of parity aid and supplemental funding with the SFRA formula. SFRA's formula contains "three major components: equalization aid, categorical aid, and adjustment aid" (Goertz & Weiss, 2009, p. 28). However, the formula calculates aid in two ways: "wealth-equalized and categorical" (New Jersey Department of Education, 2007, p. 19).

The SFRA allocates wealth-equalized aid according to a district's ability to raise enough local revenue (e.g., property taxes) based on its equalized property valuation and aggregate district income, which are indexed using the state wealth multipliers, to support its adequacy budget (Coffin & Cooper, 2017). The adequacy budget represents the resources necessary for a district to meet state-imposed standards or outcomes such as the Core Curriculum Content Standards (CCCS) and includes:

- The base amount for elementary, middle, and high school students.
- The weights for at-risk and limited English proficiency (LEP) and county vocational students.
- Two-thirds of the census-based costs for the general special education category.
- All the census-based costs for speech (New Jersey Department of Education, 2007, p. 19).

New Jersey's adequacy based school funding formula was developed in response to the Court's demands for "standard-based reforms" that "have 'judicially manageable' tools that allow them to devise effective remedial orders" (Rebell, 2002, p. 219).

Equalization aid is calculated using a "foundation formula based on an 'adequacy budget,'" that includes "funding for the regular education program and costs for student poverty ('at-risk' aid), limited English proficiency (LEP) students, and special education services" (Goertz & Weiss, 2009, p. 28). A district's adequacy budget equals the amount calculated according to the following formula:

> A district's adequacy budget equals the total of all of the base student costs plus at-risk student costs plus LEP student costs plus the combined costs of all LEP students who are also eligible for free or reduced-price lunch plus the special education census-based costs that are wealth-equalized together times the Geographic Cost Adjustment (GCA). (New Jersey Department of Education, 2007, pp. 19–20)

In contrast to wealth-equalized aid, categorical aid is not based on a district's property tax revenues. Categorical aid is calculated by multiplying the cost factor for a particular category by the number of students that qualify for the aid (New Jersey Department of Education, 2007, p. 19). The purpose of the SFRA's adjustment aid is to hold districts harmless in the short term:

> Adjustment aid is a save-harmless program for districts that receive less state aid under SFRA than they did in 2007–2008, particularly Abbott districts where state approved expenditures exceeded their SFRA adequacy budgets. For 2008–09, the state guarantees that all districts will receive a minimum of 102% of their 2007- 08 state aid. Adjustment aid will be reduced in the out-years as equalization and categorical aids grow. (Goertz & Weiss, 2009, p. 28)

On a macro level, a district's state aid equals the amount calculated according to the following formula: state aid equals a district's adequacy budget amount less the district's local fair share amount to which the district's amount of categorical aid is added (New Jersey Department of Education, 2007, p. 25).

However, the SFRA rescinded many of the court-mandated remedies such as requiring Abbott districts to have spending parity with affluent districts while it increased the "fair share" or expected local tax revenues from the Abbott districts. The local share attributed to Abbott districts under SFRA is nearly double what they currently raise in local taxes. This provision overrides the court's requirement that increases in local revenues be limited due to high levels of municipal overburden in these districts. (Goertz & Weiss, 2009, p. 31)

Thus, Abbott districts received less equalization aid because the SFRA required an increased local fair share even though Abbott districts were prevented from levying the necessary amount of property taxes to raise their local fair share beyond a four percent increase (Goertz & Weiss, 2009, p. 31).

Although the SFRA benefited most low- and middle-income non-Abbott districts but only if these districts increased their local property tax levies by the four percent state maximum, most high-income districts with DFG code I or J lost aid especially "categorical aid for special needs students" because of SFRA's wealth equalizing (Goertz & Weiss, 2009, p. 32). The New Jersey Supreme Court ruled in *Abbott XX*, 2009, that the "SFRA provides the appropriate 'measuring stick' against which to gauge the resources needed to achieve a thorough and efficient education for every child in the state" (Goertz & Weiss, 2009, p. 35).

New York State School Tax Relief (NYSTAR) program

The New York State school finance formula resembles the SFRA in terms of the ways it distributes aid: flat grants, wealth-equalized aid, and effort or expense-based aid. Wealth equalized aid is distributed by the state "in inverse proportion to local fiscal capacity to offset dramatic differences in the ability of school districts to raise local revenues" and in terms of an equalized per-pupil amount while expense-based aid is based on the state share of a district's actual approved spending (University of the State of New York & The New York State Education Department, 2010, p. 9).

Although flat per-pupil grants distribute the same amount of state aid per-pupil in every district and this aid is not wealth equalized while lump-sum grants are distributed progressively based on a district's total property value and income, the New York school finance formula's aid relies on a foundation amount. Total foundation aid equals selected foundation aid (i.e., a district's foundation aid per-pupil but not less than $500) times selected Total Aidable Foundation Pupil Units (TAFPU) (University of the State of New York & The New York State Education Department, 2010, p. 21). This aid is based on the cost of providing general education services, compared to the instructional costs of a theoretically successful school district, and is adjusted annually for the percentage increase in the consumer price index (CPI) (University of the State of New York & The New York State Education Department, 2010, p. 21).

The New York State School Tax Relief (NYSTAR) program (1997), enacted as the New York State Real Property Tax Law, is a school property tax rebate program. NYSTAR is designed to lower local school property taxes and the tax price of school property taxes to cause TPSDs to increase their spending and, thereby, the level of the educational programs and services that they provide. NYSTAR provides New York's homeowners with a partial exemption of a portion of their school property taxes that is levied only on owner-occupied primary residences. The school district will continue to receive the same amount of property tax revenue because New York State reimburses the district to make up for what would be otherwise lost revenue because of the rebate if the district maintains the existing tax rate.

The NYSTAR program has two types of exemptions: Basic NYSTAR and Enhanced NYSTAR. Basic NYSTAR is available for owner-occupied, primary residences where the owner's total income is less than $500,000. Basic NYSTAR works by exempting the first $30,000 of the full value of a home from school taxes. Enhanced NYSTAR provides an increased benefit for the primary residences of senior citizens (age 65 and older) with qualifying incomes. For qualifying seniors, Enhanced NYSTAR exempts the first $60,100 of the full value of their home from school taxes. (New York State Department of Taxation and Finance, 2011, p. 1).

Baker (2011b) concludes that NYSTAR aid is allocated inequitably and disproportionately benefits New York State's affluent school districts:

1. STAR aid is allocated to the more affluent downstate school districts.

2. STAR aid, by reducing the price to local homeowners of raising an additional dollar in taxes to their schools, encouraged increased local spending on schools.
3. When the relative efficiency of school districts is measured in terms of increases in measured test scores, given additional dollars spent, STAR aid appears to have encouraged less efficient spending. STAR aid enabled affluent suburban districts to spend on other things not directly associated with measured outcomes, but things those communities still desired for their schools.
4. STAR aid contributes to inequities across districts in a system that is already highly inequitable (p. 3).

The homeowner's property value is reduced by the amount of the NYSTAR exemption and divided by the state's equalization rate (Coffin & Cooper, 2017).

New York State's equalization rate equals the ratio of the homeowner's total assessed property value less the NYSTAR exemption divided by the homeowner's total market value whereby the district's host municipality determines assessed property values and New York State determines market values. Thus, NYSTAR is a state funded school property tax exemption that makes NYSTAR a state school financial aid program.

Foundation Aid

A district's foundation aid equals its foundation amount times the Pupil Need Index (PNI) times the Regional Cost Index (RCI) combined, less its expected minimum local contribution or what is referred to as the local fair share in New Jersey. The RCI reflects regional variations in purchasing power around New York State based on the wages of non-school professionals. The PNI reflects the costs of providing extra time and help for disadvantaged and special needs students to succeed. PNI equals one plus the district's Extraordinary Needs (EN) percentage and ranges between one and two. The PNI adjustments are based on a school district's concentrations of at-risk and disadvantaged students (University of the State of New York & The New York State Education Department, 2010, pp. 21–22).

The expected minimum local contribution is the amount that a district is expected to raise on its own and spend as its share of the total cost of general education, which equals the lesser of the two following calculations.

- The selected actual value per-pupil times a tax factor of 0.0137 times income per-pupil relative to the state average, which is capped between 0.65 and 2.00.

- The district's foundation amount times its PNI times its RCI all together times one minus its Foundation Aid State Sharing Ratio.

The foundation aid state sharing ratio compares a district's wealth measures to the state average wealth measures. It is computed by calculating the district's Combined Wealth Ratio (CWR) that is a measure of the district's fiscal capacity.

Combined Wealth Ratio

A district's CWR is calculated by multiplying a district's actual property value per-pupil and dividing that amount by $564,900, which is multiplied by 0.50. This amount is added to the total of the district's per-pupil income, which is divided by $177,200 and multiplied by 0.50 (University of the State of New York & The New York State Education Department, 2010, pp. 24–27). The state sharing ratio is the state aid to local fiscal capacity ratio that is inversely related to a district's wealth as compared to the state average and this ratio is multiplied by 1.05 only for high need/resource capacity districts (University of the State of New York & The New York State Education Department, 2010, p. 25).

APPLYING STATE SCHOOL FINANCE FORMULAE

Many states begin calculating state aid by determining a baseline foundation amount. New Jersey and New York are no exceptions. The New Jersey school finance formula, SFRA, distributes aid to school districts primarily by applying a foundation formula. Aid calculations are based on a per-pupil adequacy budget developed by the state that represents what the state believes each district should spend to provide the level of education necessary for its students to meet or exceed the state's educational standards as contained in the CCCS.

Although the New York State school finance formula seems conceptually simple, its structure is complex, which makes understanding and applying the formula challenging, especially in terms of providing an equitable distribution of state aid. Most of New York's state aid is determined by a statewide formula that calculates a foundation aid amount for each district.

SFRA Weighting

The SFRA applies weighting coefficients in calculating per-pupil baseline state aid to account for the high-need high-cost-to-educate students especially those living in poverty and with special needs. The weights are multiplied by the number of students who qualify for each of the need categories within the district and by a regional cost adjustment factor that is like New York State's calculation. The per-pupil baseline amount reflects the cost to educate a typical elementary school student and has a weighting factor of one. The weights increase for students enrolled in middle, high, and vocational school as well as for those students living in poverty.

A district's adequacy budget is funded by local property taxes and state revenues. A district's local fair share is the amount the formula dictates that the district must contribute toward funding its adequacy budget. The local fair share is based on the formula's calculation of a district's total income and property values or wealth as compared to those measures for other districts statewide, which resembles the calculations of the New York school finance formula for similar components.

The New Jersey school finance formula equalizes property values, personal income, and local property tax burdens by calculating state aid based on the wealth and the local fair share of the district (Coffin & Cooper, 2017). The formula deducts a district's local fair share from its adequacy budget level to determine the amount of state aid that the district receives, which is referred to as the district's equalization aid. However, a district only receives state equalization aid if its local fair share is less than its adequacy budget and it receives no state equalization aid if its local fair share is greater than its adequacy budget.

The SFRA compares a district's current spending level with its per-pupil adequacy budget. Although a district may spend more than its adequacy budget amount, state aid increases are capped at 10% for districts spending more than their adequacy budgets as compared to a 20% cap on those districts that are under spending their adequacy budgets. The formula requires a district to increase its property tax levies if it is falling short of providing its local fair share (Coffin & Cooper, 2017).

A district that over-spends its adequacy budget amount and whose local property tax revenues exceed its adequacy budget is subject to a two percent giveback provision (Coffin, 2021; Coffin & Cooper, 2017). In this case, the district is required to apply the amount of its state aid increase that exceeds two percent toward local property tax relief. But districts that are under-spending their adequacy budgets are not subject to the two percent giveback provision.

The New Jersey school finance formula has a disproportionately high threshold for districts to receive state aid especially categorical aid for students who are free-or-reduced-price-lunch-eligible (i.e., FRPL), special education, LEP, ELL, economically-disadvantaged, or otherwise at-risk, which results in a higher local fair share calculation. In addition, the SFRA's use of income in the calculation of a district's local fair share and measure of wealth distorts state aid distributions because it disadvantages districts that are income-rich relative to the state average for income but property-poor relative to the state average of equalized property valuation (Coffin, 2021; Coffin & Cooper, 2017).

Expected Minimum Local Contribution

A New York district's foundation aid consists of the cost of educating a pupil based on the Adjusted Foundation and the cost to the district based on the Expected Minimum Local Contribution (EMLC). New York State uses these components to equalize state aid based on a district's wealth and per-pupil need. The New York State Education Department (NYSED) analyzes the general and special education costs in theoretically successful school districts to calculate a district's foundation aid amount that approximates the average per-pupil cost of typical successful school districts' educational instruction.

Foundation aid is based on an enrollment measure called the Average Daily Membership (ADM). ADM is the maximum possible daily attendance of all students in a district divided by the number of days in which the district's schools operate (Coffin & Cooper, 2017). The foundation aid amount is calculated by using two measures of enrollment: TAFPU and Total Wealth Foundation Pupil Units (TWFPU). TAFPU is a weighted pupil count that is used to calculate the Adjusted Foundation.

The NYSED uses different coefficients for varying enrollments and types of students' needs such as 1.41 for students with disabilities, 0.50 for students declassified from special education, and 0.12 for students attending summer school. TWFPU is a weighted per-pupil amount that is used to calculate the EMLC to determine a district's relative wealth. TWFPU equals the district's students' ADM including half-day kindergarten students weighted at 0.5 plus the full-time equivalent number of resident students attending other TPSDs less the district's number of non-resident students and special education students attending BOCES.

A New York TPSD's Adjusted Foundation is the formulaic calculation of the estimated cost of educating a student in a theoretically successful school district that is adjusted for the costs of unique student needs by applying the Pupil Need Index (PNI). In addition, the Adjusted Foundation is adjusted for regional cost differences by applying the Regional Cost Index (RCI). A district's EMLC is the portion of the district's total educational cost that is funded by the district according to the state's formula. The EMLC is based on several wealth factors including the Income Wealth Index (IWI) that is based on a district's adjusted gross income for the calendar year per TWFPU and is multiplied by the state Adjusted Statewide Average School Tax Rate.

IWI is a district's average income per-student compared to the statewide average income per-student. The IWI is neither below 0.65 nor above 2.00. The IWI is flawed because the formula treats those districts whose IWI is less than 0.65 as if their IWI equaled 0.65 because the formula does not allow the IWI to fall below 0.65. Thus, the poorest districts in the state lose aid because of this flaw in the IWI.

In addition, the RCI is not as robust as New Jersey's Geographic Cost of Education Index (GCEI). This causes many of the state's poorest districts to lose aid that they would otherwise receive if the GCEI were used instead. A district's EMLC is subtracted from its gross foundation aid amount after the gross foundation aid amount is multiplied by the RCI and PNI. A district's EMLC equals a loss of state aid based on the district's wealth relative to other districts in the state.

The foundation aid amount or the baseline state aid incorporates several pupil-need-based expenditure adjustments. A district's foundation aid amount is adjusted for such factors as its per-pupil need and number of pupils living in poverty. Pupil need is determined by the PNI, which is based on a district's poverty and census data. PNI calculates a district's number of students with extraordinary needs such as those who are free-or-reduced-price-lunch eligible (i.e., FRPL), ELL, LEP, or meet the Census' poverty requirements because they are poor as well as ages five to seventeen.

Duncombe and Yinger (2004, "Cost Indexes," para. 2) use a two-year average of the number of students who qualify for free-or-reduced-price-lunches because this "variable fluctuates from year to year," meet the Census' poverty requirements, and are ages five to seventeen. Duncombe and Yinger (2004) explain the distinctions among the two primary measures of a student's economic disadvantage: qualifying for a free-or-reduced-price-lunch (i.e., FRPL) and living in poverty aged five to seventeen as well as having LEP.

The Census poverty variable cannot be manipulated by school officials, but it is not available every year, it is often excluded from data bases maintained by state education departments, and there is no evidence about its accuracy in years not covered by a census (Coffin, 2021; Coffin & Cooper, 2017). The subsidized lunch variable has the advantages that it is available every year, is included in many state data bases, and covers a broader population than does the poverty variable. This variable has the disadvantage, however, that it reflects parental participation decisions, and perhaps even school management policies.

Another difference between the two variables arises when another measure of student disadvantage, the share of students with limited English proficiency (LEP), is added to the cost model (Duncombe & Yinger, 2004, "Cost Indexes," para. 4). Although the LEP variable is significant in models that include the census poverty variable, it is not significant in models that include the FRPL variable. Thus, in the case of New York, the FRPL variable captures the cost effects of poverty and of LEP (Duncombe & Yinger, 2004, "Cost Indexes," paras. 3–4).

Although the percentage of FRPL-eligible students is commonly used to indicate a school district's poverty level or need, New York State's formula does not provide aid to offset the full cost of students participating in the FRPL program. Thus, property-tax-poor or low-income districts receive disproportionately less state aid.

School Tax Relief (STAR) Program

New York's foundation aid amount, which is provided at a given level of per-pupil need, shows that many more districts are receiving a great deal more aid than those with the same level of need. This indicates that the distribution of foundation aid is regressive. Baker (2011a) discusses the New York State school finance formula's inequitable distribution of aid:

> Like many state funding formulas, even though the first (and most logical) iteration of calculations for estimating the district state share of funding would end up providing 0% state aid to many districts, those formulas include a floor of funding—minimum guarantee of state aid.

This is the effect of New York State's minimum threshold factor on foundation aid. State share hits 0 at an income/wealth index around 1.0 in the basic calculation. First, between income/wealth ratios of about 1.0 to 2.0, the actual state share cuts the corner providing more gradually declining aid rather than going straight to 0. Then, above IWI of 2.0 it never hits 0, but rather levels off providing a minimum allotment of several hundred to about $1,000 per-pupil to even the wealthiest districts in the state (e.g., among the wealthiest in the nation).

Many state aid formulas include a variety of other types of aid, some that are distributed in flat amounts across all districts regardless of need, and some that may be even allocated in inverse proportion to what most would consider needs—either local capacity related needs or educational programming and student needs. Such is the politics of school finance.

New York State's *pièce de résistance* is a program called STAR, or School Tax Relief program. In simple terms, STAR provides state aid in disproportionate amounts to wealthy communities to support property tax relief.

> Excluding STAR aid to NYC, the aid program in 2008–09 provided $642 million in aid to districts with an income/wealth ratio over 1.0. Note that our recent report on school funding fairness . . . identified New York State (along

with Illinois and Pennsylvania) as having one of the most regressively financed systems in the nation. On average, low poverty districts have greater state and local revenue than higher poverty ones, yet the state is still allocating significant sums of aid to low poverty districts! . . . many of these wealthier communities are picking up millions in STAR aid and upwards to a thousand dollars per-pupil in basic foundation aid. Yes, the state is subsidizing the spending—quite significantly—of some of the wealthiest districts in the nation, while maintaining a regressive system as a whole. (Baker, 2011b, pp. 5–8)

New York State's distribution of foundation aid is highly regressive.

New York's formula uses a district's CWR, which is the ratio of a district's per-pupil income and property wealth to the state average for each variable that is calculated to determine a district's wealth relative to other districts. The New York formula uses CWR to wealth equalize district state aid. The CWR not only measures a district's wealth but also determines a district's ability to fund its school system relative to other districts in the state. An average wealth district will have a CWR equal to a value of one while more affluent districts will have a CWR greater than one and poor districts will have a CWR less than one.

The CWR determines a district's sharing ratio that is included within the calculation of a district's foundation aid, is the proportion of the State's aid contribution, and equals the formula of one minus the district's wealth measure (i.e., CWR) divided by the state average times the district's local contribution percentage. Although CWR measures a district's wealth using the actual valuation of the district's property and income, it does not fully account for unusual circumstances or fluctuations in a district's property valuation or income such as during times when the state averages for property wealth and income decrease while the district's wealth and income remain unchanged. This would cause the district's CWR to increase relative to the state averages causing the district to receive less state aid despite the district's property wealth and income (e.g., IRS reported income) levels remaining the same.

New York's state aid as well as the distribution of district property wealth and income relative to the respective state averages for wealth and income as compared to the measures of student need and poverty shows that the amount of combined state and local revenues funding high student need high-per-pupil-cost-to-educate or poverty school districts is disproportionately less than the total revenues funding low poverty or affluent school districts. These disparities in the distribution of state aid cause inequities in the provision of a quality education across school districts.

New York's distribution of state aid is regressive because it does not effectively equalize wealth or income among school districts. The NYSTAR aid program is the antithesis of an equitable state aid distribution system based on property wealth and income equalization. The New York State school finance formula causes large, urban, poor school districts to receive significantly less state aid than they would have otherwise received with a progressive distribution.

CONCLUSION

Although New Jersey and New York's school funding formulae are largely the result of years of litigation brought primarily by members and representatives of disadvantaged students and schools, the formulae for these states have adequacy as their goal. The SFRA and the New York school finance formula are similar in terms of the types of aid the state distributes such as foundation, wealth equalization, categorical, and specific adjustment aid. Both states use formulaic standards as the barometer against which to determine whether a district is meeting its adequacy requirements as established by the state school funding formula. New Jersey compares a district's educational outcomes to the Core Curriculum Content Standards (CCCS) while New York State uses the Regents Learning Standards.

However, components of New Jersey and New York's formulae can be politically manipulated such as New Jersey's cost indices and its formulaic restrictions on the Abbott districts' equalization aid. Several of these manipulations manifest in the SFRA's provisions that require the Abbott districts to raise their required local fair share despite the state preventing the Abbott districts from levying the necessary amount of property taxes to raise their local fair share beyond a four percent increase, which reduces state aid for the Abbott districts (Goertz & Weiss, 2009, p. 31). The SFRA raises the threshold that defines the level of need especially for students who are at-risk or otherwise disadvantaged, which contributes to a reduction of aid especially for large, urban, poor districts because these districts typically have disproportionately high levels of special needs students.

Theoretically, the SFRA's local fair share calculation is designed to compel districts to adopt the state average equalized property tax rate to equalize property wealth statewide and establish equalized district property values as the basis for a district's ability to fund its school system based on local property taxes. However, the SFRA uses a district's income and equalized property values as the primary measures of a district's ability to fund its local schools when it calculates a district's local fair share. The SFRA's reliance on income in the calculation of a district's local fair share and measure of wealth shifts the distribution of aid disproportionately away from districts having lower income but higher assessed property values as compared to the state averages for each variable.

Thus, the SFRA determines that these districts are artificially wealthier than their actual level of resources and calculates a disproportionately higher local fair share for these districts than would be otherwise the case if a district's equalized property values were the only measure of a district's ability to fund its local schools. This reinforces inequities in the state equalized property assessments and the overreliance on local property taxes stemming from inadequate tax bases as the primary basis for funding local school systems that undergird the SFRA's aid calculations.

New York's foundation funding is generated by the state aid formula as derived from an adequacy calculation based upon a successful school district model. Funding gaps in the adequacy of educational inputs result in concomitant gaps in student achievement and educational outcomes especially in underfunded and large, urban, poor school districts in New Jersey and especially in New York State.

Although New Jersey and New York's courts have frequently declared their state's formula for financing its public schools unconstitutional, each state's educational mission is to enable its public schools to provide at least an adequate education to all students statewide. As a result of many court rulings, New Jersey and New York State have struggled with how best to define the content of an adequate education, calculate formulaically the level of spending necessary to provide an adequate education based on the unique needs, costs, and resources of each district, and the appropriate measures of educational outcomes to determine whether a district is achieving its adequacy goals.

In response to the many court rulings on their state school finance formulae, New Jersey and New York State use a foundation aid approach that establishes a targeted district spending level that the state deems necessary to meet state adequacy goals. In addition, both states subsidize to the extent that a district's local fair share or local minimum contribution is below the state formula's respective minimum target level. In this way, both states attempt to address the disparities and inequities in school district spending and funding that stem primarily from differences in local property tax bases and revenues.

Achieving educational adequacy means enabling all students within a state to meet or exceed the state's educational outcome standards. Although defining educational adequacy in this way establishes a benchmark, the major obstacles preventing New Jersey and New York State from accomplishing this goal are found in the ways in which each state's school finance formula is structured, interpreted, and implemented especially in New York State. The problems inherent in each state's school finance formula could result in the following:

In the aggregate, a state's education system could be deemed adequate merely on the basis that a sufficient number of students overall achieve an adequate educational outcome—for example, 80% of all students, statewide scoring proficient or higher on state assessments. That is, adequacy, in isolation means only that a sufficient number of students perform sufficiently well, regardless of who may or may not be left out and regardless of the extent that some children far exceed the "adequacy" threshold. Significant equity concerns may arise when statewide adequacy is the exclusive focus.

At the intersection of *educational adequacy* and *equal opportunity* lies the notion that all children, regardless of their individual differences or where they attend school in a state are deserving of *equal opportunity* to achieve *adequate* educational outcomes.

Where *equal educational opportunity* provides that each child have equal opportunity to achieve any given set of outcomes, *equal opportunity* linked with *adequacy* provides that each child have equal opportunity to achieve a specific set of adequate educational outcomes. (Baker, 2011b)

New York State and New Jersey school finance formulae share a common flaw that adversely and disproportionately affects those students attending the state's large, urban, poor, or socio-economically disadvantaged school districts. Although New Jersey and New York State apply their state school funding formulae to achieve statewide TPSD adequacy and equalized funding, the flaw causes states most likely to provide an inadequate education for those students who are most in need of a quality education. Thus, high-need high-cost-to-educate primarily poor students will lack the quality of education necessary to succeed in today's knowledge-based society and economy.

REFERENCES

Baker, B. D., Green, P., & Richards, C. E. (2008). *Financing education systems.* Pearson Education, Inc.

Baker, B.D. (2011a, February 4). Where's the pork? Mitigating the damage of state aid cuts [Web log post]. Retrieved from *http://www.schoolfinance101.wordpress.com*.

Baker, B.D. (2011b, April 6). Distilling rhetoric & research on NY State education spending [Web log post]. Retrieved from *http://www.schoolfinance101.wordpress.com*.

Chambers, J. G., Levin, J. D., & Parrish, T. B. (2006). Examining the relationship between educational outcomes and gaps in funding: An extension of the New York Adequacy Study. *American Institutes for Research, 81*(21), 1–32.

Coffin, S. V. (Ed.) (2021). *Higher education's looming collapse: Using new ways of doing business and social justice to avoid bankruptcy.* Rowman & Littlefield.

Coffin, S. V., & Cooper, B. S. (Eds.) (2017). *Sound school finance for educational excellence.* Rowman & Littlefield.

Coffin, S. V., & Cooper, B. S. (Eds.) (2018). *District financial leadership today: Educational excellence tomorrow.* Rowman & Littlefield.

Duncombe, W. D., & Yinger, J. (2004). *How much does a disadvantaged student cost?* Syracuse, New York: Center for Policy Research, Maxwell School of Citizenship and Public Affairs, Syracuse University. Retrieved from http:/www.surface.syr.edu/cpr/103.

Firestone, W. A., Goertz, M. E., & Natriello, G. (1997). *From cashbox to classroom: The struggle for fiscal reform and educational change in New Jersey.* Teachers College Press.

Fusarelli, B. C., & Cooper, B. S. (Eds.) (2009). *The rising state: How state power is transforming our nation's schools.* SUNY Press.

Goertz, M. E., & Edwards, M. (1999). In search of excellence for all: The courts and New Jersey school finance reform. *Journal of Education Finance, 25*(1), 5–32.

Goertz, M. E., & Weiss, M. (2009). *Assessing success in school finance litigation: The case of New Jersey.* Columbia University Press.

Ladson-Billings, G. (2006). From the achievement gap to the education debt: Understanding achievement in U.S. schools." *Educational Researcher 35*(7) 3–12.

Ladson-Billings, G. (2009). Just what is critical race theory and what's it doing in a nice field like education? In E. Taylor, D. Gillborn, & G. Ladson-Billings (Eds.), *Foundations of Critical Race Theory in Education* (pp. 17–36).

New Jersey Department of Education (2007). *A formula for success: All children, all communities*, New Jersey Department of Education.

New York State Constitution, Article XI, Sec. 1.

New York State Department of Taxation and Finance (2011). *STAR—New York State's school tax relief Program.* New York Office of Real Property Tax Services. Retrieved from http://www.orps.state.ny.us/star/faq.htm.

Rebell, M. A. (2002). Educational adequacy, democracy, and the courts. In T. Ready, C. Edley, Jr., & C. E. Snow (Eds.), National Research Council, *Achieving high educational standards for all: Conference summary* (pp. 218–268). The National Academies Press.

Reock, E. C. Jr. (2007). *Estimated financial impact of the "freeze" of state aid on New Jersey school districts, 2002–03 to 2005–06.* Institute on Education Law and Policy, Rutgers University. Retrieved from http:/www./ielp.rutgers.edu/docs/CEIFA_Reock_Final.pdf.

Robinson v. Cahill, 303 A.2d 273 (1973).

Rundquist, J., & Calefati, J. (2011, March 23). Judge slams Christie's cuts to school aid. *The Star-Ledger*, p. 1.

Sciarra, D. G. (2008). *Certification of Dr. Ernest C. Reock, Jr. for the Supreme Court of New Jersey in support of the plaintiffs' opposition to the School Funding Reform Act of 2008.* New Jersey Education Law Center. Retrieved from http://www.edlawcenter.org/ELCPublic/elcnews_080521_Reock_Certification.pdf.

Shrader, D. W. (2007). Morse, Yinger, and the campaign for fiscal equity: School finance reform in New York. *Educational Change, 75*, Spring 2005–2007.

University of the State of New York & The New York State Education Department (2010). *State aid to schools: A primer pursuant to laws of 2010*. New York State Education Department.

PART III

Inequities in Human Resources

Chapter 5

Teachers

Adopting a Culturally Grounded Asset-Based Mindset

Corinne Brion

Learners are diverse. Age, gender, sexual orientation, socioeconomic status, physical and mental abilities, language, race, ethnicity, and creed embody cultural diversity (Gardiner & Enomoto, 2006). Diversity provides richness to PK-12 schools because learners bring their cultures with them. Cultural diversity benefits students because they experience higher learning outcomes, improve their cognitive skills, broaden their thinking, and increase their intercultural and cross-racial knowledge. Cultural diversity augments learners' empathy (Boske et al., 2017) and prepares them for employment in the global economy (Wells et al., 2016).

Increased diversity can create challenges for teachers and leaders. When teachers are unprepared to embrace and work with learners from different cultures, students can struggle academically and have higher rates of disciplinary issues while teachers can become exasperated and discouraged and families feel excluded (Wells et al., 2016). Adopting pedagogies and teaching approaches that are culturally grounded is crucial for our public schools that are serving an increasingly diverse student population (Riehl, 2000).

By 2050, the United States is forecast to become a minority majority nation with less than half of the population being non-Hispanic White (Marx, 2002). Boske et al. (2017) contend that by 2042 "communities of color will become the majority of the U.S. population with Latino and black populations comprising 45% of the 2060 U.S. population" (p. 361). Despite this diversity, scholars affirm that American schools are more segregated today than ever before (Benson & Fiarman, 2019; Kendi, 2019; Love, 2019; Singleton,

2014). Love (2019) asserts that segregation always existed because education was founded on white supremacy, anti-Blackness, and sexism. Specifically, Love suggests that "education is anchored in white rage" (p. 22). Yeskel (2008) maintains that educational systems mirror and reinforce pre-existing social status inequalities.

The author suggests that schools are segregated by their physical locations because school funding is based on property taxes. In many American cities, it is not unusual for a river or another natural boundary to separate the schools in desirable neighborhoods from the "failing schools" located in less preferred areas, where the value of properties is low. These funding inequities are accentuated when students and teachers have fewer resources. The disparities contribute to a culture of poverty among staff, teachers, and community members. Segregation can manifest itself within teaching approaches. Many educators adhere to traditional Western and Eurocentric pedagogical approaches (Hamm et al., 2016; Sue, 2015). Sue (2015) refers to this tendency as ethnocentric monoculturalism in which the curriculum represents one culture only, the White American culture and frame of reference.

To serve all students equitably, there is an urgent need for curricula and professional development (PD) that assist teachers and leaders gain an asset-based and culturally proficient mindset (Hamm, 2009; Lindsey et al., 2018). Culturally responsive teaching allows for all cultures to be recognized, embraced, valued, and celebrated. This inclusive approach stresses the need to advocate for the self-worth students bring to school rather than focusing on their families' net worth (Yeskel, 2008).

Culture and Learning

Lindsey et al. (2018) define culture as "everything you believe and everything you do that enables you to identify with people who are like you and that distinguishes you from people who differ from you" (p. 29). Love (2019) asserts that "culture reflects the educational, social, economic, political, and spiritual conditions of people" (p. 128). Influential social learning theorists explore the centrality of culture on learning (Bandura & McClelland, 1977; Vygotsky, 1962). According to these scholars, teaching and learning are social and cultural activities.

Vygotsky (1962) believes that learning occurs through social interaction and that culture affects the way we think. For Vygotsky, language is a cultural tool and a language's unique features can influence how we think and learn. Vygotsky uses the example of a speaker of a language that has different forms of address depending on social position (such as *vous* versus *tu* in French), who probably has a slightly different way of thinking about status and social position than a speaker of a language (such as English) that does not recognize this distinction.

Like Vygotsky (1962), Bandura and McClelland (1977) posit that culture affects learning and learners learn best by observing, imitating, and modeling behaviors from their social environment and culture. Freire (2000) explores the critical role culture plays in the learning process. Freire maintains that ignoring the richness that diverse students bring to the classroom keeps them oppressed. As an example, a student from the Republic of Congo, who grew up only using oral languages, will learn better using stories, songs, and dancing. For this student, being tested in writing will be extremely difficult, defeating, isolating, and perhaps traumatic.

Correspondingly, a newcomer from Kuwait who reads right to left may have a challenging time reading left to right in a timely manner while adapting to new cultural norms. Freire (2000) contends that educators should use student-centered methods as the basis of their teaching and learning approach. The merits of this approach include that students and teachers continuously learn from each other. For this co-learning to happen, students and teachers must understand that they bring their own view of the world to their learning and that their worldview is based on their culture, experiences, social class, gender, and other dimensions.

Freire believes that cultural invasion occurs when teachers, leaders, or students impose their own view of the world on others, inhibiting creativity and learning. Cultural invasion is a form of oppression. Cultural invasion occurs when educators, curriculum, policies, and practices impose their White middle-class values on students from different cultural backgrounds. This lack of cultural mindedness enlarges the achievement gap and contributes to higher drop-out rates for students belonging to certain groups such as refugees or ELL students (Blanchard & Muller, 2015; Kanu, 2008; Lindsey et al., 2018).

Schools represent the diversity of our communities. Consequently, to improve learning for all students, earn a meaningful return on investment, and create socially just educational systems schools must value students' cultures and adopt a culturally grounded asset-based mindset.

Adopting a Culturally Grounded Asset-Based Mindset

The United States' demographic profile is becoming more racially and ethnically diverse (Lindsey et al., 2018). Yosso (2005) and Moll et al. (1992) posit that diverse communities nurture cultural wealth and knowledge. Yosso (2005) asserts that communities of color provide cultural wealth through six forms of capital:

1. aspirational
2. linguistic
3. familial
4. social
5. navigational
6. resistant

These capitals build on one another to create a community's cultural wealth.

Aspirational capital pertains to the ability to hope when being confronted by difficulties. Linguistic capital refers to the intellectual, social, and communication skills gained by speaking more than one language. Familial capital deals with community spirit, collectivistic culture, and the belief that families nurture and maintain connections with the community as well as educate.

Social capital is the networks of people and community resources that provide emotional support. Navigational capital is knowing how to maneuver through social institutions, including structures that are inherently biased against people of color. Resistant capital is the knowledge and skills necessary to challenge inequities and transform oppressive structures.

When students and adults learn from each other by having genuine conversations with people from different backgrounds, experiences, and belief systems, people better understand each other's cultures. As a result, people alter their mindsets and frames of reference. However, when people do not know and do not seek to know, deficit mindsets form. Considering students' funds of knowledge and cultural wealth is the essence of culturally responsive teaching.

Culturally Responsive Teaching

Scholars study the importance of learners' cultures to improve teaching, learning, and well-being with culturally responsive pedagogy and teaching or culturally sustaining pedagogies (Gay, 2013; Hammond, 2014; Ladson-Billings, 2005; Paris & Alim, 2017; Villegas and Lucas, 2002). Knowledge is a socially constructed process that cannot be divorced from the learners' social contexts because across cultures people have different ways of communicating, interacting, and learning. Thus, learning is enhanced when educators understand cultural differences (Lindsey et al., 2018).

Culturally responsive pedagogy (CRP) has existed for over 20 years (Gay, 2013; Ladson-Billings, 1995, 2005). The premise of CRP is that our culture is central to teaching and learning and therefore, teaching and learning differ across cultures (Gay, 2010). CRP presents information in ways that learners can connect to their natural way of learning (Rychly & Graves, 2012). Ladson-Billings (1995) asserts that CRP rests on three propositions:

1. Students must experience success.
2. Students must develop or maintain cultural competence.
3. Students must develop a critical consciousness through which they challenge the status-quo of the social order.

CRP is "using the cultural characteristics, experiences, and perspectives of ethnically diverse students as conduits for teaching them more effectively" (Gay, 2002, p. 106).

According to Villegas and Lucas (2002), those characteristics include language, communication styles, learning styles, relationships, norms, values, and traditions. The authors propose that teachers who use culturally responsive pedagogy must gain sociocultural awareness, develop respect to different ways of interacting, interrupt inequitable practices, and seek ways to build strong relationships based on trust with students (Bryk & Schneider, 2003).

Educators who embrace CRP are equitable, caring, empathetic, and reflect about other cultures as well as their own. They can question their frames of reference to widen their perspectives, which promotes socially just teaching (Rychly & Graves, 2012). Hammond (2014) explores culturally responsive teaching and the brain (CRT). She describes the brain as the hardware and culture the software that programs it. According to Hammond, our cultural values program our brain to interpret the world around us. As a result, educators must create environments that the brain perceives as safe and nurturing so it can relax, let go of stress, and focus on learning. For this to happen, educators must use cultural aids that are aligned with the cultural norms and values of their learners.

CRT is not a spray and pray approach that spurts culture only during Black history month or international women's day. Rather, CRT refers to a multidimensional, student centered approach that promotes equitable excellence and serves to validate the experiences and contributions of students from various cultures and backgrounds (Hammond, 2014). Culturally responsive teaching values multilingualism because students and teachers seek to acquire knowledge about cultural diversity (Gay, 2013).

CRT focuses on reducing the achievement gap for marginalized students such as students of color and English Language Learners among others. CRT considers cultural archetypes such as individualism versus collectivism, and oral versus written culture. Some cultures are collectivistic and work best as a group (e.g., African nations). In these nations, group interdependence is critical; in-class group work or activities such as debates work very well with collectivistic cultures (Brion, in press-b). In addition, some African languages are not written, so while a student may be multilingual, he/she may experience difficulties writing.

Understanding cultural archetypes enables educators to choose curriculum and activities that reflect the cultural diversity of the school community (Nordmeyer et al., 2021). Teachers can modify expectations and facilitate strategies. For example, a refugee student with an oral native language, who just arrived in the United States, would learn best through stories, dances, and metaphors rather than completing worksheets.

Culturally responsive teachers create a safe classroom climate and environment in which every student's culture is considered. They understand how the brain works and that if a student is forced to learn in a way that is counter-cultural, the part of the brain that protects them from danger—the amygdala—will activate and their focus will be staying safe rather than learning. Culturally responsive teachers scaffold the learning, provide on-going, quality feedback, and use formative assessments. They collect and desegregate data frequently. They are willing to learn about cultural differences, their biases, and are willing to reflect and engage in critical conversations about biases and eager to widen their frames of reference.

In the Silenced Dialogue, Delpit (1988) tells the story of a student who was sharpening his pencil in class. The teacher asked him, "would you like to sit down?" to which the student responded: "no!" The student was sent to the principal's office for being defiant only to find out that the student merely answered the question the teacher had asked him. In his culture, a command would be expressed as "Please, go sit down."

Sue (2016) tells the story of a White elementary teacher in Nigeria. This story illustrates how some cultures regard the world linearly while others view it more imaginatively and creatively.

> Teacher: There are four blackbirds sitting on a tree. You take a slingshot and kill one of them. How many are left?
>
> White U.S. student (raising hand excitedly): Teacher, teacher, I know the answer! This is too easy . . . four takes away one is three!
>
> Nigerian student (interrupting): No, no, no . . . that's not right teacher! The answer is zero! (p. 67).
>
> Teacher (puzzled): I am afraid that is the wrong answer. Four takes away one is three.

Sue (2016) posits that using an empirical and linear framework the American student would be correct. However, the Nigerian student operated from an experiential reality and lived experience. To him if you "shoot one bird, the others aren't stupid enough to stay around. They will all fly away" (p. 68).

Culturally responsive teachers and leaders are aware of societal biases and systemic systems of oppression that favor specific students and are willing to dismantle these systems (Hammond, 2014). Culturally responsive teachers contribute to promoting learning opportunities regardless of social economic status, race, ethnicity, abilities, gender, sexual orientation, and creed. In doing so, they eradicate the achievement gap defined by Love (2019) as "The achievement gap is not about white students outperforming dark students, it is about a history of injustice and oppression" (p. 92).

Culturally responsive teachers and leaders help to create socially just schools by advocating for differences, recognizing funds of knowledge and cultural wealth, and promoting diversity, equity, and inclusion in the classroom, curriculum, and activities. In doing so, students' talents are recognized and celebrated, achievement increases, and communities flourish. Although all students profit from this culturally grounded asset-based mindset, marginalized students benefit the most because culturally responsive teaching ensures that they are included and valued.

Schools nationwide spend millions of dollars on professional development that has little to no impact on student learning and teacher efficacy (Hess, 2013). Consequently, culturally proficient professional development (CPPD) is necessary (Brion, in press-a). CPPD defines cultural proficiency. CPPD not only puts culture at the center of learning but also facilitates the transfer of learning or the implementation of new knowledge to the classroom, augmenting the return on investment, and improving student learning outcomes irrespective of social economic status, race, gender, or ethnicity. PD for teachers and leaders focuses on culturally responsive teaching strategies to ensure that schools are inclusive and socially just.

REFERENCES

Bandura, A., & McClelland, D. C. (1977). *Social learning theory* (Vol. 1). Prentice Hall.

Benson, T. A., & Fiarman, S. E. (2019). *Unconscious bias in schools: A developmental approach to exploring race and racism.* Harvard Education Press.

Blanchard, S., & Muller, C. (2015). Gatekeepers of the American Dream: How teachers' perceptions shape the academic outcomes of immigrant and language-minority students. *Social Science Research 51*, 262–275.

Boske, C., Osanloo, A., & Newcomb, W. S. (2017). Exploring empathy to promote social justice leadership in schools. *Journal of School Leadership, 27*(3), 361–391.

Brion, C. (forthcoming). Culturally proficient professional development." In S. V. Coffin (Ed.), *Overcoming the educational resource equity gap.* Rowman & Littlefield.

Brion, C. (forthcoming). Culture: The link to learning transfer." *Adult Learning.*

Bryk, A. S., & Schneider, B. (2003). Trust in schools: A core resource for school reform. *Educational Leadership, 60*(6), 40–45.

Delpit, L. (1988). The silenced dialogue: Power and pedagogy in educating other people's children. *Harvard Educational Review, 58*(3), 280–299.

Freire, P. (2000). *Pedagogy of the oppressed.* Bloomsbury Publishing.

Gardiner, M. E., & Enomoto, E. K. (2006). Urban school principals and their role as multicultural leaders. *Urban Education, 41*(6), 560–584.

Gay, G. (2002). Preparing for culturally responsive teaching. *Journal of Teacher Education, 53*(2), 106–116.

Gay, G. (2010). Acting on beliefs in teacher education for cultural diversity. *Journal of Teacher Education, 61*(1–2), 143–152.

Gay, G. (2013). Teaching to and through cultural diversity. *Curriculum Inquiry, 43*(1), 48–70.

Hamm, L. (2009), "I'm just glad I'm here": Stakeholder perceptions from one school in a community undergoing demographic changes on the Alberta grasslands," (unpublished dissertation), University of Calgary.

Hamm, L., Dogurga, S.L., & Scott, A. (2016). Leading a diverse school during times of demographic change in rural Canada: Reflection, action, and suggestions for practice." *Citizenship Teaching & Learning, 11(2),* 211–230.

Hammond, Z. (2014). *Culturally responsive teaching and the brain: Promoting authentic engagement and rigor among culturally and linguistically diverse students.* Corwin.

Hess, F. M. (2013). *Cage-busting leadership.* Harvard Education Press.

Kanu, Y. (2008). Educational needs and barriers for African refugee students in Manitoba. *Canadian Journal of Education, 31*(4), 915–940.

Kendi, I. X. (2019). *How to be an antiracist.* One World.

Ladson-Billings, G. J. (2005). Is the team all right? Diversity and teacher education. *Journal of Teacher Education, 56*(3), 229–234.

Lindsey, R. B., Nuri Robins, K., Terrell, R.D., & Lindsey, D.B. (2018). *Cultural proficiency: A manual for school leaders,* 4th Ed. Corwin.

Love, B. L. (2019). *We want to do more than survive: Abolitionist teaching and the pursuit of educational freedom.* Beacon Press.

Marx, G. (2002). Ten trends: Educating children for tomorrow's world. *Journal of School Improvement, 3*(1), 18–28.

Moll, L. C., Amanti, C., Neff, D., & Gonzalez, N. (1992). Funds of knowledge for teaching: Using a qualitative approach to connect homes and classrooms. *Theory Into Practice, 31*(2), 132–141.

Nordmeyer, J., Boals, T., MacDonald, R., & Westerlund, R. (2021). What does equity really mean for multilingual learners?" *ASCD, 78*(6), 60–65.

Paris, D., & Alim, H. S. (Eds.) (2017). *Culturally sustaining pedagogies: Teaching and learning for justice in a changing world.* Teachers College Press.

Riehl, C. J. (2000). The principal's role in creating inclusive schools for diverse students: A review of normative, empirical, and critical literature on the practice of educational administration. *Review of Educational Research, 70*(1), 55–81.

Rychly, L., & Graves, E. (2012). Teacher characteristics for culturally responsive pedagogy. *Multicultural Perspectives, 14*(1), 44–49.

Singleton, G. E. (2014). *More courageous conversations about race.* Corwin.

Sue, D. W. (2016). *Race talk and the conspiracy of silence: Understanding and facilitating difficult dialogues on race.* John Wiley & Sons.

Tatum, B. D. (1995). Talking about race, learning about racism. *The Black Studies Reader,* 389–412.

Villegas, A. M., & Lucas, T. (2002). Preparing culturally responsive teachers: rethinking the curriculum. *Journal of Teacher Education, 53*(1), 20–32.

Vygotsky, L.S. (1962). *Thought and language.* MIT Press.

Wells, A. S., Fox, L., & Cordova-Cobo, D. (2016, February 9). How racially diverse schools and classrooms can benefit all students. Retrieved from https://tcf.org/content/report/how-racially-diverse-schools-and-classrooms-can-benefit-all-students/?agreed=1.

Yeskel, F. (2008). Coming to class: Looking at education through the lens of class: Introduction to the class and education special issue. *Equity & Excellence in Education, 41*(1), 1–11.

Yosso, T. J. (2005). Whose culture has capital? A critical race theory discussion of community cultural wealth. *Race Ethnicity and Education, 8,* 69–91.

Chapter 6

Culturally Proficient Professional Development

Corinne Brion

THE ROLE OF CULTURE IN LEARNING

Lindsey et al. (2018) define culture as "everything you believe and everything you do that enables you to identify with people who are like you and that distinguishes you from people who differ from you" (p. 29). Learning is a social endeavor and culture affects how we interact and learn. As a result, our culture affects the implementation of knowledge and skills to the workplace, which is known as learning transfer.

Several authors have studied the importance of culture in education with culturally responsive or sustaining teaching or pedagogy (Gay, 2013; Hammond, 2014; Ladson-Billings; 2005; Villegas & Lucas, 2002). However, there is little to no mention of the impact of culture on professional development (PD) and learning transfer. The Culturally Proficient Professional Development (CPPD) framework includes a Multidimensional Model of Learning Transfer (MMLT) that aims to enhance the implementation of newly acquired knowledge. This model is a practical tool that school leaders can use to organize, plan, deliver, and evaluate their PD events to:

1. Increase their return on investment,
2. Improve student learning outcomes, and
3. Enhance teachers' efficacy and well-being.

School leaders are instructional leaders (Fullan, 2002; Marzano et al., 2005). School administrators budget large sums of money to support their teachers with PD events to increase their skills and competencies to raise their students' outcomes and well-being (Guskey, 2002; Hammond, 2014; Speck & Knipe, 2005). Because leaders work with adults from diverse cultures and because culture affects learning, school leaders must understand the role culture plays in PD. School leaders must provide PD that takes culture into consideration to optimize learning and its implementation.

Professional Development

PD is central to the practice of improvement because it develops teachers' and leaders' skills and abilities to impact student academic achievement (Desimone, 2011; Desimone & Garet, 2015; Elmore, 2002; Guskey, 1997; Koonce, et al., 2019; Reeves, 2010). PD can be delivered via workshops, conferences, college courses, and thematic institutes (Desimone & Garet, 2015; Desimone, 2011). Desimone (2011) asserts that PD can occur through coaching, formal and informal learning communities, mentoring, group discussions on students' work, study groups, teachers' networks, and book studies. This scholar posits that among the possible options, one of the most effective forms of PD happens when teachers self-reflect and observe themselves using videos. Peer learning and observation continue to be an efficient form of PD. In brief, PD is embedded in teachers' daily practices.

Desimone (2011) claims that effective PD embraces content and how students learn that content best. PD uses active learning and is coherent because it aligns with the goals of teachers, schools, and districts. In addition, PD is continuous over the academic year and is collective as well as collaborative because teachers from the same subject areas participate in the same PD.

Desimone and Garet (2015) provide a conceptual framework for successful PD. The model consists of four steps:

1. It assesses the teachers' experiences of the PD.
2. PD increases the teachers' knowledge, skills, attitudes, and beliefs.
3. Teachers use the newly acquired knowledge to improve instruction.
4. The new knowledge improves students' learning.

This framework assists school leaders in assessing if teachers learn and if they alter their practices. The model considers the implementation of new knowledge but does not account for culture as a possible enhancer or hindrance to transfer. The current lack of attention to factors that could improve the transfer of learning often leads to a low return on investment, high teacher attrition rates, and stagnating student learning outcomes.

The National Staff Development Council recommends that principals devote 10% of the school budget and 25% of teacher time to professional development (Kelleher, 2003). Although PD requires time, that time must be organized, carefully structured, and purposefully led to avoid the waste of human and financial resources (Guskey, 2003). Too often, budgets are spent on professional development activities that yield few meaningful results (Hess, 2013; Speck & Knipe, 2005).

Despite the millions of dollars spent on professional development nationally, student learning outcomes continue to stagnate or dwindle, discipline issues continue to skyrocket, and teacher moral plummets (Hess, 2013). This may be due, in part, to leaders paying little attention to culturally proficient PD that accounts for learning transfer. Successful PD should model for teachers what they ought to do in class with their diverse student population. However, frequently PD activities are lecture-based and do not account for cultural diversity. CPPD and MMLT are designed to promote cultural awareness by respecting participants' cultures when planning, organizing, conducting, and evaluating PD events.

Learning Transfer

By understanding cultural differences and using the adult learner's culture, professional development can be more effective, especially in transferring learning from the training setting to the classroom. Learning transfer, which is referred to as training transfer, is the implementation of knowledge and skills that were gained during professional learning events to the workplace.

Transferring newly acquired knowledge is the goal of teaching; however, it is the most challenging to achieve (Thomas, 2007). Although scholars have had difficulties measuring learning transfer and its impact, several authors discuss what promotes and inhibits the transfer of learning (Baldwin & Ford, 1988; Broad & Newstrom, 1992; Caffarella & Daffron, 2013; Ford, 1994; Holton et al., 2000; Hung, 2013; Illeris, 2009; Kolb et al., 2002; Knowles, 1980; Taylor, 2000; Thomas, 2007; Warr & Allan, 1998).

Baldwin and Ford (1988) were the first to categorize enhancers and inhibitors to learning transfer and organize them into three factor groups:

1. Learners' characteristics.
2. Intervention design and delivery.
3. Work environment.

Broad and Newstrom (1992) identified six factors that could hinder or promote learning transfer:

1. Program participants, their motivation and dispositions, and previous knowledge.
2. Program design and execution including the strategies for learning transfer.
3. Program content, which is adapted to learners' needs.
4. Changes required to apply learning within the organization and complexity of change.
5. Organizational context such as people, structure, and cultural milieu that can support or prevent transfer of learning including values and Continuing Professional Development (CPD).
6. Societal and community forces.

Holton et al. (2000) created, piloted, and validated a 16-factor Learning Transfer System Inventory (LTSI) based on 16 constructs (see Table 6.1) in 24 countries. The LTSI is a pulse-taking diagnostic tool for training organizers. As with Baldwin and Ford (1988) and Broad and Newstrom (1992), each of these constructs can hinder or promote learning transfer.

Despite the considerable amount of literature on the factors influencing learning transfer, a limited number of research studies examine the relationship between culture and the transfer of learning (Caffarella & Daffron, 2013; Closson, 2013; Rahyuda, Syed, & Soltani, 2014; Silver, 2000). Yang et al. (2009) assert that culture impacts training because learning is not only an individual intellectual activity but also a social process that takes place in certain cultural contexts. These authors posit that cultural factors affect training events via the content and methods chosen, the selection of facilitators, and the trainee characteristics because each culture has its learning style. Similarly, the trainers' expertise in the subject, credibility, and training style influence the trainees' motivation and learning efficiency.

Caffarella and Daffron (2013), Closson (2013), and Rahyuda et al. (2014) are among the few authors who affirm a relationship between cultural factors

Table 6.1. Learning Transfer System Inventory (LTSI).

Capability	Motivation	Work Environment
Content validity	Transfer effort: Performance expectations	Supervisor support
Transfer design	Transfer performance: Outcome expectations	Supervisor sanctions
Opportunity to use	Learner readiness	Peer support
Personal capacity	Motivation to transfer Performance, self-efficacy	Performance coaching
		Personal outcomes: Positive
		Personal outcomes: Negative
		Resistance to change

and learning transfer. Closson (2013) posits that racial or cultural differences not only impact learning (Raver & Van Dyne, 2017) and the training process (Yang et al., 2009) but also that cultural differences influence learning transfer.

Beyond an awareness of who is represented in the room socially and ethnically, Caffarella and Daffron (2013) suggest that the content of the materials should reflect the cultural differences to enable transfer. The authors assert that learning transfer should be discussed within context because context affects the way we teach, what we teach, and how we teach. Moreover, Caffarella (2002) affirms the necessity for trainers and facilitators to be culturally sensitive as well as to understand norms, traditions, and cultures to facilitate the transfer of learning. According to Caffarella (2002), the planning phase of a training is when facilitators can deliberately include culturally responsive approaches and determine how prominent his or her own cultural identity is in the training.

Some scholars argue that there is a need for a comprehensive, multidimensional, and unifying model of learning transfer that considers culture plays a key role in learning transfer (Raver & Van Dyne, 2017). Brion (2020) merged and extended existing models of culturally proficient leadership and learning transfer by proposing the Multidimensional Model of Learning Transfer (MMLT). This model is intended to help school leaders organize, deliver, and evaluate their PD while enhancing learning transfer. This model is salient for all schools and districts and should be of particular interest to school leaders who serve a diverse student and staff population.

Multidimensional Model of Learning Transfer

The MMLT is based on data collected, analyzed, and synthesized over six years in educational institutions in five African nations (Brion, 2017; Brion & Cordeiro, 2017). Even though the data was collected in Africa, the findings apply to all nations because culture is a predominant force in people's lives and organizations. The MMLT (Brion, in press; Brion, in peer review; Brion, 2020) is a research and culturally grounded model inspired by the seminal work of Broad and Newstrom (1992).

Brion (2020) combined two of Broad and Newstrom's (1992) factors, namely organizational context and societal community forces, into one category called Context and Environment. The author posits that the Context and Environment categories encompass Broad and Newstrom's (1992) ideas by including the micro and macro contexts of organizations and societies. The author provides two additional dimensions to learning transfer: pretraining interventions and follow-up.

These new dimensions complement Broad and Newstrom's (1992) learning transfer framework. For the MMLT this author refers to *Culture* with a capital letter because it includes individual, sectional, departmental, organizational, regional, and national cultures as well as cultures related to a continent. Brion (2020) asserts that Culture is the predominant enhancer and inhibitor to transfer and that Culture affects the entire learning transfer phenomenon (Brion, in press).

MMLT is composed of seven dimensions: Culture, Pretraining, Learner, Facilitator, Material and Content, Context and Environment, and Post-Training (Figure 6.1). In the MMLT, Brion (in press, 2020) proposes that culture is the overarching factor that affects all dimensions of learning transfer. Ignoring cultural issues in schools presents numerous risks including reinforcing stereotypes, increasing intolerance, raising misunderstandings, escalating

Figure 6.1. The Multidimensional Model of Learning Transfer.

frustrations and defensiveness as well as learners' and facilitators' withdrawals (Williams & Green, 1994). The author asserts that pretraining and posttraining play a key role in promoting the implementation of knowledge. A description of the MMLT elements is provided below.

Culture

Culture incorporates the differential effects of age, gender, race, ethnicity, social class, religion, sexual orientation, and abilities. School leaders must become culturally proficient so that they can teach teachers as well as students and build a school culture that is inclusive, equitable, and respectful of all cultures represented in their communities (Lindsey et al., 2018).

Pretraining

As Figure 6.1 indicates, pretraining includes the orientation of facilitators and key stakeholders so that they can support the professional learning. Pretraining includes communicating expectations to facilitators and learners, explaining who will benefit from training, and stating that participants are accountable to implement new knowledge (Yang et al., 2009). In addition, pretraining includes sharing the schedule, goals, and information that is perceived as mandatory (Baldwin et al., 1991).

Brion (in peer review) found that in some African cultures, pretraining plays a key role in the learning transfer process because people in these societies prefer knowing in advance and in writing what will happen during the training, how it will be led, and by whom. With these details in mind, leaders and PD organizers can adapt accordingly and enhance the learning transfer process.

Learner

Learners are the participants in the professional development programs. This dimension refers to understanding the learners' motivation, cultural background of the facilitators and participants, and how history and social events affect stakeholders, including self, facilitator, peers, and colleagues. The learner category includes understanding cultural differences in learning styles as well as language and writing differences (Lindsey et al., 2018).

A learner is comprised of the participants' beliefs and attitude toward their job whether they have the freedom to act, and the positive consequences of that application (Yelon et al., 2013). Finally, it involves the participants' belief of the efficacy of the knowledge and skills learned (Yelon et al., 2013). In this dimension, leaders and PD organizers seek to understand how the learners learn best, learn about the participants' experiences, and how they intend to use the new information in their context.

Facilitator

Effective facilitators must understand the cultural background of the participants and themselves. It includes how history and social events affect stakeholders (including self, students, peers, and colleagues). In addition, facilitator refers to the understanding of language and writing differences, setting goals, and the selection of participants (Yang et al., 2009). Leaders and facilitators should examine the biases they may have towards certain groups of people before teaching and gathering materials for the PD event. Principals should hire facilitators who have a culturally proficient mindset as to promote learning transfer.

Content and Materials

The professional development content and information uses evidence-based, culturally relevant, and contextualized materials. It involves using a pedagogical approach based on andragogy, or how adults learn best (Knowles, 1980; Mezirow, 2000). Material and content involves using symbols and meaningful artifacts to cue and help recall (Debebe, 2011). In this dimension, culturally proficient leaders ensure that the content reflects the participants' needs and cultural backgrounds. For example, if the PD event is about communicating with parents and families at school, the principal and facilitators should ensure that participants from different cultural backgrounds share what is or is not appropriate in their cultures and contexts.

Context and Environment

Context and environment comprise the training and work environments (i.e., micro and macro cultures within context), sociocultural context, transfer climate, peer contact, and social networks. It refers to having enough time to transfer knowledge, support for action, resources, freedom to act, and peer support (Burke & Hutchins, 2008; Facteau et al., 1995). Finally, context and environment refers to training incentives: intrinsic incentives such as providing educators with growth opportunities, and extrinsic incentives, such as reward or promotion (Facteau et al., 1995). For this dimension, leaders and facilitators would consider the organizational culture.

Follow-up

Although post-training is often overlooked, it is necessary to avoid skill decay and training relapse. Examples of follow-up include tutor-facilitated networks via mobile technology (Brion, 2018), micro-learning using mobile technology, coaching, testimonials, Professional Learning Communities (PLCs), Community of Practice (COPs), apprenticeships, coaching, and E-coaching (Speck & Knipe, 2005; Wang & Wentling, 2001).

Trainees' reports and assessing transfer help to create a culture where learning and its application are valued (Bates, 2003; Saks & Burke, 2012). For example, follow-up can be done during teacher-based meetings or PLC. It should consider the participants' preferred styles of learning and communicating.

Understanding how the various cultures of PD participants impact the dimensions of the MMLT could help leaders and teachers implement new knowledge, and improve student learning outcomes and well-being while supporting a better return on schools' PD investments. In his seminal work on professional development, Guskey (1977) identifies three main reasons for the lack of quality PD and implementation. First, the author asserts that there is confusion about what is effective PD. Second, Guskey affirms that the effects of PD on student learning vary widely as a function of differences in program content, structure, and format of the experience, and the context and culture in which implementation occurs. Finally, the author indicates that often school leaders focus on the quantity of PD offered rather than the quality.

To provide quality PD, Guskey (1977) recommends that leaders focus on evaluating three components. The first component measures knowledge and skills that participants acquire from professional development. This information helps to improve program format, content, and organization. In the MMLT, this is accomplished during the pretraining and within the content and materials dimensions.

The second element measures the participants' use of knowledge and skills that they have gained and incorporate the new knowledge and skills into practice. In the MMLT, the transfer of knowledge can be evaluated in the follow-up dimension. Lastly, the third element focuses on measuring the impact of participants' changes in knowledge and skills on student learning. Improving student outcomes and well-being by providing culturally proficient PD that accounts for learning transfer is the MMLT's goal.

Implications for Practice

The author has two recommendations for school leaders to increase the skills and abilities of adult learners: (1) enhance learning transfer post-PD and (2) earn a return on investment that positively affects students' outcomes. To provide PD that accounts for culture before, during, and after PD events, school leaders should use the MMLT and its rubrics to organize, prepare, and evaluate their PD offering.

The rubrics are designed to help practitioners think through the seven dimensions of the MMLT before, during, and after the training. Within each of these dimensions, there are several items practitioners can self-assess. For example, during the pretraining phase, school leaders and PD organizers should reflect on the culture of their participants and how they learn best. Leaders should conduct a needs assessment and offer culturally proficient PD that is relevant and individualized to each teacher's needs. Because learning is a social endeavor, the MMLT and its rubrics enable leaders to take culture into consideration for each of the MMLT dimension for maximum learning transfer and impact on student learning.

Second, facilitators must remain flexible and open to learning about different cultures and adjust their practices accordingly without prejudgment. Facilitators should reflect on the impact that their culture has on participants and colleagues in terms of language, history, and traditions. When organizing PD, principals should carefully select the facilitators, brief them on team members, and provide them with the MMLT.

Conclusion

Culture plays a key role in students' and adults' ability to learn and implement new knowledge because learning is a social endeavor (Gay, 2013; Hammond, 2014; Ladson-Billings, 2005; Lindsey et al., 2018). Current PD offerings seldom consider the culture in the learning transfer process. Because of the lack of attention placed on learning transfer, PD does not often generate changes in practice. By forgetting to account for learning transfer in the organization, delivery, and follow-up of PD events, teachers and leaders often become frustrated and lose interest in the professional learning.

PD offerings would be most impactful and earn a meaningful return on investment if all dimensions of the PD took culture into consideration (Yang et al., 2009). CPPD is a framework grounded in culture that enhances the learning transfer by using the MMLT. The MMLT serves as an innovative lens that school leaders can use to prepare, organize, and evaluate the trainings to promote learning transfer and earn a positive return on investment.

The rubrics derived assist principals and training organizers in enhancing learning transfer before, during, and post-training.

Understanding the role culture plays in PD and the learning transfer process promotes the transfer of learning in schools and contributes to better academic outcomes and well-being for students, teachers, and leaders regardless of race, ethnicity, gender, religion, sexual orientation, language, abilities, or cultural backgrounds. In this way, MMLT promotes equity.

If teachers and leaders received culturally proficient quality PD, they would be better equipped to implement in their classrooms the newly acquired knowledge and model the importance of culture. As a result, students would be more equitably served because teachers would be more aware of the impact of culture on learning. Providing an equitable education to students from all walks of life and students who embrace all cultural identities would create socially just educational systems and societies.

REFERENCES

Baldwin, T. T., & Ford, J. K. (1988). Transfer of training: A review and directions for future research. *Personnel Psychology, 41*(1), 63–105.

Baldwin, T. T., Magjuka, R. J., & Loher, B. T. (1991). The perils of participation: Effects of choice of training on trainee motivation and learning. *Personnel Psychology, 44*(1), 51–65.

Bates, R. A. (2003). Managers as transfer agents: Improving learning transfer in organizations. In E.F. Holton III & T.T Baldwin (Eds.), *Improving learning transfer in organizations* (pp. 243–270). Jossey-Bass.

Brion, C., & Cordeiro, P. A. (2017). Learning transfer: The missing link to learning among school leaders in Burkina Faso and Ghana. *Frontiers in Education, 2*(69), 1–12. http://doi.org/10.3389/feduc.2017.00069.

Brion, C. (2017). Low-fee private schools in West Africa: Case studies from Burkina Faso and Ghana [Doctoral dissertation. University of San Diego].

Brion. (2018). Keeping the learning going: Using mobile technology to enhance learning transfer. *Educational Research for Policy and Practice*, 1–16.

Brion, C. (2020). Learning transfer: The missing linkage to effective professional development. *Journal of Cases in Educational Leadership, 23*(3), 32–47. https://doi.org/10.1177/1555458920919473.

Brion, C. (in peer review). The use of culturally proficient professional development to enhance learning transfer. *Journal of School Leadership*.

Brion, C. (in press). Culture: The link to learning transfer. *Adult Learning*.

Broad, M. L., & Newstrom, J. W. (1992). *Transfer of training: Action-packed strategies to ensure high payoff from training investments*. Da Capo Press.

Burke, L. A., & Hutchins, H. M. (2008). A study of best practices in training transfer and proposed model of transfer. *Human Resource Development Quarterly, 19*(2), 107–128.

Caffarella, R. S. (2002). *Planning programs for adult learners: A practical guide for educators, trainers, and staff developers.* The Jossey-Bass Higher and Adult Education Series. Jossey-Bass.

Caffarella, R. S., & Daffron, S. R. (2013). *Planning programs for adult learners: A practical guide.* Wiley & Sons.

Closson, R. B. (2013). Racial and cultural factors and learning transfer. *New Directions for Adult and Continuing Education, 137,* 61–69.

Debebe, G. (2011). Creating a safe environment for women's leadership transformation. *Journal of Management Education, 35*(5), 679–712.

Desimone, L. M. (2011). A primer on effective professional development. *Phi Delta Kappan, 92*(6), 68–71.

Desimone, L. M., & Garet, M. S. (2015). Best practices in teacher's professional development in the United States. *Psychology, Society and Education, 7*(3), 252–263.

Elmore, R. F. (2002). Bridging the gap between standards and achievement: The imperative for professional development in education. *Secondary lenses on learning participant book: Team leadership for mathematics in middle and high schools,* 313–344.

Facteau, J. D., Dobbins, G. H., Russell, J. E., Ladd, R. T., & Kudisch, J. D. (1995). The influence of general perceptions of the training environment on pretraining motivation and perceived training transfer. *Journal of Management, 21*(1), 1–25.

Ford, J. K. (1994). Defining transfer of learning: The meaning is in the answers. *Adult Learning, 5*(4), 22–30.

Ford, J. K., Yelon, S. L., & Billington, A. Q. (2011). How much is transferred from training to the job? The 10% delusion as a catalyst for thinking about transfer. *Performance Improvement Quarterly, 24*(2), 7–24.

Fullan, M. (2002). The change. *Educational Leadership, 59*(8), 16–20.

Gay, G. (2013). Teaching to and through cultural diversity. *Curriculum Inquiry, 43*(1), 48–70.

Guskey, T. R. (1997). Research needs to link professional development and student learning. *Journal of Staff Development, 18,* 36–41.

Guskey, T. R. (2002). Does it make a difference? Evaluating professional development. *Educational Leadership, 59*(6), 45–51.

Guskey, T. R. (2003). What makes professional development effective? *Phi Delta Kappan, 84*(10), 748–750. https://doi.org/10.1177/003172170308401007.

Hammond, Z. (2014). *Culturally responsive teaching and the brain: Promoting authentic engagement and rigor among culturally and linguistically diverse students.* Corwin.

Hess, F. M. (2013). *Cage-busting leadership.* Education Press.

Holton III, E. F., Bates, R. A., & Ruona, W. E. (2000). Development of a generalized learning transfer system inventory. *Human Resource Development Quarterly, 11*(4), 333–360.

Hung, W. (2013). Problem-based learning: A learning environment for enhancing learning transfer. *New Directions for Adult and Continuing Education, 137,* 27–38.

Illeris, K. (2009). Transfer of learning in the learning society: How can the barriers between different learning spaces be surmounted, and how can the gap between learning inside and outside schools be bridged? *International Journal of Lifelong Education, 28*(2), 137–148.

Kelleher, J. (2003). A model for assessment-driven professional development. *Phi Delta Kappan, 84*(10), 751–756. https://doi.org/10.1177/003172170308401008.

Knowles, M. (1980). My farewell address: Andragogy no panacea, no ideology. *Training and Development Journal, 34*(8), 48–50.

Kolb, D. A., Boyatzis, R. E., & Mainemelis, C. (2002). Experiential on cognitive, learning, and thinking styles. *Perspectives Learning Theory: Previous Research and New Directions*, 227–248.

Koonce, M., Pijanowski, J. C., Bengtson, E., & Lasater, K. (2019). Principal engagement in the professional development process. *NASSP Bulletin, 103*(3), 229–252. https://doi.org/10.1177/0192636519871614.

Ladson-Billings, G. J. (2005). Is the team all right? Diversity and teacher education. *Journal of Teacher Education, 56*(3), 229–234.

Lindsey, R. B., Nuri Robins, K., Terrell, R.D., & Lindsey, D.B. (2018). *Cultural Proficiency: A Manual for School Leaders*, 4th Ed., Corwin.

Marzano, R. J., Waters, T., & McNulty, B. A. (2005). *School leadership that works: From research to results*. ASCD.

Mezirow, J. (2000). *Learning as transformation: Critical perspectives on a theory in progress*. The Jossey-Bass Higher and Adult Education Series. Jossey-Bass Publishers.

Paris, D., & Alim, H. S. (Eds.) (2017). *Culturally sustaining pedagogies: Teaching and learning for justice in a changing world*. Teachers College Press.

Reeves, D. B. (2010). *Transforming professional development into student results*. Association for Supervision and Curriculum Development.

Saks, A. M., & Burke, L. A. (2012). An investigation into the relationship between training evaluation and the transfer of training. *International Journal of Training and Development, 16*(2), 118–127.

Silver, D. (2000). Songs and storytelling: Bringing health messages to life in Uganda. *Education for Health, 14*(1), 51–60.

Speck, M., & Knipe, C. (2005). *Why can't we get it right? Professional development in our schools*. Corwin.

Taylor, M. C. (2000). Transfer of learning in workplace literacy programs. *Adult Basic Education, 10*(1), 3–20.

Thomas, E. (2007). Thoughtful planning fosters learning transfer. *Adult Learning, 18*(3–4), 4–9.

Villegas, A. M., & Lucas, T. (2002). Preparing culturally responsive teachers: Rethinking the curriculum. *Journal of Teacher Education, 53*(1), 20–32.

Wang, L., & Wentling, T. L. (2001, March). The relationship between distance coaching and the transfer of training. In *Proceedings from the Academy of Human Resource Development Conference. Tulsa, Oklahoma.*

Williams, T., & Green, A. (1994). *Dealing with difference: How trainers can take account of cultural diversity*. Gower.

Yang, B., Wang, Y., & Drewry, A. W. (2009). Does it matter where to conduct training? Accounting for cultural factors. *Human Resource Management Review*, *19*(4), 324–333.

Yelon, S. L., Ford, J. K., & Golden, S. (2013). Transfer over time: Stories about transfer years after training. *Performance Improvement Quarterly*, *25*(4), 43–66.

Chapter 7

Special Education

Keith Dewey and Stephen V. Coffin

The authors focus on special education's evolution from America's system of public, private, religious, charter, magnet, and vocational K-12 education school system. Our early educational and political leaders worked to develop an informed, literate, and enlightened citizenry (Franklin and Masur, 1993). Mansfield and Winthrop (2000) describe Alexis de Tocqueville's amazement at the power of education that enabled ordinary citizens "to lift themselves up by their own bootstraps (p. 90)." Robinson and Aronica (2015) describe special education's evolution:

> Personalizing education might sound revolutionary, but this revolution is not new. Its roots are deep in the history of education. In the seventeenth century John Locke advocated the simultaneous education of the body, character, and mind—in other words, the whole person. Many different individuals and types of institutions have carried the torch of personalized forms of education that follow the natural grain of children's development, and the importance of these forms of education for more equitable and civilized societies. (p. 254)

Education transforms students, and special education enables special needs students to succeed, which would not be otherwise possible (Braxton et al., 1997; Pascarella & Terenzini, 2005).

The authors begin with an overview of general education as well as special education's development and specialization. Second, the authors highlight major historical developments in general education, including pedagogical trends as well as strategies for providing special education. Third, the authors discuss how these factors affect general and special education populations. Fourth, the authors discuss special education equality and equity issues. The authors suggest ways for administrators, teachers, parents, and policymakers to provide more equitable and equal educational services and programs for special education students.

General Education Overview

Education's primary purpose is to develop democratically minded, informed, and thoughtful citizens (Franklin & Masur, 1993). Hirsch (2020) asserts that "schooling in a democracy is not just schooling. It's also citizen making" (p. 19). Noah Webster, an early American schoolmaster, declared that "The Education of youth is, in all governments, an object of the first consequence. The impressions received in early life usually form the characters of individuals; a union of which forms the general character of a nation" (Hirsch, 2020, p. 9).

Tocqueville et al. (2000) recommended that other nations adopt the Americans' propensity to unite for educational purposes. He believed that this was a healthy and progressive form of social development. Jurgen Habermas (1992) drew from Tocqueville's *Democracy in America* in writing *Gemeinschaft*. In addition, Kronman (2019) highlights Tocqueville's view and forecast for the role of race in American society.

> The existence of a caste order among the races poses a unique threat to the integrity of American egalitarianism. Tocqueville could see no obvious solution. The Indians, he thought, would eventually be exterminated, or absorbed into the White world. In their case, the problem would simply disappear. By contrast, the condition of Blacks presents what Tocqueville viewed as an insoluble dilemma. At the time of his visit to America, the overwhelming majority of Blacks were slaves. He could not conceive their being freed without a monumental struggle. Even if they were freed, he believed, the racial barrier between Whites and Blacks would remain insurmountably high. Tocqueville noted that in 1831 in the North, as Blacks achieved legal equality, prejudice against them hardened. The history of the next fifty years proved him right, though the struggle he predicted took a different course than the one that he imagined. (p. 68)

Rise of Primary Education

Primary education developed differently from the educational foundation provided by Franklin and Tocqueville following the Civil War. Webster, like Horace Mann, the founder of the common school movement in the 1830s, experienced opposition.

Consistently in our history, the push for commonality in the United States has been resisted by two factions: first, by those who feel left out of the dominant culture; and second, by those whose who are opposed in principle to dull, unproductive uniformity (Hirsch, 2020, p. 11).

Hirsch (2020) addressed those who feared excessive Protestant influence or uniformity in early education, noting that:

> Commonality in the means of communication and in the valuation of liberty is consistent with high diversity in the use to which such commonality is put. Alexander Hamilton was right to make the dollar the common national currency. Similarly, Webster was dead right that we also need a common intellectual currency. (p. 11)

Reconstruction left former slaves without economic or political power, "the slave went free; stood a brief moment in the sun; then moved back again toward slavery" (Kronman, 2019, p. 68). According to Picower (2021), teacher preparation programs must be redesigned to emphasize that "racism operates at four levels: ideological, institutional, interpersonal, and internalized" (p. 85).

Rise of Pragmatism and Progressive Schools

John Dewey and Henry James might be surprised by the extent to which their ideas have flourished:

> David Steiner, the executive director of the Johns Hopkins Institute for Education Policy and New York's former education commissioner, defines progressive education as "a movement that champions child-based, experiential learning, and enlists schools as agents of building a democratic society characterized by public intelligence based on the free-flow of knowledge across all social sectors." (Pondiscio, 2019, p. 50)

Providing progressive education is difficult when the free flow of knowledge is impeded.

Rise of Normalcy

The rise of normalcy after World War II was America's returning to family, investing time and resources in peaceful endeavors, and owning homes in safe neighborhoods with good schools. In addition, it was time during which many Whites exited urban centers and moved to the suburbs, which is known as white flight. As Kronin (2019) writes, "A regime of legal apartheid reinforced caste relations between whites and blacks in ways unknown even in the age of slavery. A long fight for basic civil rights followed, culminating in *Brown v. Board of Education*, and a decade later the Civil Rights and Voting Rights Acts of the Johnson Administration" (p. 68).

Academics have written about philosophical, epistemological, and pedagogical problems of public education, such as Bloom's (1987) argument against relativism in *The Closing of the American Mind*, and Boyer's (1990) advocacy for new standards of scholarship in *Scholarship Reconsidered*. However, public education needed Kozol's 1991 ground-breaking study of East St. Louis public schools and poverty to expose the *Savage Inequalities* that exist in America.

Computers, Internet, and New Technologies

Issues centering on class, ethnicity, and race persist and manifest in Internet and technology access creating a digital divide. Kronman (2019) acknowledges:

> The Second Reconstruction fizzled too. Blacks continued to be concentrated in inner city ghettos. They still enjoyed dramatically fewer economic and educational opportunities than their white counterparts, even those whose economic status was roughly the same. Race remained, and remains to this day, a special barrier to advancement and success, independent of class. (p. 68)

The digital divide exacerbates opportunity and equity gaps in general as well as special education.

Although technology is not a panacea, education must innovate using cutting-edge technology to meet the twenty-first century challenges. Wagner (2012) supports this goal:

> What we urgently need is a new engine of economic growth for the twenty-first century. The solution to our economic and social challenges is the same: creating a viable and sustainable economy that creates good jobs without polluting the planet. And there is general agreement as to what that new economy must be based on. One word: innovation. (p. 2)

Wagner and Dintersmith (2015) echo the need for innovation in education.

> Today, assessment in our schools has become the bitter enemy of learning. It is perverting the school agenda. It is killing curiosity and motivation. It is driving our best teachers from the profession. Assessment in our schools has become the single biggest threat to our nation's long-term national security. It is corroding our nation's education and society in the same way invasive species like kudzu or snakehead fish drive healthy species from our environment. (p. 206)

Wagner (2014) adds:

The lack of adequate teacher preparation and support is considered the primary cause for the astounding public school teacher attrition rate. Studies show that nearly one in two teachers, who start in the classroom, leave after just five years! (p. 146)

Wagner concludes that the future of K-12 innovative teaching is at risk without a major infusion of cutting-edge technology.

General Education Implications for Special Education

However, many school districts face pedagogical, operational, educational, and technological challenges. Pondiscio (2019) focuses on a network of controversial New York City charter schools founded by Eva Moskowitz. Pondiscio (2019) doubts Moskowitz's claims that she has "created something unprecedented in American education: a way for large numbers of engaged and ambitious low-income families of color to get an education for their children that equals and even exceeds what wealthy families take for granted" (p. 1).

In challenging Moskowitz's claim that her model is "Catholic school on the outside, Bank Street on the inside," Pondiscio (2019) describes it as "a label that encompasses the old-school uniforms, routines, and strict classroom management that makes possible the kind of teaching championed by the Bank Street School for Children, a one-hundred-year-old-citadel of progressive education" (p. 152). Pondiscio (2019) argues:

> If John Dewey, the intellectual father of the progressive education movement, were to set foot in Bronx 1, he might run screaming into the street and across the Third Avenue Bridge, not breaking stride until he was safely back at Columbia University, a few miles and a world away. Success Academy's curriculum and pedagogy is simply not "progressive" in the way that most educators understand and use the term. (p. 153)

A common objection to "charter schools and publicly financed vouchers is that school choice siphons resources from traditional public schools" (Coffin & Cooper, 2017, p. 105).

Pondiscio (2019) laments that "well-intentioned efforts to leverage schools as a means of ending generational poverty are perversely doomed to perpetuate it—unless we allow like-minded parents to self-select into schools in the greatest numbers possible" (p. 278). In opposition to this approach, Ravitch argues that for those who advocate traditional public schools (TPSs) the "movement that is dedicated to protecting public schools from those who are funding privatization and who believe that America's schools should be run like businesses and that children should be treated like customers or products"

(Ravitch, 2020, p. 11). However, the charter school business model such as the one employed by Moskowitz's Success Academy that "systematically weeds out special education students and the hardest to teach" has a much more adverse impact on special education students (Ravitch, 2020, p. 86).

Special Education Learning Differences

Using his theory of multiple intelligences, Gardner (2000) argues that different students learn differently. Some students are visual learners who learn best using their eyes. For visual learners, new material and information must be presented visually for them to learn. Gardner (2000) argues that humans are most capable of remembering "chunks of information," which helped Americans to remember phone numbers (p. 322). While a visual learner would best remember a phone number by writing it down repetitively, an audio learner might best recall it by hearing it repeatedly, as repetition is a key component of most forms of learning. A tactile learner might best learn math and science if it can be made concrete and tangible or be associated with a laboratory or practicum field experience.

Attention spans differ among different grade levels of students as well as "between general education and special education students, especially those with attention disorder deficit (ADD), hypertension, hyperactivity, or autism" (Gardner, 2000, p.123). English as a second language (ESL) learners and English language learners (ELLs) learn differently than English proficient students (Gardner, 2000).

Supporting Special Education Students

Teachers are under increasing pressure to differentiate instruction (Danielson, 2012; Marzano, 2003). Marzano (2003) argues that "public school teachers must deal with all of America's children" (p. 45). Teachers face additional challenges educating students with attention deficit and hyperactivity disorder, depression, eating disorders, homelessness, missing guardians or parents, poverty, and non-traditional gender orientation (Marzano, 2003, p. 49).

Gabriel (2005) focuses on developing leadership qualities, building teams, enhancing communication, overcoming obstacles, and differentiating instruction for special education teachers. Tomlinson and Strickland (2005) provide best practices, resource guides, and techniques for differentiating the special education classroom.

New Special Education Strategies

Culturally and linguistically responsive teaching and learning empowers underserved populations (Hollie, 2018). Culturally and linguistically responsive teaching and learning enables students to quickly change assumptions and paradigms with implications for special education assistive technologies as well as new developments in artificial intelligence (Hammond, 2015). New approaches include Problem Based Learning (PBL), instructional rounds, Socratic circles, and literary circles (City et al., 2016).

Poverty's Impact

Students living in poverty face emotional and social challenges, acute and chronic stressors, cognitive lags, and health and safety issues that, when combined, "present an extraordinary challenge to academic and social success" (Jensen, 2009, pp. 14–15). Jensen (2009) argues that "these factors present an extraordinary challenge to academic and social success" for special education students (p. 15). Downey (2020) asserts that poverty hinders our understanding of how special education students learn. Burgess (2012) argues for increased use of technology to help offset poverty's impact in teaching special education students.

Policy Recommendations

The following policy recommendations should help to improve special education.

- Special education students must have equal access to cutting-edge technology as well as all educational resources including more technological training for administrators and teachers (Wexler, 2019).
- Special education teachers must have more advanced training (Wagner, 2012, 2014, 2020).
- Implement Palmer's (2017) five proposals:
  - We must help our students debunk the myth that institutions possess autonomous, even ultimate, power over our lives.
  - We must validate the importance of our students' emotions as well as their intellect.
  - We must teach our students how to mine their emotions for knowledge.
  - We must teach them how to cultivate community for the sake of both knowing and doing.
  - We must teach—and model for—our students what it means to be on the journey toward an undivided life (p. 205).

The authors suggest that adopting the strategies and lessons learned provided in this chapter will help to close the educational resource and achievement gaps among regular and special education students. Adopting these strategies and lessons learned will enable administrators and policymakers to allocate financial, material, and human educational resources more efficiently and equitably among students based on need and cost-to-educate (Coffin, 2021).

REFERENCES

Alger, H. (1985). *Ragged Dick and struggling upward.* Penguin Books.

Braxton, J. M., Sullivan, A. V., & Johnson, R. M. (1997). Appraising Tinto's theory of college student departure. In J. C. Smart (Ed.), *Higher education: Handbook of theory and research.* (Vol. XII, pp. 107–164). Agathon Press.

Burgess, D. (2012). *Teach like a pirate: Increase student engagement, boost your creativity, and transform your life as an educator.* Dave Burgess Consulting, Inc.

City, E. A., Elmore, R. F., Fiarman, S. E., & Teitel, L. (2016). *Instructional rounds in education: A network approach to improving teaching and learning.* Harvard Education Press.

Coffin, S. V. (Ed.) (2021). *Higher education's looming collapse: Using new ways of doing business and social justice to avoid bankruptcy.* Rowman & Littlefield.

Coffin, S. V., & Cooper, B. S. (Eds.) (2017). *Sound school finance for educational excellence.* Rowman & Littlefield.

Danielson, C. (2012). Observing classroom practice. *Educational Leadership. 70*(3), 32–37.

DeBoer, F. (2020). *The cult of smart: How our broken education system perpetuates social injustice.* All Points Books.

Dewey, J. (1938). *Experience & education.* Kappa Delta Pi Lecture Series. Free Press, Simon & Schuster, Inc.

Downey, D. B. (2020). *How schools really matter: Why our assumption about schools and inequality is mostly wrong.* University of Chicago Press.

Franklin, B., & Masur, L. P. (1993). *Autobiography of Benjamin Franklin.* Bedford Books of St. Martin's Press.

Gardner, H. (2000). Using multiple intelligences to improve negotiation theory and practice. *Negotiation Journal. 16*(4), 321–324. https://doi.org/10.1111/j.1571-9979.2000.tb00760.x.

Gabriel, J. G. (2005). *How to thrive as a teacher leader.* ASCD.

Goldstein, D. (2014). *The teacher wars: A history of America's most embattled profession.* Anchor Books, A Division of Penguin Random House LLC.

Habermas, J. (1992). *The structural transformation of the public sphere.* New York: Polity Press.

Hammond, Z. (2015). *Culturally responsive teaching and the brain: Promoting authentic engagement and rigor among culturally and linguistically diverse students.* Corwin Press.

Hirsch, E. D. (2020). *How to educate a citizen: The power of shared knowledge to unify a nation.* Harper, An Imprint of Harper Collins Publishers.

Hollie, S. (2018). *Culturally and linguistically responsive teaching and learning: Classroom practices for student success.* Shell Educational Publishing, Inc.

Jensen, E. (2009). *Teaching with poverty in mind: What being poor does to kids' brains and what schools can do about it.* ASCD.

Kozol, J. (1991). *Savage inequalities: Children in America's schools.* Broadway Books, An Imprint of the Crown Publishing Group, a division of Random House, Inc.

Kronman, A. (2019). *The assault on American excellence.* Free Press.

Marzano, R. J. (2003). *Classroom management that works: Research-based strategies for every teacher.* ASCD.

Matera, M. (2015). *Explore like a pirate: Engage, enrich, and elevate your learners with gamification and game-inspired course design.* Dave Burgess Consulting, Inc.

Pascarella, E. T., & Terenzini, P. T. (2005). *How college affects students: A third decade of research.* Jossey-Bass.

Picower, B. (2021). *Reading, writing, and racism: Disrupting whiteness in teacher education and in the classroom.* Beacon Press.

Pondiscio, R. (2019). *How the other half learns: Equality, excellence, and the battle over school choice.* Avery, An Imprint of Penguin Random House LLC.

Ravitch, D. (2020). *Slaying Goliath: The passionate resistance to privatization and the fight to save America's public schools.* Vintage Books, A Division of Penguin Books, Random House LLC.

Robinson, K., & Aronica, L. (2015). *Creative schools: The grassroots revolution that's transforming education.* Penguin Books, An Imprint of Penguin Random House LLC.

Rollins, Q. (2016). *Play like a pirate: Engage students with toys, games, and comics to make your classroom fun again!* Dave Burgess Consulting, Inc.

Schneider, J., & Berkshire, J. (2020). *A wolf at the schoolhouse door: The dismantling of public education and the future of school.* New Press.

Tocqueville, A., Mansfield, H. C., & Winthrop, D. (2000). *Democracy in America.* University of Chicago Press.

Tomlinson, C. A., & Strickland, C. A. (2005). *Differentiation in practice: A resource guide for differentiating curriculum: Grades 9–12.* ASCD.

Wagner, T. (2012). *Creating innovators: The making of young people who will change the world.* Scribner.

Wagner, T. (2014). *The global achievement gap: Why even our best schools don't teach the new survival skills our children need—and what we can do about it.* Basic Books, A Member of the Perseus Books Group.

Wagner, T. (2020). *Learning by heart: An unconventional education.* Viking, An Imprint of Penguin Random House LLC.

Wagner, T., & Dintersmith, T. (2015). *Most likely to succeed: Preparing our kids for the innovation era.* Scribner.

Welcome, A. (2018). *Run like a pirate: Push yourself/get more out of life*. Dave Burgess Consulting, Inc.

Wexler, N. (2019). *The knowledge gap: The hidden cause of America's broken education system—and how to fix it.* Avery, An Imprint of Penguin Random House LLC.

Chapter 8

Resource Inequities among Deaf and Hard-of-Hearing Students

Thomas Barger

America's first deaf school, the American School for the Deaf, was established in 1817 in Hartford Connecticut by Thomas Gallaudet, Dr. Mason Cogswell, and a deaf teacher from France, Laurent Clerc. The school was originally called the Connecticut Asylum for the Deaf and Dumb. The state of Connecticut has funded the school since its inception.

Deaf student education has three types of K-12 schools:

- Residential schools
- Day schools
- Mainstream schools with a deaf program

America's 53 residential schools have students who live on campus year-round but go home for the holidays. The 47 day-schools teach classes using oral instruction or American Sign Language. Traditional public schools (TPSs) have deaf programs in which deaf students are taught in self-contained classes or mainstreamed in classes with general education students. Enrollment in these schools depends on the child's needs or parental preference.

About 75 percent of deaf and hard-of-hearing students are mainstreamed in public school programs with an interpreter or an itinerant (i.e., hearing teacher) to assist with education and hearing issues as they arise in the classroom (Deaf and Hard-of-Hearing Students in the Mainstream, 2014). Deaf and hard-of-hearing students need assistive technology such as hearing aids, cochlear implants, and digital transmitters that allow aids to pick up clear sounds and cancel noise for better reception by teachers. Additional accommodations include a sign language interpreter, notetaker, or CART (Captioning by Remote Technology) as well as captioning on videos.

Deaf students typically fall behind general education students because children born deaf or hard of hearing lack their peers' language and cognitive development. Most are born to hearing parents, who lack the skills to communicate with them. In addition, some parents cannot afford hearing aids or parents do not realize that their children have a hearing impairment until late in their development. New Jersey passed a law that established a newborn hearing screening program in 2000:

> N.J. Rev. Stat. § 26:2-103.1 et seq states that prior to the discharge from any hospital or birthing center, all newborns are to be given a hearing screening examination and the parents or legal guardians of the newborn shall be provided with literature describing the normal development of auditory function (Newborn Hearing Screening State Laws, 2011).

The Individuals with Disabilities in Education Act (IDEA), which was passed in 1975 as the Education for All Handicapped Children Act, requires schools to provide a free appropriate public education (i.e., FAPE) to children with educational disabilities. IDEA requires schools to identify and evaluate students with disabilities (i.e., Child Find), and develop an Individualized Education Plan (IEP), at no charge to the parents. Beginning at age three, children are entitled to special education services and an IEP.

A child study team (CST) evaluates each student with disabilities. Typically, a CST consists of one or more teachers, psychologists, disabilities consultants, speech therapists, occupational therapists, language therapists, and social workers. In addition, a CST includes one or more hearing providers who determine the accommodations necessary to address hearing loss.

The placement of a deaf child depends on the answers to such questions as:

- Where do they live?
- Should they attend a deaf school?
- Should they attend a mainstream classroom with general education students in a traditional public school (TPS)?
- Should they attend a self-contained class in a TPS?

The CST aims to develop an IEP that will require quality special educational services for each student who is educationally disabled in a school setting and will provide the educational services in the least restrictive environment.

The two basic modes of communication in teaching deaf/hard-of-hearing children are:

- Total communication
- American Sign Language.

Total communication is a form of sign language that uses different means of communications: fingerspelling, gestures, voice, and lipreading. Deaf and hard-of-hearing students may wear hearing aids and/or cochlear implants to listen to the speaker. Students may have speech training in their school program. The sentence is signed word for word verbatim. The latter is American Sign Language (ASL) where words are interchanged in sign and the syntax is in a different format. There is no voice used during this method. Students may wear hearing aids depending on the severity of their hearing loss.

Interpreters interpret information between teachers and students. The Registry of the Deaf (RID) certifies interpreters. The RID was established in 1964 to ensure ethics and professionalism in the field of interpreting. Under the Americans with Disabilities Act (ADA), any public entity, including public schools, must provide interpreters. Certification depends on individual state laws.

Teachers who sign are not generally certified per se but must pass the American Sign Language Proficiency Interview (ASLPI) while earning their degree in deaf education. Up until recently, teachers of the deaf only needed to earn a deaf education degree rather than a subject content degree. New York City now requires dual certification in the subject matter plus a deaf education degree to teach deaf children. Not all states require dual certification to educate deaf children. All they need is a degree in deaf education. Teachers with the dual certification are more qualified because of the content knowledge in their field, such as math, science, and ELA as well as the instructional skills to teach deaf children.

4201 Schools

New York State has two types of programs for day and residential students:

- State supported schools (SSS)
- State operated schools (SOS)

The 4201 schools are primarily state funded and nonprofit. New York State has 10 privately operated SSS, which are funded by the state. SSS are residential or day schools that provide services to the deaf, blind, and physically challenged.

In January 2021, the 4201 School Association proposed a budget to the fiscal committee of the New York legislature requesting $93.7 million, of which

$84.7 million was allocated for students' tuition. In addition, they requested funds for Wi-Fi for low-income families due to the pandemic.

> Many of the children we serve need specialized hardware and software to access digital learning and life needs. These extras are often costly, and students need training to use these devices effectively. We support efforts to ensure broadband access to all students and their families. (The 4201 Schools Association testimony presented to the fiscal committees of the New York legislature hearing on the FY 2021–2022 executive budget. New York Institute for Special Education, 2021, para. 10).

SOS are operated by the New York State Department of Education and have similar admission processes for the deaf and blind. In both programs, parents or the Committee of Special Education (CSE) from the home district can initiate or refer the child to these school programs. In April 2021, part of the state budget was approved for 4201 schools. A short summary of the provisions totaled approximately $136 million including $93.7 million for tuition to districts with students attending a 4201 school and $30 million for health and safety capital projects. The remainder of the funding was for general support for deaf children under three and residential services for students who stay on campus.

The 4201-school association takes pride in guiding its core mission for all students to succeed. They offer a rigorous and quality education that focuses on constructive learning. Many of their students graduate, attend college, or go to vocational training.

Deaf Is Not a Disability

Disability means a person with a physical or mental condition that limits movement, senses, or activities. Children who are born deaf or hard of hearing lack critical language skills causing them to fall behind their hearing peers. This language delay causes their reading and math skills to fall below their grade level peers. Most hearing parents of deaf children seek medical technology such as cochlear implants or hearing aids to improve their child's hearing along with speech therapy. The use of these devices does not improve their hearing. It only amplifies the sound that transmits via the sensory nerves to the brain.

During the 1960's and 1970's, deaf children wore headsets while the teacher wore a microphone around his/her neck. Oral communication was used but sign language was not permitted because this approach was believed to be more beneficial for student learning. Although some deaf schools still follow this practice, most mainstream classrooms use total communication.

The deaf child can acquire language unless they have an actual physical or mental disability, for example, a learning disability, dyslexia, or autism. Noam Chomsky introduces the idea that children can learn a first language through acquisition.

> Therefore, the acquisition of language is not a passive act by which children simply soak up information they hear in the environment. It is an active act by which children construct unconscious principles that permit them to receive information, produce novel utterances, and use language in a variety of forms (Cruz, 2015, p. 3).

Noah Chomsky believes that children have the capacity to learn languages. Despite critics of Chomsky's work, language can be learned innately, and children normally have access to language by their second month (Cruz, 2015, pp. 12–13).

Deaf children born to hearing parents don't have access to sign language because hearing parents typically don't know how to sign while deaf children born to deaf parents do well. Comparing these two groups of deaf children, children with deaf parents do exceedingly well on math and reading. Deaf bilingual programs benefit students academically as well as socially. These programs, however, are declining nationwide.

The trend has been for states and local school districts to place deaf and hard-of-hearing students in public schools with little to no support or access in sign language. Deaf children need a "language rich environment such as ASL/English classes, including direct access to peers and teachers using sign language" (American Bilingual, 2016, para. 11).

Laws Impacting Deaf Learners

- IDEA—Individuals with Disabilities Education Act (IDEA)
- ADA—American with Disabilities Act
- Section 504

These federal regulations protect the rights of students who have disabilities, including deaf students. They provide equal access to public schools, universities, and public institutions. The IDEA provides students with a free appropriate education in the least restrictive environment (LRE).

The accommodations are provided through the Individual Educational Plan (IEP), for special education children who need services to help with their learning. The LRE is a law designed to allow students with disabilities to transfer from the general education classroom to a self- contained classroom. The ADA ensures that students with disabilities have the accommodations or services to help to perform in school or on the job without discrimination or barriers. The 504 plan of the Rehabilitation Act gives students with disabilities a waiver of the IEP written plan and full access of the school (Johnson, 2017, pp. 8–9).

Parents must decide whether their children should attend a mainstream school or deaf school. Curriculum is more standardized at the mainstream level while deaf schools' curriculum is more flexible and customized. Deaf schools have more deaf teachers than mainstream schools and use sign language more often while interpreters are included in mainstream schools. Because most deaf and hard-of-hearing students attend mainstream schools, many of them are in inclusion classes.

In New York City, one deaf school and approximately six public schools have self-contained deaf classes. A few of these self-contained classes have closed due to low enrollment. As a result, these students have gone back to their home school district with an interpreter and/or itinerant teacher. With mainstream classes, these students require more services such as tutoring, speech services, note-taking, and captioning.

In public schools, interpreters are hired through the board of education or outside agencies. New York has no licensing requirement and certification requirements for educational interpreters vary by school district. New Jersey has no licensing requirement and certification is mandatory. The average annual salary for interpreters in New York and New Jersey is $66,250 and $55,298 respectively (ZipRecruiter, 2021).

Deaf Bill of Rights

New Jersey's deaf bill of rights (2019) ensures that deaf students who attend public schools have equal access to education. Language access must start as early as possible through sign language or other communication. In Bergen County, the special services school district operates programs for deaf and hard-of-hearing students. They offer two academic tracks based on communication modes. One uses total communication/ASL while the other uses auditory and spoken language.

> We intertwine them to provide customized programs based on students' needs utilizing the most current research and technology in the field of Deaf education. (New Jersey Joint Council of County Special Services, January 14, 2020).

Seventeen states' standards include a Deaf Bill of Rights, which brings deaf culture to classrooms and increases deaf cultural awareness.

Deaf Black Students

An achievement gap exists between Black and White deaf students. Although many deaf Black students successfully graduate from elite colleges and hold senior positions in major companies, like their hearing peers in the Black community, they are often underperforming. Deaf Black students perform below grade level, and their graduation rates are low. Little research has been found on successful Black students in high school and college (Williamson, 2007, p. 3).

Many issues stem from how Black deaf students are perceived. They are often placed in special education classrooms because they are labeled at risk, which has a negative connotation. Black deaf students are perceived as being at risk based on low academic performance, socioeconomic status, and differing cultural and family backgrounds compared to White norms. However, many programs designed to close the academic achievement gap have not succeeded (Williamson, 2007, p. 5). Deaf students are classified as being in special education classes because of a disability based on their IEPs.

According to the National Center for Education Statistics in 1996, only 5 percent of deaf Black students entered a two- or four-year college compared with their deaf White peers at 85 percent. The reasons for the achievement gap include:

- Acceptance of African Americans to deaf schools
- School enrollment in programs for the deaf
- Preschool enrollment
- Dropping out (e.g., feelings of despair)

Black students faced racial discrimination and discrimination for being deaf. In the classroom, hearing Black students do not feel as respected as their White counterparts, feel that they get called on less, and feel that their White teachers assume that they do not want to learn.

Black deaf students face cultural and implicit bias. Implicit bias expands across gender identity, racial identification, sexual preference, and workplace roles. Implicit bias treatment of marginalized people can be derogatory, hurtful, or offensive. Some may not realize the existence of implicit bias in the various areas of life.

For example, a culturally or racially non-Black teacher may not call on Black students in the classroom as much as they call on students of their same culture or race. Perhaps the teachers thinks that students are not interested in learning the class material or have unconscious bias of African American students. In addition, there is a presumption that Asians are intelligent and excel in math and science; however, some teachers may assume that people of color are lazy and do not participate in class. Microaggression is often unintentional harm. While implicit bias expresses negativity straightforwardly, microaggression expresses negativity in a subtext format.

In terms of testing, White and Asian students achieve higher SAT scores than minorities (e.g., Black and Hispanic students). Samuels (2020) surveyed students, parents, and teachers with more than 20 years of experience, involving ordering a set of factors (genetics, discrimination, school quality, income levels, and home environments) from most to least impactful to student success. Samuels (2020) found that students and parents ranked self-motivation, home life, and income levels as the most important (Samuels, 2020, para. 9).

Samuels (2020) realized that wealth is one of the main factors separating racial groups. Implicit bias suggests that low-income minority students perform less well than White students from high-income families. She found that school quality influenced student performance. For example, she found disparities in the distribution of wealth across different districts. "Right now, majority-minority school districts get $23 billion less in funding nationally than majority-White school districts" (Samuels, 2020, para. 16).

Closing the achievement gap requires new policies, more funding, and a cohesive school community. There is a large discrepancy between the number of Black and White teachers. Teachers may regard Black students as having low expectations and invoke stereotypes that classify them as social needs students. This causes them to be placed in special education remedial classes (Samuels, 2020, para. 19).

Until the 1970s, Black and White deaf students were segregated. Prior to the landmark *Brown v. Board of Education* (1954) ruling, some deaf schools began integrating Black students with their White counterparts. One example was the Kendall school in Washington D.C. In 1857, a separate residential building was built on campus for Black students while the classrooms for Blacks and Whites were integrated. Even though the classrooms were integrated, their sleeping facilities were separated. When the historic landmark decision passed, all deaf students were placed together. Although the school was the first to accept deaf Black students it continued to follow the separate but equal practice.

The separate and equal 1896 *Plessy v. Ferguson* ruling impacted many Black schools because these schools were underfunded. In 1952, a Washington D.C. parent of a Black deaf child wanted to move her son to a different deaf school because she felt that the Maryland school did not offer adequate instruction. She requested to have her son attend the Kendall School, but the Washington D.C. Board of Education denied her request. Although she requested, again, to send him to a Pennsylvania school, her request was denied. She sued the Board of Education in federal court, stating that other states pay for deaf children to attend out of state deaf schools.

Two years later, in 1954, everything changed when the separate but equal clause was ruled unconstitutional (Separate But Equal, 2018). Edward Gallaudet believed in educating all deaf children regardless of their background.

> Gallaudet continued to receive letters in the late 1800s regarding orphaned Black students found abandoned in alleys, sponsored by church groups and other social agencies. He continued to respond positively to these requests for assistance for poor, Black deaf youth in need of training and accepted all who were sent. (Stapleton, 2014, p. 24).

Multiculturalism in Deaf Education

In rural and urban areas, deaf students of different ethnic or racial backgrounds from poor immigrant communities struggle with low academic achievement. Deaf children who have emigrated may not have a sense of identity of their own cultural background along with deaf culture.

> Deaf children are already developing the skills needed to be bilingual and bicultural, as they have to navigate both deaf and hearing culture but individuals who are both deaf and members of racial or ethnic minority groups must navigate three or more sets of norms, traditions, etc. (Hernandez, 2020, para. 3).

Occasionally, teachers of the deaf and hard of hearing overlook students' cultural values, which may lead to misinterpretations in the classrooms. Cultural sensitivity and responsive training is recommended to create a well-balanced multicultural curriculum. In rural areas, it is more challenging to find others of similar culture than in urban areas.

Hearing aid technology has improved greatly transitioning from analog to digital. More frequencies are available to adjust wanted sound absorption from all directions while minimizing background noise. Cochlear implants were introduced around 1975, which were only used for adults with latent hearing loss. The cochlear implants were made available for children as young as two around 1990 as well as to 12-month-olds by 2000.

Research has shown that for deaf education using the bilingual, or bimodal, method is most promising (Sparks, 2016). Deaf children who have not been exposed to sign language by age three fall behind those who have acquired ASL (Sparks, 2016). Cognitive development varies among children with cochlear implants between three and six years of age.

- group 1: deaf children, who have acquired ASL by age of 3,
- group 2: deaf children, who are not exposed to ASL by age of 3,

- group 3: deaf children, who have cochlear implants between the ages of 3 and 6.

One difference lies in the development of executive function skills: the set of skills to process, break down, and resolve problems. For example, solving a math word problem, more components of the executive function skills are needed compared to rote adding/subtracting of numbers. There is a set of skills that is needed to "unpack" the word problem. The problem utilizes complex layers of executive function skills. The child must decipher the information given, determine what the questions is asking for, organize which information comes first or needed, utilize short-term and long-term memory, and constantly self-check to complete the math word problem (Hall, et al., 2018, p. 1971). Those students ages six and up, who are language deprived will have serious implications and will fall behind grade level in reading, writing, and math.

In 1965, the Bilingual Education Act provided students, who have a language and cultural identity, to use ASL to build up on their cognitive abilities while learning sign language and English gradually (Tanner, 2017, p. 29). Bilingual teachers should be trained in ASL and deaf culture as well as proficiency in their subject area knowledge.

Schools with bilingual programs benefit deaf children with a strong ASL foundation. For those with cochlear implants, families want their children to be in an oral/auditory school environment. Different schools offer different programs across the nation. It can be just a bilingual environment, strictly oral/auditory, or both.

One of the keys for an effective deaf curriculum is to build a strong family-school relationship that involves strong parental engagement. This success often increases student achievement. Parents have a voice and develop good partnerships with their children's school. Social efficacy and role construction of the families are positive indicators that children can do well in school.

Many low-income families do not or cannot come to school for meetings or other activities due to time constraints, financial burdens, lack of transportation, language barriers, or feeling defensive or inadequate. Some deaf children are immigrants and dual interpreters in ASL/Spanish are needed.

One of the goals of parental engagement is for families to take home the learning skills needed to help their deaf child improve. For example, parents attended orientation at the school to teach their children how to problem solve or do critical thinking skills. Another example is family nights during which parents can learn more about deaf culture or learn ASL with their children in after-school programs.

Surveys and questionnaires can be used to evaluate program effectiveness. Funding is needed to develop strategies for parents to help their deaf children learn how to work with their hearing aids as well as guiding children with study skills. Some of the family members of deaf children need ASL/ESL help, so schools need funding to provide programs.

Technology Services

Providing assistive technology resources is costly for deaf and hard-of-hearing children. Besides hearing aids and cochlear implants, students require other tools like strobe lights, communication boards, closed captioning, ASL videos, CART services (Remote Captioning), and Frequency Modulated (FM) systems. The FM system uses a transmitter and receiver to create a loop system using a frequency. It is a wireless system like Bluetooth. The FM receivers' boots are connected to the hearing aids and receive the signal from the FM transmitter. The receivers can block out most of the sound and focus more of the speech sounds coming from the speaker. The sound waves can travel up to 60 feet in the classroom or out in the hallway. Students are responsible to make sure that the FM is charged and stored away at the end of the day.

As of this writing, the replacement of one FM system costs close to a thousand dollars. New York City provides this equipment for students to use and must return at the end of the year. Under the IDEA, Students with an IEP or 504 plan are eligible for this assistive equipment. The school system pays for the assistive technology system, which is budgeted from the state budget (Musgrove, 2020, para. 1).

Families can purchase hearing aids and cochlear implants. Health insurance can cover hearing aids and cochlear implants but for low-income families who can't afford health insurance, the school system can provide assistive technology. The microphone on the hearing aid receives the sound and then the sound is amplified through a speaker. Deaf children with profound deafness have sense neural loss. The nerves in the ear are not functional. Hearing aids often come with some issues such as feedback, static, and buzzing noises.

The New Jersey Deaf Education Advisory Group (NJDEAG) governs the New Jersey Deaf Education program that covers approximately 720,000 individuals with hearing loss with an $800,000 budget and six employees (Sullivan, 2020). The Advisory Board, NJDEA, recommends at least a $1,000,000 budget increase for deaf education. (Sullivan, 2020). The U.S. Department of Education ranked New Jersey on the Poor Report Card as twenty-ninth in high school completion, forty-fifth in college degrees, and thirty-third in deaf employment.

The state report cards show how poverty levels affect college readiness and attendance in school districts. There is a correlation between poverty and low scores on college admission tests. Research shows that increased funding does increase student achievement (Baker et al., 2018, p. 1). For deaf schools in high poverty districts, more funding is needed to close the achievement gap.

> School funding reform also leads to improvements far beyond test scores. A study of school finance reforms of the 1970s and 80s finds that increased spending led to higher high school graduation rates, greater educational attainment, higher earnings and lower rates of poverty in adulthood (Baker et al., 2018, p. 1).

Baker and his colleagues found unfair funding systems in many states, which impact high poverty districts disproportionately.

Deaf children placed in their own neighborhood schools may be not be cost effective because more resources for qualified teachers, interpreters, technology equipment, and services are needed to support their learning. The cost of schooling for high needs students in one school district can crush a school budget in a smaller community, with a school district with fewer students. Geographically speaking, more funding and resources are given to students in highly urban school districts than in very rural areas.

Currently, there is a shortage of teachers of the deaf and hard of hearing in rural and urban areas. Deaf schools and mainstream schools are constantly looking for well qualified teachers of the deaf and hard of hearing. For the next decade, there will be a 20 percent growth in demand for special education teachers (DeafJobWizard, 2019). The reasons for the teacher shortage include:

- Teacher preparation deaf programs are inadequate.
- Deaf programs lack the appropriate resources to prepare teachers of deaf students from different cultural backgrounds.
- High rates of teacher turnovers are due to low retention.
- Low pay, lack of administrative support, and poor work environments. (DeafJobWizard, 2019).

Newly hired teachers are placed in classes with difficult students or in classes that are outside their certified subject area. Part of their job is to complete IEP documents annually and monitor progress goals for their students. Lastly, some teachers of the deaf and hard of hearing have minimal American Sign Language (ASL) skills with which to teach deaf students.

In New Jersey, there are 365 educational interpreters with no method of evaluating them using some type of standardized test. The New Jersey Department of Education requires interpreters to take the Educational Interpreter Performance Assessment (EIPA) exam.

The EIPA is a tool that evaluates the voice-to-sign and sign-to voice skills of interpreters who work in the elementary through secondary classroom using videotape stimulus materials and a procedure that includes a comprehensive rating system. (Qualifications of Educational Interpreters - Administrators: Classroom Interpreting.org, 2021, para. 1)

The rating system requirements range from one to four. A rating of three and above is considered meeting the standards. Interpreters who are not qualified are not able to provide the interpreting skills and knowledge to help deaf students succeed in the classroom.

States across the country, with federal and state funding, can provide strong teacher programs such as deaf bilingual programs. Teachers and interpreters should be qualified in ASL using a scoring guide to evaluate their knowledge of sign language. Increasing the EIPA score from a 3 to a 3.5 would ensure that more qualified interpreters and teachers meet strict standards of competency and skills to increase deaf student achievement in the classroom. The training of teachers to better understand the IEP process and Section 504 will help to fulfill the needs of deaf and hard-of-hearing children. Teachers of the deaf and hard of hearing should examine achievement data for their students and use the data to improve instruction.

A professional learning community (PLC) is a great solution for grade level teams to collaborate on culturally responsive teaching. A characteristic of a high performing PLC is a "Shared mission (purpose), vision (clear direction), values (collective commitments) and goals (indicators, timelines, and targets), which are focused on student learning" (Dufour & Fullan, 2013, p. 14). Strong school-family partnerships increase student achievement and enhance two-way communications.

Funding in Deaf Education

More money is needed for special education. The material resources for deaf students to succeed require appropriate funding. Students are entitled to a free adequate public education (FAPE). The amount of funding and how it's distributed affects student achievement. Higher poverty districts receive less funding, therefore fewer resources than affluent districts. Special education services in high poverty districts tend to have more low-income families and immigrants.

In New Jersey, the Abbott school districts (i.e., Special Needs Districts) have high poverty, which requires more funding for deaf children. One deaf school, the Bruce Street School, situated in Newark, New Jersey, enrolls about 600 deaf students, who are all minorities. State testing shows that these students underperform compared to the state average and average per pupil spending is around $44,000.

The New Jersey School Funding Reform Act (SFRA) needs increased funding for high poverty school districts as well as for hiring experienced teachers and interpreters. "Equitable and adequate financing is a prerequisite condition for a thorough and efficient school system" (Weber & Baker, 2021). Lower funding levels will result in limited resources in terms of hiring qualified teachers/interpreters and having the necessary technology services to support learning. State formulae must provide more funds to high need special education students.

One problem facing very young deaf and hard-of-hearing children in closing the achievement gap with their hearing peers is language delay. One proposed remedy is to provide early intervention for deaf and hard-of-hearing infants and toddlers in the language they need. This allows young deaf children to get a head start on executing functioning and improving their cognitive skills. To accomplish this goal, early intervention specialists are essential in providing these skills for them. Specialists must understand that language deprivation among young deaf and hard-of-hearing children will have a negative impact in their future.

On October 21, 2021, the U.S. Department of Education awarded a federal grant of $1.25 million to Iona College in New Rochelle, New York. The funds provide specialist training in early childhood deafness. Forty graduates are selected in the certificate program to work with deaf and hard-of-hearing children for the next five years. The certificate program will take two summers and one academic year to complete.

This certificate program needs government support because while there are relatively few deaf and hard-of-hearing children, those who do not have access to high-quality specialists may experience profound linguistic, social, and cognitive delays due to lack of language access (*Awarded $1.25 Million Grant to Train Specialists in Early Childhood Deafness, Filling a Critical Need*, 2022).

The federal grant would provide the resources that professionals need to support deaf and hard-of-hearing children. The condition of the grant is once the graduates are certified, they must fulfill their obligations to serve two years of work with deaf and hard-of-hearing children or pay back the scholarships. This is a true endeavor to ensure graduates today get the proper training to educate our young deaf children in language literacy.

The U.S. Department of Education awarded a $1.1 million grant to the Deaf Education and Hearing Science Program based at The University of Texas Health Science Center at San Antonio to improve deaf education. Currently, there is a shortage of teachers of the deaf and hard of hearing nationwide. Students in this program undergo nine hours of educational psychology along with six hours of deaf education as part of the master's degree program. This enables future educators to analyze test results to better inform practice (Sansom, 2021, para. 4).

Higher Education

Many college-bound deaf students benefit from financial aid like Pell grants or loans. Deaf students who attend the National Institute of Technology (NTID) at Rochester Institute of Technology receive financial support. NTID tuition assistance is granted to any student with a hearing loss. The Gallaudet University in Washington D.C. is federally funded. Both colleges by law must charge the same amount of tuition because they are federally funded, which allows students to choose a college based on educational need rather than affordability.

Many grants are available for deaf and hard-of-hearing students that are based on type of disability or mode of communication such as congenital deafness, blindness, or progressive hearing loss. Grants range from $1,000 to $10,000. These programs offer several scholarships for full-time students who are deaf and hard of hearing and use listening and spoken language, and who are pursuing a four-year undergraduate degree or a graduate degree at an accredited college or university. To be eligible, spoken communication must be the applicant's primary mode of communication (Scholarships.com, 2022, para. 2).

There are no IEP or 504 plans for deaf and hard-of-hearing students in college. The IDEA Act does not apply to higher education. Both private and public colleges and universities must offer equal access for students that follows the Section 504 Rehabilitation Act of 1973 and offer disability services for students with disabilities.

Vocational Rehabilitation

Vocational rehabilitation (VR) is a federal funded state program that assists students with disabilities including deaf and hard-of-hearing students. Many deaf and hard-of-hearing students receive funding from their state Vocational Rehabilitation (VR) agencies. This includes financial help with tuition, books, technological aids, and other information (*Financial Aid for Students: Vocational Rehabilitation*, 2021, para. 2). Eligibility is based on hearing loss and family income. If accepted, students must apply for financial aid and VR will cover just a portion of their college expenses. Each state VR has their own rules for how students with disabilities are processed.

State Lotteries

The State Lottery offers funding relief to schools as it "generates, on average, about 3% of total state revenues" (Brady & Pijanowski, 2007, p 20). The New Jersey Lottery that began in 1970, in 2012 provided $950,000,000 to support educational programs and institutions. In 2014, the ticket sales collected provided close to 30 percent to state programs. A portion of the lottery provided funding for the Marie Katzenbach School for the Deaf (MKSD). The MKSD is a state school, with tuition that is about $45,000 per-pupil and provides special services and accommodations. MKSD receives about $2,000,000 annually from the New Jersey lottery (Mega Millions, 2013).

State Funding

Two deaf schools in Fremont and Riverside, California have high per-pupil spending. However, does higher spending result in higher achievement? Deaf students have been underperforming or below proficiency in reading and writing in the elementary grades. Lisa Snell, a director of education at the Reason Foundation, in California, suggests that special needs scholarships offer the best solution (*The Price Tag for Schools for the Deaf*, NYTimes.com, 2011).

Although Florida and Kentucky provide families with vouchers, New Jersey and New York do not offer these programs for students with disabilities. However, the Alliance scholarship is for graduates with disabilities who enter a certain post-secondary field or vocational training. (*Alliance Scholarships*, 2021). This program is offered only to students in central and northern New Jersey. They offer financial support for those who graduate from a public school and want to pursue post-secondary education. This includes financial support for disabilities with an IEP or 504 program. This scholarship is limited to ten counties in New Jersey.

Another type of scholarship is offered by the Hearing Loss Association of America. It is one of the leading organizations that represents people with hearing loss and their families. The organization has state and local chapters nationwide. Applicants must be New York City residents, have applied to a college, be between the ages of 17 and 20, wear a hearing aid or cochlear implant, and have a minimum academic average of 80 or grade point average of 3.0 or better. A $5,000 scholarship is for a high school senior with hearing loss and is to be used toward the pursuit of a college degree. The scholarship is a one-time award. Financial need is not a consideration.

Although most of the deaf schools are state funded, the number of deaf schools is decreasing. For example, deaf schools in rural areas are expensive to maintain compared to mainstream schools. In addition, medical and technological advances such as cochlear implants are done at an earlier age, which allows deaf children to enroll in mainstream schools, but decreases student enrollment in certain deaf schools.

The Vermont School for the Deaf, which closed in September 2014, was independently owned and school districts paid tuition for deaf and hard-of-hearing students to attend. The educational philosophy and mode of communication were primarily bilingual-bicultural approaches. After the closure, due to low enrollment and lack of funds, most deaf and hard-of-hearing students were transferred to their home public school districts and specialized independent schools.

The public schools in Vermont still had access to a range of services; however, the specialized independent schools' services were sporadic. The state of Vermont provides a grant of $1 million to an outside agency to provide these services. The agency contracts out for these services based on student needs. There have been some negative reviews from parents and associations, while the state believes this new agency will "cover a wide, diverse variety of services" (D'Auria, 2021).

We must find ways to get more from federal, state, and local resources for public schools. These funds must be allocated appropriately to alleviate inequities in our public schools that includes the deaf and hard-of-hearing student population.

REFERENCES

America the Bilingual. (2016, September 6). Children of a Silent God: A Bilingual Journey Through American Sign Language. https://www.americathebilingual.com/children-of-a-silent-god-a-bilingual-journey-through-american-sign-language/.

Alliance Scholarships. (2021). The Alliance. https://specialeducationalliancenj.org/alliance-scholarships/.

Awarded $1.25 Million Grant to Train Specialists in Early Childhood Deafness, Filling a Critical Need. (2022, February 18). Iona College. https://www.iona.edu/news/iona-college-awarded-125-million-grant-train-specialists-early-childhood-deafness-filling.

Baker, B., Farrie, D., & Sciarra, D. (2018, February). Is School Funding Fair? A National Report Card. Education Law Center. Retrieved from: https://edlawcenter.org/assets/files/pdfs/publications/Is_School_Funding_Fair_7th_Editi.pdf.

Brady, K., & Pijanowski, J. (2007). Maximizing State Lottery Dollars for Public Education: An Analysis of Current State Lottery Models. https://files.eric.ed.gov/fulltext/EJ809436.pdf.

Cruz, Z. (2015, May). First Language Acquisition: Is Children's Knowledge of Language Innate? www.Skemman.Is. Retrieved from: https://skemman.is/bitstream/1946/21346/1/BA_Essay_Zulaia_loka_2.pdf.

D'Auria, P. (2021, December 9). A $1 million state grant for deaf, hard of hearing and deaf-blind education in Vermont schools draws criticism. VTDigger. https://vtdigger.org/2021/12/08/a-1-million-state-grant-for-deaf-hard-of-hearing-and-deaf-blind-education-in-vermont-schools-draws-criticism/.

Deaf and Hard-of-Hearing Students in the Mainstream. (2014, January 1). Raising and Educating Deaf Children. http://www.raisingandeducatingdeafchildren.org/2014/01/01/deaf-and-hard-of-hearing-students-in-the-mainstream/.

DeafJobWizard.com. (2019, January 1). Overcoming Shortage of Teachers of the Deaf and Hard of Hearing. https://www.deafjobwizard.com/post/overcoming-shortage-of-teachers-of-the-deaf-and-hard-of-hearing

Dufour, R., & Fullan, M. (2013). Cultures Built to Last Systemic Places at Work. Solution Tree Press.

Financial Aid for Students: Vocational Rehabilitation. (2021, November 22). Gallaudet University. https://www.gallaudet.edu/financial-aid/vocational-rehabilitation.

Hall, M. L., Eigsti, I.-M., Bortfield, H., & Lillo-Martin, D. (2018). Executive Function in Deaf Children: Auditory Access and Language Access. *Journal of Speech, Language, and Hearing Research.* https://doi.org/10.1044/2018_JSLHR-L-17-0281.

Hernandez, L. (2020, January 10). Multicultural Deaf Education in Rural Communities. American Society for Deaf Children. https://deafchildren.org/2020/01/multicultural-deaf-education-in-rural-communities/.

Johnson, S. L. (2017). Deaf Education: Bicultural Bilingual Education and Total Communication in General Education. Encompass. https://encompass.eku.edu/honors_theses/450/.

Mega Millions. (2013). Mega Millions. https://www.megamillions.com/Winners-Gallery/2013/New-Jersey-Lottery-Mega-Millions-Players-Claim-Jac.aspx.

Musgrove, M. (2020, October 22). Who Pays for Assistive Technology? Parents or Schools? Understood. https://www.understood.org/articles/en/who-pays-for-assistive-technology-parents-or-schools.

Newborn Hearing Screening State Laws. (2011, May). NCSL.Org. https://www.ncsl.org/research/health/newborn-hearing-screening-state-laws.aspx.

NJ Joint Council of County Special Services. (2020, January 14). Special Services School Districts Ready to Meet High Standards of New Jersey's Deaf Student's Bill of Rights | NJ Joint Council of County Special Services School Districts. New Jersey Special Services. https://njspecialservices.org/special-services-school-districts-ready-to-meet-high-standards-of-new-jerseys-deaf-students-bill-of-rights/.

Qualifications of Educational Interpreters-Administrators-Classroom Interpreting. (2021). Classroom Interpreting. https://www.classroominterpreting.org/Admin/qualifications.asp.

Samuels, C. A. (2020, December 29). Who's to Blame for the Black-White Achievement Gap? Education Week. https://www.edweek.org/teaching-learning/whos-to-blame-for-the-black-white-achievement-gap/2020/01.

Sansom, W. (2021, October 19). Deaf Education and Hearing Science Program attracts $1.1 million grant from U.S. Department of Education. UT Health San Antonio. https://news.uthscsa.edu/deaf-education-and-hearing-science-program-attracts-1-1-million-grant-from-u-s-department-of-education-2/.

Scholarships.com. (2022). Disability Scholarships - Scholarships.com. https://www.scholarships.com/financial-aid/college-scholarships/scholarships-by-type/disability-scholarships/.

Separate But Equal. (2018, October). LII / Legal Information Institute. https://www.law.cornell.edu/wex/separate_but_equal.

Sparks, S. (2016). Studies on Deafness Yield Broader Benefits. Education Week. https://www.edweek.org/teaching-learning/studies-on-deafness-yield-broader-benefits/2016/02.

Stapleton, L. (2014). The unexpected talented tenth: Black Deaf students thriving within the margins. Lib.Dr.Iastate.Edu. https://lib.dr.iastate.edu/cgi/viewcontent.cgi?article=4898&context=etd.

Sullivan, C. (2020, August). New Jersey Commission for the Deaf, Deaf-Blind and Hard of Hearing: New Jersey Deaf Education Advisory Group Recommendations for Improvements in Deaf Education. NJ.Gov.Edu. https://www.njleg.state.nj.us/legislativepub/budget_2021/Senate_Budget_Testimony/Sullivan_C.pdf.

Tanner, K. (2017). An examination of home, school, and community experiences of high-achieving deaf adults. Repository.Wesu.Edu. https://repository.wcsu.edu/cgi/viewcontent.cgi?article=1024&context=educationdis.

The Price Tag for Schools for the Deaf - NYTimes.com. (2011, July 31). NY Times. https://www.nytimes.com/roomfordebate/2011/07/31/do-states-need-schools-for-the-deaf/the-price-tag-for-schools-for-the-deaf/.

The 4201 Schools Association Testimony Presented to the Fiscal Committee of the New York Legislature Hearing on the FY 2021–2022 Executive Budget. The New York Institute for Special Education. (2021). Nyise.Org. https://www.nyise.org/apps/news/article/1376662.

Weber, M., & Baker, B. (2021, August 19). School Funding in New Jersey: A Fair Future for All. New Jersey Policy Perspective. https://www.njpp.org/publications/report/school-funding-in-new-jersey-a-fair-future-for-all/.

Williamson, C. E. (2007). Black deaf student: A model for educational success. Gallaudet University Press.

ZipRecruiter. What Is the Average Sign Language Interpreter Salary by State in 2021? (2021). https://www.ziprecruiter.com/Salaries/What-Is-the-Average-Sign-Language-Interpreter-Salary-by-State.

PART IV
Inequities in Crucial Services

Chapter 9

State Preschool Education

Karin A. Garver

Unpacking resource inequities for state-funded preschool programs reveals an often overwhelmingly complex system of program delivery with issues unique from that of the public K-12 education system. Public preschool education lies within a larger system of programs and services generally termed Early Care and Education (ECE). In addition to state-funded preschool, the ECE spectrum includes programs and services such as Head Start, Early Head Start, childcare, subsidized childcare, and home visiting. While each has a unique set of goals and standards, they are often brought together in one building to provide comprehensive services to children from birth to at least age five.

ECE programs can be found in a wide variety of locations, most commonly public schools, Head Start agencies, private childcare providers, and family childcare providers. Although this chapter focuses on inequities within state-funded preschool programs serving three- and four-year-old children, it is essential to recognize that these programs operate within a layered system of ECE, where each layer endures both individual and shared resource inequities.

Most U.S. states offer at least one state-funded preschool program. As of 2020, 44 states, Washington, D.C., and Guam support educationally based and publicly funded preschool programs serving three- and/or four-year-old children (Friedman-Krauss et al., 2021). Twelve states offer more than one program operating under separate policies, resulting in a total of 63 state-funded preschool programs offered throughout the country (Friedman-Krauss et al., 2021). Just six states (Idaho, Indiana, Montana, New Hampshire, South Dakota, and Wyoming) have other programs and services in place for preschool-aged children, but do not offer a state-funded preschool program (Friedman-Krauss et al., 2021).

Much like public kindergarten, public preschool programs operate under a set of learning and development standards and almost all require use of a curriculum aligned to those standards (Friedman-Krauss et al., 2021). Unlike public kindergarten, most states with public preschool fund and regulate the program separately from the K-12 educational system, leaving state preschool vulnerable to stark inequalities in both program funding and access. Inequalities between preschool and K-12 are further exacerbated for many programs by competing policies, priorities, and goals across various ECE programs.

To illustrate the unique resource inequalities observed in state preschool programs, this chapter first explores how states approach funding for public preschool and the resulting differences in per-child allocations between state preschool programs and K-12 public education. The impact of inadequate preschool funding is described through the layers of eligibility requirements states use to limit program access and how low levels of funding impact policies to support program quality. Finally, we explore how poor policy alignment across ECE initiatives limits the ability of program administrators to balance inadequate resources by combining funding across sectors of the ECE system. Program providers in New Jersey serve as a case study for these issues.

State Preschool Funding Methods and Revenue Sources

Understanding the significant disparities between the resources states dedicate to public preschool and K-12 education requires an explanation of the funding methods and revenue sources states use to determine preschool funding levels. While public K-12 education is funded as an entitlement in every state, public preschool is funded as a discretionary program in all but a few states. To fund K-12 education, almost every state in the nation uses either a foundation formula, a resource-allocation model, or a hybrid of the two (Dachelet, 2019).

Foundation formulas start with a base rate for each child, to which weights are added to support children with unique needs, and resource-allocation models provide funding based on the achievement of specific goals (e.g., employing enough teaching staff to meet an established teacher/child ratio) (Dachelet, 2019). Regardless of the approach, state K-12 funding is intended to provide local education agencies with an appropriate level of funding to meet the basic educational needs of all children, once capacity to contribute local resources is taken into account (Barnett & Kasmin, 2018).

Funding for most state preschool programs does not operate this way. In fact, just 11 states use their K-12 funding formula to determine support for preschool (Barnett & Kasmin, 2018). Even among those 11 states, most modify the formula in some way, for example using only base per-child rates without added weights or capping the total number of children who may be served each year (Barnett & Kasmin, 2018).

Whether states follow the K-12 formula exactly, preschool programs that are incorporated into the state K-12 funding formula tend to have more stable funding over time, even through economic downturns (Barnett & Kasmin, 2018). Yet despite the increased stability associated with including preschool in the state K-12 funding formula, most states use a form of discretionary grant to determine state preschool allocations, and more than half of preschool programs award funding only on a competitive basis (Barnett & Kasmin, 2018; Friedman-Krauss et al., 2021).

Regardless of how preschool funding is allocated, the revenue used to support preschool is generated in most states through state legislative appropriations, property taxes, and lottery revenues, with the overwhelming bulk of revenues coming from annual or bi-annual state legislative appropriations (Barnett and Kasmin, 2016; Friedman-Krauss et al., 2021). This means that support for state preschool is constantly in competition with other state initiatives and subject to both political whims and state economic stability in ways from which K-12 funding is more protected (Barnett and Kasmin, 2016).

In addition to, or instead of, legislative appropriations from the state general fund, some states use a dedicated revenue stream to fund public preschool programs. At least five states use revenue from major lawsuits to fund preschool. The 1998 Tobacco Master Settlement Agreement requires tobacco companies to compensate 46 states for the extraordinary medical costs incurred from treating residents with smoking and other tobacco-related illnesses, and Arizona, Connecticut, Kansas, and Missouri use a portion of their revenues to support state preschool (Barnett and Kasmin, 2016; Friedman-Krauss et al., 2020; Lester and Cork, 2020). Similarly, revenues from a casino lawsuit contribute to preschool program costs in Ohio (Friedman-Krauss et al., 2021). State lottery revenues provide the entire state budget for preschool in Virginia and Georgia, and a portion of the funding in North Carolina (Friedman-Krauss et al., 2020). South Carolina is the only state that uses a dedicated state sales tax to generate revenue for public preschool (Barnett and Kasmin, 2016; Friedman-Krauss et al., 2020).

Although having a dedicated revenue stream may imply that funding for state preschool is stable, all these revenue sources lack long-term stability. Revenue from each of the settlement agreements is ultimately time-limited and, in some cases, not entirely ear-marked for preschool. Revenues from state lotteries and sales taxes can fluctuate from year to year and are subject to consumer behaviors. Even taking into account the inequalities that prevail within state school funding formulas, incorporating preschool into the state funding formula appears to ensure the greatest amount of stability over time, and yet still few states employ this method.

The patchwork way state preschool programs are funded underscores the point that, in many states, preschool is treated as an initiative outside the realm of public education. Funding levels are determined not based on what is needed to meet specific educational standards or desired child outcomes, but rather based on what state leaders believe is affordable. Total funding is often based on an arbitrary per-child rate and a politically acceptable number of seats, leaving state preschool programs significantly underresourced.

STATE PRESCHOOL RESOURCES

Looking nationally at state-funded preschool education, program costs are supported through a combination of local, state, and federal funding, just like its public K-12 counterpart, but the proportion of funding coming from each source, and how much overall, looks quite different. On average, K-12 public education is funded 10% by federal funding, with remaining support divided equally between state and local resources (Barnett & Kasmin, 2016; Friedman-Krauss et al., 2021).

By contrast, state early childhood administrators report that just 4% of state preschool funding comes from the federal government, 9% comes from the local level, and the remaining 87% comes from the state (Friedman-Krauss et al., 2021). Even if federal and local resources are underreported for public preschool, there is a clear difference in how states approach K-12 versus preschool funding. This difference in approach has clear implications for total resources dedicated to state preschool and the extent to which children and families have access to high-quality preschool programs that meet their needs.

State Funding for State Preschool

Nationwide, states spent just over $9 billion in state funding on public preschool in FY2020 (see Table 9.1), amounting to just under $5,500 per-child (Friedman-Krauss et al., 2021). In an annual survey of state preschool programs conducted by the National Institute for Early Education Research (NIEER) in 2020, 19 states (41%) reported only, or were only able to report, state funding to support preschool programs (see Table 9.1). That is, these states reported no federal or local funding dedicated to support state preschool. Only 11 states (24%) reported a combination of state, federal, and local funding used to operate state preschool. Remaining states reported a combination of state and federal funding (6 states, 13%) or state and local funding (10 states, 22%).

Maine, Mississippi, Nebraska, and Oklahoma serve as rare outliers, each reporting that state funding constitutes less than half of total state preschool spending (Friedman-Krauss et al., 2021). For Maine, Mississippi and Nebraska, state statute requires substantial local matching funds which, in the case of Nebraska, can include tuition payments from families (Friedman-Krauss et al., 2021).

Federal Funding for State Preschool

Although 29 states with state-funded preschool (63%) did not report, or were not able to report, an amount of federal funding used towards the program, all but 10 states with state-funded preschool report that at least some source of federal funding is used (Friedman-Krauss et al., 2021). Funding from Title I, Head Start, the Individuals with Disabilities Education Act (IDEA), and the Child and Adult Care Food Program (CACFP) are the most commonly referenced federal funding sources, but states also reference using Temporary Assistance to Needy Families (TANF), Childcare and Development Fund (CCDF), McKinney-Vento, Title II, Social Services Block Grant, and Title III funding (Friedman-Krauss et al., 2021).

This large discrepancy between the number of states reporting that federal funding is used for state preschool (36) and the number of states actually able to report an amount of federal funding dedicated to state preschool (17) suggests that states do a poor job of collecting data on federal spending for state preschool. In addition, it appears that states are able to identify which federal sources programs are permitted to use to support preschool expenses, but not necessarily which sources are actually used or to what extent.

Regardless of which issue is at play, this mismatch in reporting illustrates the likelihood that $413.7 million in reported FY2020 federal spending (about $250 per-child, see Table 1) is an underrepresentation of federal contributions (Friedman-Krauss et al., 2021). In spite of this probable underestimation, given current state spending levels, reported federal funding would need to increase by almost $1.6 billion (284%) nationwide to reach the same proportion of support provided for K-12.

Local Funding for State Preschool

Thirteen states have at least one state preschool program with policies requiring some level of matching funds at the local level, but policies wary widely (Friedman-Krauss et al., 2021). North Carolina and Connecticut's Smart Start program do not specify how much programs must contribute to matching funds, but states like Alabama, Arkansas, Iowa's Shared Visions Program, and Mississippi stipulate a minimum percentage or require a one-to-one match (Friedman-Krauss et al., 2021).

Programs in Colorado, Maine, Tennessee, and Virginia all require local matching funds, but use weight-adjusted formulas to determine how much each locality must contribute (Friedman-Krauss et al., 2021). In-kind support is permitted to satisfy at least some of the local match requirement in Alabama, Arkansas, Mississippi, Tennessee, and Virginia (Friedman-Krauss et al., 2021).

Although 13 states require matching funding for public preschool programs, only 11 can report exact local funding levels (Friedman-Krauss et al., 2021). However, an additional 10 states report non-required local funding contributed to public preschool programs (Friedman-Krauss et al., 2021). In total, 21 states reported just $947.7 million in required and non-required local funding spent on state preschool programs in FY2020 (see Table 9.1), amounting to less than $600 per-child nationwide (Friedman-Krauss et al., 2021). Although there is evidence that states significantly underreport the level of direct and/or in-kind support provided at the local level, given current state spending levels, reported local funding would need to increase by over $8.1 billion (751%) nationwide to reach the same proportion of support provided for K-12.

Total State Preschool Funding

Looking at FY2020 figures reported by 44 states, Washington D.C., and Guam including all known funding sources (state, federal, and local), spending totaled $10.4 billion for 1.6 million preschoolers (see Table 9.1).

Average per-child spending was just $6,325 compared to $15,513 for K-12 (Friedman-Krauss et al., 2021; National Education Association, 2020). Even if federal and local spending for state preschool increased to match the proportion of spending they contribute to K-12 education, preschool per-child

Table 9.1. Reported State Preschool Funding by Source, as Percent of Total and Spending per-child FY2020

	FY2020 Total Spending[1]	FY2020% of Total	FY2020 Spending Per-child[1]	Spending to Match K-12 Proportion	New % of Total	New Per-child	% Increase
State	$9.01 B	87%	$5,495	$9.01 B	45%	$5,495	0%
Local	$947.7 M	9%	$578	$9.01 B	45%	$5,495	751%
Federal	$413.7 M	4%	$252	$2.0 B	10%	$1,221	284%
Total	$10.4 B		$6,325	$20.0 B		$12,210	

[1] *Source*: Friedman-Krauss et al. (2021).

spending would still be 27% lower than K-12 per-child spending at current state preschool enrollment levels ($12,210 per-child for preschool versus $15,513 for K-12). Of course, one could argue that K-12 spending levels are higher because first through twelfth grades are provided consistently in a full-day setting, where many state preschool programs are provided for only a half-day. In addition, one could argue that low per-child rates for state preschool prevent programs from expanding to full-day and that low per-child rates and half-day services force program providers to mix funding from multiple ECE initiatives to meet the needs of the children and families they serve (Wallen & Hubbard, 2013).

Average total and per-child spending figures provide helpful context for the status of state preschool spending in the United States, but these figures mask the massive disparities in state preschool spending across states. In FY2020, per-child spending ranged from a high of $19,463 in Washington, D.C. to a low of $527 in North Dakota (Friedman-Krauss et al., 2021). Only six states (13%) exceed $10,000 per-child (New Jersey, North Carolina, Oregon, Rhode Island, West Virginia, and Washington, D.C.). By contrast, only two states with state-funded preschool programs (Utah and Mississippi) do not exceed $10,000 per-child in K-12 spending (National Education Association, 2020). Low total and per-child funding for state preschool leads states to create policies that result in massive inequalities in program access and quality.

INEQUALITIES IN PROGRAM ACCESS

States offer public education universally, such that all school-age children are entitled to attend the public K-12 system in the locality where they reside. Families can move in and out of different localities, even from state to state, and their children will have access to public K-12 education wherever they go. This is not to suggest that K-12 program quality is comparable wherever children attend school, only that public K-12 education exists universally. Not only is state-funded preschool not offered in every state, but inadequate resources limit access within the states that do fund programs. Scarce preschool resources lead states to use eligibility policies to limit access to public preschool by geography, age, income, and child and family characteristics.

These policies are typically designed to ensure that children with the greatest need receive first access to programs, but rarely result in access for all high-need children, and certainly not for all preschool-age children. Taken together, policies restricting state preschool program eligibility result in low national enrollment rates such that only 20% of US three- and four-year-olds are served in state preschool programs (Friedman-Krauss et al., 2021). These policies limit which children can attend public preschool, but policies around program duration limit access in terms of the number of hours per day and days per year children are served, and insufficient funding also leads to inadequate policies to support program quality.

Geography

In the 45 states (including Washington, D.C.) offering public preschool, only seven require the provision of at least one state-funded preschool program in every locality (i.e., school district, county, parish or town, depending on the state) (Friedman-Krauss et al., 2021). Nine additional states report that public preschool is available in every locality despite not being required (Friedman-Krauss et al., 2021). Outside of these 16 states, policies limiting geographic availability of state preschool vary substantially from state to state. For example, Illinois and Mississippi both offer preschool program funding to localities on a competitive basis, but while the state preschool program in Illinois is offered in 101 of 102 counties (99%), in Mississippi state preschool is available in only 24 out of 144 school districts (17%) (Friedman-Krauss et al., 2021).

In the 12 states with multiple public preschool programs, it is difficult to judge program access geographically. Pennsylvania supports four state-funded preschool initiatives, two awarding funding to school districts on a competitive basis and two providing funding to any school district choosing to offer the program (Friedman-Krauss et al., 2021). None of the four programs is currently offered in 100% of school districts but overlap suggests that at least one program is likely offered in every district. Regardless, geographical limitations are the first way states put limits on preschool programs, creating the initial layer of inequality in program access.

Age

Age is the second layer of eligibility restriction imposed by states. Twenty-six of 64 current public preschool programs restrict preschool eligibility to only four-year-old children (Friedman-Krauss et al., 2021). The remaining 38 programs allow the enrollment of three-year-olds either though explicit state policy, or by allowing age-eligibility determinations at the local level (Friedman-Krauss et al., 2021). However, because limited seats are often reserved first for four-year-olds, 19 states do not serve any three-year-old preschoolers (including the six states with no public preschool program), and most states that do enroll three-year-olds serve very few (Friedman-Krauss et al., 2021).

After Washington, D.C., and Vermont, which enroll 73% and 59% of three-year-olds, respectively, the states with the highest access for three-year-olds are Illinois (22%) and New Jersey (21%) (Friedman-Krauss et al., 2021). Twenty-one states serve fewer than 10% of their three-year-old preschoolers (Friedman-Krauss et al., 2021). As a result, only 6% of three-year-old children are served in state preschool programs nationwide (Friedman-Krauss et al., 2021). Access for four-year-olds is better, but reaches only 34% of the population, illustrating the impact of other policies in place to restrict equal program access (Friedman-Krauss et al., 2021).

Income

After age, many states look to income as a third eligibility layer. Thirty-five state preschool programs restrict program access to children from low-income families, limiting enrollment to preschoolers living at or below a designated income level (Friedman-Krauss et al., 2021). Overwhelmingly, states rely on the federal poverty level (FPL) as the yardstick against which income eligibility is measured. Seventeen programs use a specific percentage of the FPL to determine eligibility (e.g., at or below 200% of the FPL), another 13 use free and reduced lunch eligibility, which is already premised on families living at or below 185% of FPL, and two use Head Start guidelines which are also premised on FPL (Friedman-Krauss et al., 2021). The remaining three programs use state median income (Friedman-Krauss et al., 2021).

Unlike public K-12 programs, some states have policies allowing public preschool programs to charge families tuition for at least some children attending the program. Six programs explicitly require programs to charge tuition, and another 13 allow program providers to determine locally whether families must contribute towards enrollment (Friedman-Krauss et al., 2021). Although almost all programs are restricted from charging the lowest income families, it is those families living just above income eligibility guidelines who are most at risk of not being able to afford tuition costs and losing program access for their children. As a result, in addition to income eligible, tuition serves as an additional, albeit indirect, way states foster unequal access to preschool programs.

Child and Family Characteristics

After program access is limited by geography, age, and income, 34 state programs allow or require consideration of additional risk factors to determine which children are eligible for public preschool (Friedman-Krauss et al., 2021). These additional risk factors vary from program to program but most commonly include homelessness, foster care, disability, or developmental delay, and having a home language other than English (Friedman-Krauss et al., 2021). Over 70% of programs that consider additional risk factors look at these characteristics (Friedman-Krauss et al., 2021).

Less commonly considered is whether the child is at risk of not being prepared for kindergarten and whether the child has a parent on active military duty, but over 40% of programs that look beyond geography, age, and income use these characteristics at least in part to determine program eligibility (Friedman-Krauss et al., 2021). While it makes sense for states to ensure that the children with the greatest need receive first access to public preschool programs, it is the overall lack of appropriate resources that forces states to exclude other children.

Program Duration

Not all state preschool programs operate following a traditional school calendar or academic year like their K-12 counterpart programs. Over one-quarter of state programs allow providers to determine their annual operating schedule locally, leaving it up to providers to decide whether to align with the local school calendar year (Friedman-Krauss et al., 2021). In terms of weekly operating schedules, 32 state programs require providers to operate five days per week, while most remaining state programs allow local providers to determine how many days per week the program is offered (Friedman-Krauss et al., 2021). Only 17 state programs require providers to offer services for at least four hours per day, while the remaining 46 programs allow fewer hours either through a specific minimum requirement, or through local determination (Friedman-Krauss et al., 2021). Together, these state regulations mean that even preschoolers who get to enroll in public preschool may not have access to classroom time equal to their 1st grade-12th grade counterparts.

Allowing preschool programs to operate outside of public school schedules adds an additional barrier to access in that it can have a negative impact on working parents' ability to choose state preschool as an option and for their children to maintain proper attendance if they do enroll. Low-income families in particular experience more difficulty getting children to preschool regularly when hours offered per week are low, as well as when the preschool schedule conflicts with parents' working hours, is different from school hours for other children in the household, or diverges from supplemental childcare provider schedules (Ansari & Purtell, 2018; Ehrlich et al., 2014; Susman-Stillman, et al., 2018). These issues prevent some parents from enrolling children who are eligible and contributes to the chronic absenteeism observed among preschool aged children, both serving to reduce their overall program access.

It is important to pause here and acknowledge that not all kindergarten-age children receive equal services across the U.S. either. In fact, nine states do not require local entities to offer kindergarten at all (Alaska, Florida,

Idaho, Michigan, Minnesota, New Hampshire, New Jersey, New York, and Pennsylvania) and of the remaining states, only 17 mandate a full-day kindergarten program (Education Commission of the States, 2020).

INEQUALITIES IN PROGRAM QUALITY

Inadequate funding does not just impact access to state-funded preschool, but also the quality of the programming offered to children who do gain access. NIEER developed ten quality standards benchmarks to track state policies associated with minimum preschool program quality. Through an annual survey of state early childhood program administrators, NIEER evaluates the extent to which each state program meets the ten quality standards benchmarks (Friedman-Krauss et al., 2021). The benchmarks include policies for teacher and teacher assistant credentials, class size, teacher/child ratio, professional development, early learning standards, support for developmentally appropriate curricula, child screening and referral, and systems for continuous quality improvement (Friedman-Krauss et al., 2021).

As of the 2019–2020 school year, only five states (Alabama, Hawaii, Michigan, Mississippi, and Rhode Island) had policies in place to meet all ten quality standards and, combined, these states serve just 3.8% of children in state-funded preschool programs (Friedman-Krauss et al., 2021). At the same time, California, Florida, and Texas serve almost 40% of the children in state preschool programs while meeting fewer than half of the quality standards benchmarks (Friedman-Krauss et al., 2021).

Although it is not one of NIEER's quality standards benchmarks, compensation for preschool teachers is a critical component of overall program quality. Poor compensation is linked to lower teacher education and credentials, higher teacher turnover, and lower teacher morale, all of which are associated with low preschool program quality (Barnett, 2003; Bellm et al., 2002). Only four states require all public preschool teachers with a bachelor's degree and early childhood certification to be paid comparably to their K-3 peers in public schools (Friedman-Krauss et al., 2019).

As a result, state-funded preschool teachers in public school settings are paid, on average, almost $7,500 less per year than similarly credentialed K-3 teachers, and state-funded preschool teachers in private settings are paid, on average, more than $17,700 less (Friedman-Krauss et al., 2019). Greater resources for state-funded preschool would allow programs to support teachers in pursuit of higher degrees and credentials and provide a level of compensation appropriate to retain preschool teachers and increase overall program quality.

CHALLENGES OF BLENDING AND BRAIDING ECE FUNDING

Understanding K-12 public education finance requires knowledge of how federal, state, and local funding streams are used together to support the delivery of a comprehensive education. Although specific funding may be generated or designated to support specific populations of children (e.g., state funding formula weights to support dual language learners), state and local K-12 funding ultimately gets blended together to support cohesive program delivery meeting basic state and local program standards, while federal funding supplements state and local aid to meet the unique needs of special populations of children (e.g., low-income children through Title I and children with disabilities through IDEA). It would be impossible to identify the specific funding stream used to support an individual child's time in the classroom because funding streams for K-12 education are pulled together to achieve the unifying goal of educating children.

ECE funding streams, on the other hand, are not always unified toward a single goal (IOM, 2015; National Academies of Sciences, Engineering, and Medicine, 2018; Wallen & Hubbard, 2013). A 2018 report from the National Academies of Sciences, Engineering, and Medicine underscores the point that for each source of local, state, and federal early childhood funding, there is a unique set of program goals (National Academies of Sciences, Engineering, and Medicine, 2018). While state preschool programs focus primarily on child development, other ECE programs are concerned with combating generational poverty or enabling parents to reenter or remain in the workforce (National Academies of Sciences, Engineering, and Medicine, 2018).

Regardless of their stated goal, few ECE funding streams (including state preschool) provide funding at a level adequate to support the full-day care working families need. To meet the unique needs of each child and family, local program administrators are forced to cobble together ECE funding from a multitude of different sources to fully support program costs. The result for local program administrators is a burdensome tangle of different and frequently conflicting eligibility requirements, quality standards, allowable or required services and related expenditures, and accountability measures (IOM, 2015; LPI, 2021; Wallen & Hubbard, 2013). This can be particularly challenging when ECE program eligibility requirements are set in such a way that children phase in and out of eligibility from year to year or even month to month (Wallen & Hubbard, 2013). Even when program administrators successfully blend funding for state preschool with funding for other ECE funding initiatives, the unfortunate result for children and families can still be wide variation in program quality and potential disruptions in the services they receive (Wallen & Hubbard, 2013).

New Jersey

Examples from the State of New Jersey illustrate the often-territorial nature of regulations controlling ECE funding and the burden they place on program administrators to provide seamless ECE programming without breaking the rules governing any one funding stream. State funding for New Jersey's preschool program, Preschool Education Aid (PEA), is appropriated each year by the state legislature based on state-established per-child funding rates and state-approved enrollment projections in a specific group of districts (Friedman-Kraus et al., 2021). Only about 180 of the state's 591 school districts (30%) are funded to provide the state preschool program (Friedman-Kraus et al., 2021). Although most of the 180 districts are permitted to serve all resident three- and four-year-old children, few are funded to do so and not all are provided with adequate funding to support a full-day program (Friedman-Kraus et al., 2021).

PEA-funded districts may choose to serve children in school district buildings, but they are also permitted to contract with local Head Start agencies and other private providers to increase capacity and ensure that all eligible children are served (Division of Early Childhood Education, 2019a; Friedman-Kraus et al., 2021). The New Jersey Department of Education, Division of Early Childhood Education (DECE) regulates how children are served in the state preschool program, as well as the relationship between school districts and their contracted preschool sites. There are both unique and shared challenges across providers in school districts, Head Start agencies, and private childcare providers who operate within the state's public preschool system and attempt to blend funding across multiple ECE initiatives.

New Jersey School Districts

PEA is allocated to school districts to serve only general education preschoolers (DECE, 2019a; Wolock & Scott, 2011). Preschoolers with identified disabilities are funded separately through the state's K-12 funding formula calculation of base aid for elementary school students, as well as special education funding (Wolock & Scott, 2011). School districts are required to blend revenue streams when serving preschoolers with disabilities and general education preschoolers within the same classroom and are prohibited from using any PEA funding to serve preschoolers with disabilities (DECE, 2019a; Wolock & Scott, 2011).

In fact, PEA is restricted for use only in preschool classrooms and may not be used to support any K-12 program costs (DECE, 2019a; Wolock & Scott, 2011). While this successfully protects state preschool funding from being pilfered to support other grade levels, it reinforces the separation between the preschool program and the K-12 education system within school districts.

In addition to restricting the use of PEA funding to general education preschoolers, districts are restricted from using PEA funding to serve non-resident children. Even if the district has space available, it may not serve children from neighboring school districts unless those children live in a school district that is also funded for the state preschool program (DECE, 2019a; DECE, 2019b). The children of teachers or other staff members are also required to pay tuition for their children to attend the program if they are not residents of the school district (DECE, 2019b).

New Jersey Head Start Providers

New Jersey Head Start grantees may partner with their local school district to serve preschool-age children in a blended program of Head Start and state preschool. The goal is to provide Head Start-eligible children with the best aspects of both programs, including the higher educational standards required by the state (e.g., smaller class sizes, increased teacher qualifications) and the higher health, social, and family services required by Head Start.

To participate in the program, the Head Start agency must contract with a school district receiving PEA and agree that state funding is used only to supplement and not supplant the grantee's existing Head Start funding (DECE, 2021b). Contracted grantees are required by both the state and the federal government to prove that no state preschool funding is spent on a Head Start activity and no federal funding is spent on a state preschool activity (DECE, 2021b).

For example, the grantee is required to use Head Start funding to pay each teacher the salary he or she would receive as a Head Start teacher, and then use state funding to increase it to what he or she would make as a public school teacher. If a participating Head Start grantee's catchment area allows for the enrollment of children from a school district that is not funded by the state to provide preschool, those children may not be enrolled in the same classroom as children supported by PEA, and no PEA funding may be used to support programming for those children. Head Start grantees are subject to financial and program reviews from both the state and the federal government and are penalized for non-compliance (DECE, 2021b).

New Jersey Childcare Providers

A non-Head Start private childcare provider may contract with a New Jersey school district to serve children in the state preschool program. Resident children are supported in full by state funding for a six-hour preschool day during the 180-day school year. Of course, many families need programming throughout the year and for longer hours to meet the demands of work schedules. For children enrolled in summer or wraparound care, the private provider must ensure that no state preschool funding goes to support the cost of serving children during time periods outside of the state-funded preschool program day (DECE, 2021a; DECE, 2021c).

Providers are required to show proof, for example, that expenditures for facilities costs are prorated for the number of days the state preschool program operates within the total calendar year (DECE, 2021a). Like Head Start grantees, preschool children from school districts without state preschool may not be enrolled in the same classroom as preschool children who are eligible for state preschool. In some centers, this means that classrooms of children within the same building, and the staff within those classrooms, receive vastly different levels of resources. Rules governing PEA also require program administrators to maintain complicated records of which children are supported by each revenue stream (PEA, state childcare subsidy, parent tuition, state wraparound funding) and for what portion of the day or year in order to satisfy strict auditing rules (DECE, 2021a; DECE, 2021c).

Although New Jersey provides one of the highest per-child funding rates for state preschool, that funding does not ensure uniformity of access, program duration, or quality for children throughout the state. It also does not ensure a seamless system of program delivery for children who need services beyond the scope of the state preschool program. Instead, conflicting eligibility requirements and restrictions around the use of specific funding streams breed a sense of exclusivity among programs and services with overlapping, or at least highly related, goals. At the very least, the constraints around blending together multiple sources of ECE funding is a disincentive for program administrators to undertake such an onerous task.

CONCLUSION

Eligibility restrictions distinguish public preschool from public K-12 in part because the former restricts participation where the latter does not, but the true distinction between public preschool and K-12 is the reason why eligibility is restricted for one and not the other: highly inadequate resources. The K-12 system is funded on the premise that once children reach age eligibility for compulsory school (in some states not until first grade), all children not otherwise engaged in private or home school programs must enroll. On the other hand, public preschool enrollment is widely restricted through eligibility policies and rarely funded with the idea that even all eligible children will enroll.

States typically restrain preschool program participation either by limiting total funding to the program or by limiting the total number of seats that may be filled in a given year. State and local program administrators may attempt to alleviate public preschool resource inequities by blending together various sources of ECE funding, but highly restricted program regulations often make it difficult to combine resources effectively.

As the U.S. begins to recover from the COVID-19 pandemic, the importance of a strong ECE system is being examined in a new light. Along with this new appreciation for a stable and affordable ECE system, rekindled federal attention has ECE positioned well for important and necessary policy changes. Secure and adequate levels of funding across the entire ECE system requires an examination of goals and policies across programs and services at the federal, state, and local level. With so many ECE initiatives funded across the US, no one initiative needs to meet every need for every child, but more closely aligned priorities would allow the programs and services already in place to provide children and families more effectively and efficiently with the critical services that they need.

REFERENCES

Ansari, A., & Purtell, K. M. (2018). Absenteeism in Head Start and children's academic learning. *Child Development*, 89(4), 1088–1098. https://doi.org/10.1111/cdev.12800.

Barnett, W. S. (2003). Low wages = low quality: Solving the real preschool teacher crisis. *Preschool Policy Matters*, 3, 1–8. https://nieer.org/wp-content/uploads/2016/08/3.pdf.

Barnett, W. S., & Kasmin, R. (2016). *Funding landscape for preschool with a highly qualified workforce.* National Institute for Early Education Research. https://nieer.org/wp-content/uploads/2018/10/Funding-Landscape-for-Preschool-with-Highly-Qualified-Workforce_December2016.pdf.

Barnett, W. S., & Kasmin, R. (2018, January). *Fully funding pre-k through K-12 funding formulas.* National Association of State Boards of Education.

Bellm, D., Burton, A., Whitebook, M., Broatch, L., & Young, M. P. (2002). *Inside the Pre-K Classroom: A Study of Staffing and Stability in State-Funded Prekindergarten Programs.* Center for the Childcare Workforce. https://www.fcd-us.org/assets/2016/04/InsideThePKClassroom.pdf.

Dachelet, K. (2019). *50-State Comparison: K-12 Funding*. Education Commission of the States. https://www.ecs.org/50-state-comparison-k-12-funding/.

Division of Early Childhood Education. (2019a). *2020–2021 District budget planning workbook instructions*. New Jersey Department of Education. https://www.nj.gov/education/ece/budget/2019-2020%20Private%20Provider%20Budget%20Expenditure%20Guidance.pdf.

Division of Early Childhood Education. (2019b). *Preschool expansion aid frequently asked questions*. New Jersey Department of Education. https://www.nj.gov/education/ece/budget/2020-2021%20Preschool%20Expansion%20Aid%20(PEA)%20Frequently%20Asked%20Questions.pdf.

Division of Early Childhood Education. (2021a). *2019–2020 Private provider budget expenditure guidance*. https://www.nj.gov/education/ece/budget/2019-2020%20Private%20Provider%20Budget%20Expenditure%20Guidance.pdf.

Division of Early Childhood Education. (2021b). *Preschool education program contract for head start grantees school year 2021–2022*. New Jersey Department of Education. https://www.nj.gov/education/ece/budget/.

Division of Early Childhood Education. (2021c). *Preschool education program contract school year 2021–2022*. New Jersey Department of Education. https://www.nj.gov/education/ece/budget/.

Education Commission of the States (2020). *State K-3 policies; Does the state require the district to offer kindergarten and if so, full or half day?* https://reports.ecs.org/comparisons/state-k-3-policies-07.

Ehrlich, S. B., Gwynne, J. A., Pareja, A. S., & Allensworth, E. M. (2014). *Preschool attendance in Chicago public schools: Relationship with learning outcomes and reasons for absences: Research summary*. University of Chicago Consortium on Chicago School Research. https://files.eric.ed.gov/fulltext/ED553158.pdf.

Friedman-Krauss, A. H., Barnett, W. S., Garver, K. A., Hodges, K. S., Weisenfeld, G. G., & DiCrecchio, N. (2019). *The state of preschool 2018: State preschool yearbook*. National Institute for Early Education Research. Retrieved on May 29, 2021, from https://nieer.org/wp-content/uploads/2019/08/YB2018_Full-ReportR3wAppendices.pdf.

Friedman-Krauss, A. H., Barnett, W. S., Garver, K. A., Hodges, K. S., Weisenfeld, G. G., & Gardiner, B. A. (2021). *The state of preschool 2020: State preschool yearbook*. National Institute for Early Education Research. https://nieer.org/wp-content/uploads/2021/04/YB2020_Full_Report.pdf.

Lester, J. M., and Cork, K. (2020). A complex achievement: The tobacco master settlement agreement. In Macbeth, H. T. (Ed.), *Looking back to move forward: resolving health and environmental crisis* (pp. 41–75). Environmental Health Institute.

National Academies of Sciences, Engineering, and Medicine. 2018. *Transforming the financing of early care and education*. The National Academies Press. https://doi.org/10.17226/24984.

National Education Association. (2020). *Ranking of the states 2019 and estimates of school statistics 2020*. https://www.nea.org/sites/default/files/2020-07/2020%20Rankings%20and%20Estimates%20Report%20FINAL_0.pdf.

Susman-Stillman, A., Englund, M. M., Storm, K. J., & Bailey, A. E. (2018). Understanding barriers and solutions affecting preschool attendance in low-income families. *Journal of Education for Students Placed at Risk,* 23 (1–2), 170–186. https://doi.org/10.1080/10824669.2018.1434657.

Wallen, M., & Hubbard, A. (2013). *Blending and braiding early childhood program funding streams toolkit: Enhancing financing for high-quality early learning programs.* The Ounce of Prevention. http://qrisnetwork.org/sites/default/files/resources/mrobinson%40buildinitiative.org/2014117%2011%3A36/Blending%20and%20Braiding%20Early%20Childhood%20Program%20Funding%20Streams%20Toolkit.pdf.

Wolock, E., & Scott, P. C. (2011). *Funding and accounting for preschool program costs for children with disabilities and preschool general education children.* New Jersey Department of Education. https://www.nj.gov/education/finance/fp/af/AccountingClarificationMemorandum.pdf.

Chapter 10

School-based Healthcare Services

Camille A. Clare and Tanya O. Rogo

SCHOOL-BASED HEALTH CENTERS AND SERVICES

For over 40 years, in a partnership between schools and community health organizations, school-based health centers (SBHCs) have provided a full range of age-appropriate health care services, applying a comprehensive model of care for children and adolescents (Keeton et al., 2012). SBHCs are clinics that provide health services to students in pre-kindergarten through the 12th grade either on site at a school-based center or off-site at a school-linked center (Knopf, et al., 2016). These services include primary medical care; behavioral and mental health services; dental and oral health care; health education and promotion; substance abuse counseling; case management; and education on nutrition. Dental, vision, and hearing screening, and the management of acute illnesses, such as the flu, as well as chronic conditions such as diabetes, mental health disorders, and asthma, may occur in a school-based setting.

In addition, SBHCs deliver preventive care, such as immunizations; provide reproductive health services for adolescents; and improve the academic performance of adolescents (Keeton et al., 2012). This model of health care may be utilized to advance health equity by providing a health care "safety net" for children who are uninsured, underinsured, or represent special populations who do not regularly access health care (Kjolhede et al., 2021).

SBHCs improve health care access for children in rural and remote areas, increase time spent learning in school by reducing travel to regular health appointments, improve follow-up compliance, and better serve adolescents (Arenson et al., 2019). SBHCs have been associated with improved educational (i.e., grade point average, grade promotion, suspension, and completion rates) and health-related outcomes (i.e., vaccination and other preventive services, asthma morbidity, emergency department use and hospital admissions, contraceptive use, prenatal care, birth weight, illegal substance use, and alcohol consumption) (Knopf, et al., 2016).

Although SBHCs are not in all school systems throughout the United States, some benefits to this health care model include increased access to care, improved health and education outcomes, and high levels of satisfaction (Keeton et al., 2012). Increased services and more hours of availability are associated with greater reductions in emergency department overuse (Knopf, et al., 2016). Community needs and resources dictate that school-based services are provided in collaboration with the community, school district, and health care providers.

The "Whole School, Whole Community, Whole Child," or WSCC model, is the CDC's framework for addressing health in schools by emphasizing the role of the community in supporting schools, the connections between health and academic achievement, and the importance of evidence-based school policies and practices (Centers for Disease Control and Prevention [CDC], 2021). The community health organizations involved in school-based health care include local health departments (15%), community health centers (28%), and hospitals (25%) (Keeton et al., 2012). However, this breakdown may not be based on current nationwide trends. For example, in New York State (NYS), school-based health care is represented by diagnostic and treatment centers (59%) and by hospitals (41%) (NYS Department of Health, n.d.). In addition, despite their proven success, SBHCs often have difficulty securing adequate funding for operating costs and developing effective financial systems for billing and reimbursement (Keeton et al., 2012).

In 2013, the School Based Health Alliance census reported 2,300 SBHCs, which represented 1.8 percent of the public and private schools (Knopf, et al., 2016). The Health Resources and Services Administration (HRSA) Health Center Program funds 20 percent of school-based health centers, and the Patient Protection and Affordable Care Act in 2010 appropriated $200 million in capital grants through 2013 for their improvement and expansion. In addition, 440,000 more patients (i.e., reaching a total of 1,230,000) were served by $95 million provided by HRSA to 278 SBHCs in July 2011 (Health Resources and Services Administration, 2017).

School districts receive Medicaid reimbursements for providing Early Periodic Screening Diagnostic and Treatment (EPSDT) benefits, which finance Medicaid-eligible children under age 21 with a variety of diagnostic and treatment services. In 2015, Medicaid paid for more than $3 billion in school-based health care services, including special education and additional EPSDT services outside of special education.

Some districts depend on Medicaid reimbursements to purchase and update specialized equipment (e.g., walkers, wheelchairs, exercise equipment, special playground equipment, and equipment to assist with hearing and vision), and assistive technology for students with disabilities to learn with abled peers. School-based health services generate healthcare savings, better health outcomes, and reductions in hospitalizations, non-urgent emergency department visits, and race-based healthcare disparities (American Psychological Association, n.d.).

Providers

SBHCs use three staffing models:

1. A single clinician may provide primary care services
2. Clinical staff who provides primary care and mental health services
3. Clinical staff who provides medical and mental health services with expanded services that involve an interdisciplinary team of social workers, health educators, vision and dental providers (Kjolhede et al., 2021).

School Nurses

Nurses in schools originated on October 1, 1902, when Lina Rogers, the first school-based nurse, was placed to reduce school absenteeism due to the high burden of communicable diseases. Her efforts led to evidence-based nursing care after one month of successful interventions in New York City schools. The school nurse has served a pivotal role in health care assessment, intervention, and follow up in the school setting (National Association of School Nurses, 2018).

According to the National Survey of Children with Special Healthcare Needs, 11.2 million U.S. children are at risk for chronic physical, developmental, behavioral, or emotional conditions. School nurses address social determinants of health, which are responsible for 80% of health concerns, including housing, income, transportation, access to health insurance, and environmental health. Nearly one quarter of children attending school in the United States live below the federal poverty level. Children from low-income families may not be able to access regular medical care for chronic health conditions (National Association of School Nurses, 2018). Therefore, school-based nurses fulfill these unmet health care needs.

Grounded in community and public health, school nurses focus on health promotion and disease prevention. They provide health education to enhance physical and mental health; inform healthcare decisions; prevent disease; enhance school performance in a primary prevention model; and promote health equity. School nurses also teach developmentally appropriate health topics pivotal to a child's learning needs and ability to learn. Such topics include healthy lifestyles, risk reducing behaviors, activities of daily living, and self-care to prevent disease and illness (National Association of School Nurses, 2018).

School nurses offer care management and the coordination of care between the medical home, family, and school, utilizing a continuous quality improvement framework to assess, identify an issue, develop a plan of action, implement that plan, and evaluate the outcome using available data collection tools. These approaches are student-centered in the context of the school community and the student's family (National Association of School Nurses, 2018).

School Physicians

According to the American Academy of Pediatrics (AAP) Council on School Health, a school physician is a physician who serves in any capacity for a school district, such as an advisor, consultant, medical director, volunteer, team physician, medical inspector, or district physician. This role is not limited to physicians in school-based health centers or community pediatricians, who are private providers to school-based children.

Dating back to the 1800s, the school physician came into being when parents and school officials recognized the need for national systemic medical inspection in schools. These roles expanded to the containment of prevalent infectious diseases of children and the management of universal immunization. Modern school physicians focus on the needs of individual children and the school community by accommodating students who have special health care needs, managing acute and chronic illness, and overseeing emergency response, environmental health and safety, health promotion, and education (American Academy of Pediatrics, 2013).

Physicians are not consistently involved in schools throughout the United States, even though typically children spend seven hours per day and 180 days in school annually. Children may only see their medical home once per year. As a result, they have varying levels of medical support and safety. School physicians serve to create evidence-based policies and practices for the coordination of school-based teams. There are no single universal set of national laws regarding school health (American Academy of Pediatrics, 2013).

According to the Primary Care Collaborative, the medical home is "a model or philosophy of primary care that is patient-centered, comprehensive, team-based, coordinated, accessible, and focused on quality and safety" (Primary Care Collaborative, n.d.). The medical home is not a physical location, but a model for health care delivery, focused on achieving primary care excellence so that "care is received in the right place, at the right time, and in the manner that best suits a patient's needs" (Primary Care Collaborative, n.d.).

This philosophy of health care delivery encourages providers and care teams to meet patients where they are, so that they are treated with respect, dignity, and compassion, and that strong and trusting relationships are developed between patients and providers and staff. In 2007, the major primary care physician associations developed and endorsed the Joint Principles of the Patient-Centered Medical Home (Primary Care Collaborative, n.d.).

School physicians bring value to the quality of health services. In addition, they save school districts money by reducing liability via physician oversight of school health programs. Costly litigation against school districts may be prevented as school physicians are involved in school physician–coordinated concussion management programs, climate standards for outdoor activity, or guided anaphylaxis management protocols to reduce morbidity and mortality and improve outcomes. Schools are funded based on student attendance so reductions in absenteeism by school physician advocacy and education on asthma or diabetes management, for example, are critical roles for them (American Academy of Pediatrics, 2013).

School physicians may have a professional relationship with schools as part-time or full-time employees, independent contractors, or volunteers on a school advisory board. Establishing clear expectations for compensation of goods and services in agreement with laws governing school districts and including indemnification and liability are crucial.

State laws regarding whether a school district has an obligation to hire a medical director should be understood by the school physician with notification by his or her professional liability insurance company of involvement in school-based health activities in writing. Compensation by the school district allows for school physician consistency and quality of services (American Academy of Pediatrics, 2013).

School Psychologists

Approximately 43,570 psychologists work in elementary and secondary schools. SBHCs provide preventive care and diagnosis, assessment, treatment, and monitoring of physical and behavioral health conditions by school psychologists. This is funded by Medicaid, which reduces the provision of costlier medical services. In addition, school psychologists help improve childhood academic achievement (American Psychological Association, n.d.).

According to the U.S. Department of Health and Human Services, one in five children and adolescents experience a mental health problem during their school years, including stress, anxiety, bullying, family problems, depression, learning disability, and alcohol and substance abuse. Serious mental health problems, such as self-injurious behaviors and suicide, are increasing, especially among young people. Approximately 3.8 million adolescents ages 12–17 years reported a major depressive episode in 2019, but nearly 60% did not receive any treatment, according to a 2019 report by the Substance Abuse and Mental Health Services Administration.

The COVID-19 pandemic exacerbated the mental health crisis in children, as evidenced by increased emergency room visits for children's mental health emergencies (Leeb et al., 2020). Nearly two thirds of adolescents who need mental health services do so only in school (National Association of School Psychologists, 2021). The National Association of School Psychologists (NASP) recommends a ratio of one school psychologist per 500 students, but the national ratio for the 2020–2021 school year was one school psychologist per 1,162 students (National Association of School Psychologists, n.d.).

School-employed mental health professionals (i.e., school psychologists, school counselors, school social workers, and school nurses) who know the students, parents, and other staff, contribute to the accessibility of services. Students are more likely to seek counseling when services are available in schools. In some rural areas, schools provide the *only* mental health services in the community.

Comprehensive, culturally responsive school mental health services address inequities in access and reduce the stigma associated with receiving mental health services. Increased access to mental health services in schools improves the physical and psychological safety of students and schools and addresses academic performance and problem-solving skills. Improving staffing ratios for these professionals is important to adequately supporting students' mental and behavioral health (National Association of School Psychologists, 2021).

School districts use Medicaid funds to expand the availability of physical and mental health services for over 20 million students living in poverty, who often lack consistent access to healthcare. While children comprise almost half of Medicaid beneficiaries, less than one in five dollars spent by Medicaid is consumed by children.

In 2017, 69 percent of school superintendents reported the use of Medicaid funding to support health professionals on staff, in addition to paying for students' health services. However, only 22 percent of schools have a full-time psychologist. Currently, schools receive less than one percent of the federal Medicaid allocation (American Psychological Association, n.d.). The low numbers of school psychologists are woefully inadequate to address the behavioral health needs of students in the SBHCs.

Since 1988, Medicaid has permitted payment to schools for certain medically necessary services provided to children under the Individuals with Disabilities in Education Act (IDEA) through an individualized education plan (IEP) or individualized family service plan (IFSP). In a 2017 survey of school districts, two-thirds of district officials reported using Medicaid funds to pay the salaries of health professionals and other specialized instructional support personnel (e.g., audiologists, school psychologists, and nurses), who provide comprehensive health and mental health services to students (American Psychological Association, n.d.).

Programs and Services

Basic Healthcare and Wellness Services

School based health centers (SBHCs) must provide primary health care on site (school-based) or off site (school-linked). Health services are given to students from pre-kindergarten through high school with parental consent. Certain types of services may not be provided including reproductive health care and mental health services. Services may be provided only during some school days or hours or non-school hours either by a single provider for primary care or multi-disciplinary teams for more complex services.

Primarily located in low-income communities, SBHCs may provide services to school staff, student family members, or others within the community (Community Preventive Services Taskforce, n.d.). Students with access to the SBHCs are more likely to report having a regular health care provider and awareness of confidential services, support for health services in their school, and a willingness to use those services (Gibson et al., 2013).

SBHCs are increasingly providing care in rural and frontier areas via the use of remote telehealth visits. In 2017, 823 SBHCs were in rural locations throughout the United States (Rural Health Information Hub, n.d.). Services include vaccinations, health and mental health screenings, prevention and peer group education, vision, hearing, and dental services, substance use treatment and prevention services, and reproductive health services. Common youth behavioral issues may be addressed in the setting of SBHCs including stress, personal safety, depression and anxiety, and other social risk factors that impact academic success and overall well-being (Rural Health Information Hub, n.d.).

SBHCs also provide an avenue for increased access to care by adolescents. Teenagers may be reluctant to seek care in traditional medical settings because of cost, and concerns about confidentiality and parental involvement (Kjolhede et al., 2021). Low-income adolescents with access to SBHCs are more likely to have received a health maintenance visit and vaccines (Allison et al., 2007).

Sexual Education within the School System

Public support for sexual education in schools originated during the 1970's due to concerns about adolescent pregnancy and subsequently HIV and AIDS. General requirements for sex education and HIV/AIDS vary among the states (Guttmacher Institute, 2021). There are several reasons why sexual education is needed in schools.

A 2017 Centers for Disease Control and Prevention (CDC) survey indicated that nearly 40 percent of all high school students reported having had sex, and 9.7 percent of high school students have had sex with four or more partners during their lifetime. Among students who had sex in the three months prior to the survey, 54 percent reported condom use and 30 percent reported the use of another birth control method during their last sexual encounter.

The birth rate for women aged 15–19 years was 18.8 per 1,000 women in 2017, a drop of seven percent from 2016. A higher number of teens abstain from sexual activity, and there has been an increased use of birth control in teens who are sexually active. Nevertheless, the United States has the highest teen birth rate in the industrialized world (National Conference of State Legislators, 2021).

The social and economic costs to society from a teen pregnancy are astronomical. The National Campaign to Prevent Teen and Unplanned Pregnancy estimates that teen childbearing costs taxpayers at least $9.4 billion annually. Between 1991 and 2015, the teen birth rate dropped 64%, resulting in approximately $4.4 billion in public savings in one year alone (National Conference of State Legislators, 2021). The costs of treating for sexually transmitted infections is nearly $16 billion annually with costs associated with HIV infection accounting for more than 81% of the total cost. Twenty-one percent of new HIV diagnoses were in young people ages 13–24 years in 2017 (National Conference of State Legislators, 2021).

The Centers for Disease Control and Prevention's (CDC) Division of Adolescent and School Health (DASH) has established an evidence-based approach to sexual education in schools to prevent adolescent HIV, sexually transmitted infections, and pregnancy. In delivering quality sexual health education, schools can provide the essential knowledge and skills to reduce sexual risk behaviors. This curriculum includes medically accurate and developmentally appropriate content to promote healthy sexual development.

Unfortunately, only 43 percent of high schools and less than one-fifth of middle schools (18%) teach key topics for sexual health education based on the CDC guidelines (Centers for Disease Control and Prevention, 2020). In addition, CDC funding has been utilized to implement school-based programs and practices designed to reduce HIV and other sexually transmitted infections among adolescents. It has also strengthened sexual health education, increased adolescent access to key sexual health services, and established safe and supportive environments for students (Centers for Disease Control and Prevention, 2020).

According to the Guttmacher Institute, state laws and policies as of June 1, 2021, include the following: 39 states and the District of Columbia (DC) mandate sex education and/or HIV education; 28 states and DC mandate both sex education and HIV education; two states only mandate sex education; and nine states only mandate HIV education. Other requirements include 30 states and Washington D.C. mandate that, when provided, sex and HIV education programs meet certain general requirements; 18 states require program content to be medically accurate; 26 states and Washington D.C. require instruction to be appropriate for the students' age; nine states require the program to provide instruction appropriate to students' cultural background and not biased against any race, sex or ethnicity; and three states prohibit the program from promoting religion (The Guttmacher Institute, 2021).

Parental involvement in sex education, HIV education, or both is required in 40 states and the District of Columbia as follows: 25 states and Washington D.C. require parental notification that sex education or HIV education will be provided; five states require parental consent for students to participate in sex education or HIV education; and 36 states and Washington D.C. allow parents the option to remove their child from instruction. Other restrictions to sex education in schools include discussions of types of contraception and abstinence, healthy romantic and sexual relationships, intimate partner violence, sexual orientation, teen dating violence, and sexual violence (The Guttmacher Institute, 2021).

Maternity Care for Pregnant Students

School absenteeism and missing prenatal care appointments are common for pregnant teenagers. One program to address this is the Prenatal Care at School (PAS) program, a model of prenatal care involving local health care providers and school personnel to reduce the need for students to leave school for prenatal care. In this pilot program, in 2010, there was a 14.2 percent increase in school attendance among students enrolled compared to peers enrolled the previous year, a 5.7 percent increase compared to a local teen clinic attendance to the group prenatal care program, and a 42 percent increase in pregnancy and childbirth knowledge. Participants reported that PAS helped prepare them for labor and delivery in satisfaction surveys, and 92 percent felt encouraged to stay in school. This pilot program benefited pregnant teens by increasing school educational time, improving preparation for labor and delivery, and increasing participation with prenatal care (Griswold et al., 2013).

Other benefits of school-based adolescent pregnancy classes include reductions in late presentation to prenatal care because of pregnancy denial and school absenteeism. Faculty, school, and support person encouragement in adolescent participation can increase parental confidence after childbirth and the continuation of school. These learning environments, which are already established for education, allow for earlier initiation of prenatal care in the first trimester, assurance of childbirth education in these high-risk groups, and early contact with the childbirth educator who serves as a liaison with school administration.

Free day care in school helps to encourage returning to school after childbirth. Parenting classes on crying, infant safety, and feeding are available. Counseling for the adolescents is focused on raising self-esteem, teaching decision-making and refusal skills, and substance abuse treatment. These program strategies may allow for breaking the cycle of poverty, low educational skills, and adolescent pregnancy in a multigenerational approach (Podgurski, 1993).

School Psychologist and Psychological Services

The National Association of School Psychologists (NASP) state that a multitiered system of supports (MTSS) enables schools to promote mental wellness for all students, and identify and address problems before they escalate or become chronic. MTSS provides increasingly intensive, data-driven services for individual students as needed. This approach facilitates collaboration while ensuring that services provided in school are appropriate to the learning context.

School psychologists have specialized training in child development, mental health, learning, diversity, culturally responsive services, and school systems and the law. Their unique expertise includes how these elements interact to shape children's behavior, learning, and adjustment (National Association of School Psychologists, n.d.).

Furthermore, according to NASP, "culturally responsive school mental health supports that encompass social–emotional learning, mental wellness, behavioral health, resilience, and positive connections between students and adults are essential to creating a school culture in which students feel safe and empowered to report safety concerns, which is proven to be among the most effective school safety strategies. Additionally, in the aftermath of a crisis, school-employed mental health professionals provide supports that facilitate a return to normalcy, are sustainable, and can help to identify and work with students with more intense or ongoing needs" (National Association of School Psychologists, n.d.).

To address the national shortage in mental health services for children, the American Rescue Plan Act, passed in March 2021, included $170 billion for school funding, which many schools used to hire mental health workers. Another strategy employed to address the mental health staffing shortage is to use school psychologists to train teachers to address mental health concerns among their students (Abramson, 2022). Curricula for teachers on trauma-informed practices can help teachers identify signs of trauma in students and how to refer to appropriate resources.

Endogenous Factors

Impact of Free-and-Reduced-Price Meals

There are several programs mitigating hunger available through schools. The National School Lunch and National School Breakfast Programs provide meals at low-cost or no cost to students who qualify. The federal government provides income eligibility scales annually to determine the eligibility for free and reduced-price (i.e., FRPL; a proxy for poverty) meals in schools (United States Department of Agriculture, Food and Nutrition Services, n.d.). In 1998, the National School Lunch Program was expanded to include coverage for snacks served to children in after-school educational and enrichment programs.

The Healthy, Hunger-Free Kids Act (Pub L No. 111–296) passed in 2010 established the Community Eligibility Provision, which allowed schools in high-poverty areas to offer breakfast and lunch at no charge to all students. The Summer Food Service Program (SFSP) serves children during the summer and in day care when schools are not in session. Through SFSP, children can receive free meals and snacks at approved community sites. However, participation in SFSP is far below the number of children eligible for the program and below the number enrolled in school meals during the school year, reflecting the challenge of reaching some populations in rural and urban areas where transportation or safety is difficult (AAP Council on Community Pediatrics & Committee on Nutrition, 2015).

In 2016, approximately 30.3 million children participated in the National School Lunch Program (NSLP) and 14.5 million children participated in the School Breakfast Program (SBP) each day school was in session. Seventy-three percent of all lunches and 85 percent of all breakfasts were served at the free and reduced-price rate.

State and local educational agencies (LEAs) accurately determine, certify, and verify children's eligibility for free and reduced-price school meals and free milk using the Eligibility Manual for School Meals. The goals of these guidelines are to protect the privacy of students and to verify the eligibility for students to participate. Eligibility is also determined for other meal programs, including the Summer Food Service Program (SFSP) for children and adult participants in the Child and Adult Care Food Program (CACFP) (United States Department of Agriculture, Food and Nutrition Services, n.d.).

Schools participating in NSLP or SBP must make free and reduced-price meals available to all eligible children. All eligible children should receive free milk in schools and institutions participating in the free milk option of the School Milk Program. The public should be notified that these free and reduced-price meal options are available in schools not only at the beginning of the school year, but also throughout the year. The goal of these programs is to avoid discrimination based on race, color, national origin, or disability.

Other eligibility categories for which students might qualify include the following: homelessness, migrant status, being a runaway or foster child, or enrollment in a federally funded Head Start or comparable State- or Indian Tribal Organization-funded Head Start or pre-kindergarten program. Households are sent an information letter regarding the option to participate in the program based on reduced price guidelines and for incomes at or below the reduced-price income limit (United States Department of Agriculture Food and Nutrition Services (USDA), n.d.).

Healthy Meals and Clean Water

The National School Lunch Program (NSLP), operating in nearly all public schools, requires "that schools make potable water available and accessible without restriction to children at no charge in the place where lunches are served during the meal service" (Hecht, 2018). State plumbing codes also require a certain number of drinking fountains per capita. Smart Snacks protections restrict the availability of sugar-sweetened beverages sold on campus and permit the sales of bottled water in schools (Hecht, 2018).

Ninety percent of schools in the U.S. receive their water from a local public water utility or from their own well. The Centers for Disease Control and Prevention (CDC) records of utility compliance with the U.S. Safe Drinking Water Act (SDWA) indicate that about 95% of utilities provide water that meets standards for contaminants including arsenic, nitrates, and disinfection by-products. In many areas of the country, especially rural ones, these quality standards are violated, and there is sparse data on well water quality. Drinking water sources in schools may be contaminated by several potential sources including lead-containing plumbing, pipes, or fittings, especially true of older schools (Hecht, 2018). This was illustrated most prominently with contaminated water supplies in Flint, Michigan (Jacobson et al., 2020).

The U.S. Environmental Protection Agency standards set 15 parts per billion (ppb) of lead in a liter of water as the level for which corrective action must be taken. The American Academy of Pediatrics recommends a goal of one ppb for lead in school drinking water. The public must demand improvements in tap water quality through the regulation of emerging contaminants and increased protections for source waters (e.g., groundwater, rivers, lakes, watersheds) (Hecht, 2018). School communities may advocate for safe drinking water in a variety of ways including voluntary testing programs for lead in school tap water for school districts; access to quality tap water as a part of School Wellness Policies; National Drinking Water Alliance resources to build effective access to water in schools; education of school communities about the health benefits of switching to water as "First for Thirst" instead of sweetened sugary beverages; and the promotion of drinking water in schools (Hecht, 2018).

Health Impact of School Policing

School resource officers (SRO) began during the 1950s and became widespread during the 1990s with increased zero tolerance policies in schools. The U.S. Department of Justice's Office of Community Oriented Policing Services program heavily subsidized the hiring of SROs. The widespread use of zero tolerance disciplinary practices, especially in schools with predominantly students of the global majority (previously described as "of color"), led students into the criminal justice system instead of the classroom. The school-to-prison pathway (previously known as pipeline) is dependent on federal, state, and local education and public safety policies that include school-based policing and the presence of SROs. More SROs were noted in large schools (1,000+ students) or in schools in urban or high-poverty areas (Lindberg, 2015).

During the 2011–2012 school year, the U.S. Department of Education (DOE) reported that 260,000 students were referred to law enforcement and 92,000 were subjected to school-based arrests. National data is lacking, but community-level reports from Colorado, Ohio, and New York, for example, indicate that the presence of police directly resulted in larger numbers of arrests for disorderly conduct, which is five times higher than in schools without SROs. A 2013 report of the National Center for Education Statistics' Indicators of School Crime and Safety stated that the percentage of students aged 12 to 18 years reporting the presence of security guards and/or police officers in their schools increased from 54 percent in 1999 to 70 percent in 2003.

Students of the global majority, those with disabilities, gender non-conforming and LGBTQIA+ students are most likely to be targeted with police actions and referrals to the juvenile and criminal justice systems. Students' feelings of alienation, distrust of authority, disengagement, and lower educational attainment were more likely when subjected to school-based referrals, tickets, arrests, and policing for minor disciplinary offenses (Lindberg, 2015).

Solutions to reduce the utilization of SROs abound. For example, in 2013, the Denver Public Schools and the Denver Police Department signed an intergovernmental agreement (IGA) to redefine the role of SROs in public schools. This led to restorative approaches to disciplinary policies, SRO training in child and adolescent development and psychology, and best practices for improving school climate and for creating safe spaces for LGBTQIA+ youth. Alternative methods for disciplinary action by administrators and school officials are sought to avoid the use of SROs unless necessary.

Advocacy efforts as offered by the Council of State Governments' Justice Center suggest the development of memorandums of understanding between schools and policing agencies; the establishment of a working group to express concerns around school based policing; research sharing on why school based policing should not be routinely engaged in discipline; data collection and annual sharing on school-based policing by administrators; evidence based approaches to restorative justice and school-wide positive-behavioral interventions and supports; and improvements in the school climate with a movement towards trauma centered schools (Lindberg, 2015).

Exacerbating Factors

Impact of Family Food Insecurity, Hunger, and Malnutrition

In 2013, almost fifty million people (14.3 percent) were food insecure in the United States. About one-third of these people have a more serious level known as "very low food security" (Gundersen & Ziliak, 2015). In distinguishing between the types of food insecurity, low food security means food insecurity without hunger, but reduced quality, variety, or desirability of diet. Those with very low food security have hunger, and at times during the year, eating patterns of one or more household members became disrupted and food intake reduced because the household lacked money and other resources for food (Children's Health Watch Research Brief, n.d.).

Food-insecure children are at least twice as likely to report being in fair or poor health and at least 1.4 times more likely to have asthma, compared to food-secure children. Food insecurity, a condition in which households lack access to adequate food because of limited money or other resources, is a leading health and nutrition issue in the United States.

The United States Department of Agriculture (USDA) measures food insecurity via responses to a series of eighteen survey questions and statements fielded to roughly 45,000 households in the Food Security Supplement of the Census Bureau's Current Population Survey (CPS-FSS). The first item addresses worry about food running out, while the remaining items address possible reductions in food intakes because of financial constraints. Eight of the items are focused on children (Gundersen & Ziliak, 2015).

Most of the research on food insecurity has been on children. The negative outcomes are especially significant in this group. For example, food insecurity is associated with an increased risk of some birth defects, anemia, lower nutrient intake, cognitive problems, aggression, and anxiety. It is also associated with higher risks of being hospitalized and poorer general health, as well as with having asthma, behavioral problems, depression, suicide ideation, and worse oral health.

In a 1998 study of over 40,000 children younger than age four from the Children's Health Watch of five large urban hospitals, compared to children in fully food-secure households, those in marginal-food-secure households were more likely to be in fair or poor health and more likely to have a mother who reported one or two substantial concerns about the child's development on the Parent's Evaluation of Developmental Status (Gundersen & Ziliak, 2015).

Food insecurity can damage children's health and brain development by years prior to the time of entering school. By kindergarten, food-insecure children often are cognitively, emotionally, and physically behind their food-secure peers. Food-insecure children are also more likely to suffer from common illnesses such as gastrointestinal illnesses, headaches, and colds when they reach preschool age. Due to the increased risk for developmental delays, many food-insecure children have greater difficulty acquiring the social and academic skills necessary to successfully transition to pre-school or kindergarten. Food insecurity predicts poor performance during a child's first years at school which has implications for future academic success (Children's Health Watch Research Brief, n.d.).

Appropriate evaluation for food insecurity in the schools that have children with poor academic performance should be considered. Federal programs, such as the Supplemental Nutrition Assistance Program (SNAP, formerly the Food Stamp Program), the Special Supplemental Nutrition Program for Women, Infants, and Children (WIC), and the Child and Adult Care Food Program (CACFP) help young children to overcome the negative effects of food insecurity on school readiness by supporting their health and development through healthy nutrition at home and at school (Children's Health Watch Research Brief, n.d.).

Food insecurity is linked to poor childhood development including the development of basic motor and social skills, and developmental delays, especially with iron-deficiency anemia in young children. Food insecure infants and toddlers are two thirds more likely than those without food insecurity to be at risk for developmental delays. Family hardships, such as food-insecurity, placed on a young child physically alter the development of crucial brain structures controlling memory and psychosocial functioning. The basic capacity to learn and interact productively with others are critical development skills in early childhood. Disruptions to this period may diminish children's ability to acquire complex school and later, job skills (Children's Health Watch Research Brief, n.d.).

Food insecure children ages 6 to 11 years were more likely to have lower scores than their peers on intelligence tests, to have seen a child psychologist, had more problems getting along with others, repeated a grade, as well as have lower math and general achievement test scores. Data from the 1999 National Survey of American Families found that food insecurity predicted poor school engagement since these children tend to be in poor emotional and physical health. In a longitudinal study, other researchers found that food insecurity as early as kindergarten was associated with poor reading performance and impaired social skills in later grades (Children's Health Watch Research Brief, n.d.).

Lack of Access and Proximity to Available and Affordable Healthy Food

Structural barriers are major factors for the development of food insecurity in school aged children and adults. For example, 2012–2013 data showed that the average distance for US households to the nearest supermarket was 2.19 miles. Persons without vehicles or access to convenient public transportation are further limited in terms of healthy choices for food venues within walking distances.

In a study of people living in predominantly Black low-income neighborhoods in Detroit, Michigan, individuals traveled an average of 1.1 miles farther to the closest supermarket compared to those living in predominantly white low-income neighborhoods. Therefore, transportation and distance to sources of healthy foods have an adverse impact on low-income and rural communities (Office of Disease Prevention and Health Promotion, n.d.).

Low-income areas have mostly convenience stores and small food markets, which carry foods of poor nutritional quality compared to larger supermarkets. These food deserts have limited or no food sources. Lack of access to food sources that support healthy eating habits is noted primarily in low-income, racial, and ethnic minoritized and rural communities. Residents of these communities are more likely to be affected by poor access to supermarkets, chain grocery stores, and healthy food products.

Predominantly Black and Hispanic neighborhoods have fewer large chain supermarkets than predominantly white and non–Hispanic neighborhoods, further decreasing access to healthy food options for minoritized populations. Low-income groups often rely on inexpensive, conveniently accessible foods that are low in nutrient density, compared to fresh fruits and vegetables and other healthier items, which are often more expensive at convenience stores and small food markets than in larger chain supermarkets and grocery stores. Smaller stores may also charge more for healthier options, such as fresh produce (Office of Disease Prevention and Health Promotion, n.d.).

Impact of Family Housing Instability

Housing instability profoundly affects children and their families. This instability is characterized by "couch hopping," homelessness, and frequent moves. Lundberg and Donnelly in "A Research Note on the Prevalence of Housing Eviction Among Children Born in American Cities," reported that children born in 20 large U.S. cities between 1998 and 2000 from disadvantaged backgrounds were most likely to experience eviction in their lifetime. About 25 percent of children who were born into deep poverty were evicted from their homes by age 15.

Brown and Thurber in "What Explains Differences in How Homelessness and Housing Interventions Affect Child Well-Being," conducted 80 semi-structured interviews with mothers, and found that housing instability and shelter use were often related to increased family stress and school instability. Children are further disrupted by unfamiliar restrictions on their daily schedules in the shelter environment, including the lack of privacy, which plays a critical role in shaping children's behavior. Brown further notes that connecting families to stable, independent housing can reduce parental stress and negative side effects for children (HUD User, n.d.).

Homelessness

It is estimated that there are 500,000 to two million homeless adolescents in the United States. Homeless adolescents have particularly poor health compared to the general population and experience higher rates of sexually transmitted infections, human immunodeficiency virus, pregnancy, depression, and injuries. If these adolescents also self-identify as members of the LGBTQIA+ community, then they may also be at additional risk for depression and suicide.

Compared to shelter-based homeless youth, those seeking care from school-based health centers as their location of last use had lower rates of risk-taking behaviors (early sexual initiation, forced sex experiences, higher rates of multiple sex partners, and increased drug use behaviors) and more positive health experiences compared to their peers who did not attend SBHCs. These homeless adolescents were more likely to seek care in emergency rooms or hospital clinics compared to SBHCs (Ensign & Santelli, 1998).

The U.S. Department of Education reported that in 2013–2014, public schools served a total of 1.36 million homeless youth, who are also at significant risk of diseases, injuries, and developmental delays with lifelong consequences. The Health Care for the Homeless (HCH) and other service providers have developed strategies for engaging homeless youth in systems of care to reduce a lifetime risk of homelessness and minimize poor health (School Based Health Alliance, 2016).

Lack of Housing

Lack of housing leads to poor health, including environmental concerns, neighborhood factors (e.g., lack of walkability, safety, access to affordable supermarkets), and the psychosocial stress of financial instability. Housing instability stems from increasing rents, inadequate housing availability, and poor access to legal resources to fight evictions.

Research that has examined foreclosures and its relationship to health has found significant relationships between foreclosures and higher body mass index, higher systolic blood pressure, a greater frequency of psychological distress, poorer reported health, a higher number of positive depression screens and self-reported anxiety attacks, an increased number of service calls about domestic violence, higher rates of suicide, increased number of emergency visits and hospitalizations, higher rates of alcohol dependence, lower rates of health insurance, higher rates of cost-related unmet health needs, and higher rates of cost-related prescription non-adherence (Gill, 2018).

This adversely affects people of the global majority in the United States. For example, 54.7% of Black households were categorized as rent burdened in 2015, compared to 42.7% of white households. Persistent residential segregation may explain racial health disparities including chronic disease burdens, cancer rates, mortality, and geographic access to health care.

In a randomized controlled trial, conducted in five cities in the 1990's focusing on providing financial support to families to move out of impoverished neighborhoods, researchers demonstrated that these families had significantly lower rates of diabetes, obesity, and psychological distress. Children who participated in the study at the time of the move were more likely to attend college, had higher average earnings, and lower rates of single parenthood. Another study showed that children who experienced a period of homelessness in utero were more likely to have fair or poor health and to be at risk for developmental delays (Gill, 2018).

Absenteeism

Approximately 13% of students, which represents more than 6.5 million children in the United States, experience chronic absenteeism by missing 15 or more days of school annually as defined by the U.S. Department of Education's Office of Civil Rights. These rates vary by state, community, and school. There are disparities in absenteeism based on race, ethnicity, and income. African American, Latino/a/e/x, American Indian, and Pacific Islander students experience higher rates of chronic absenteeism than their white and Asian American peers. Chronic school absenteeism, starting as early as preschool and kindergarten, puts students at risk for poor school performance and dropping out of school, leading to unhealthy behaviors as adolescents and young adults, as well as poor long-term health outcomes (Allison & Attisha, 2019).

Poverty, unstable housing conditions, and poor parental health are associated with poor child health outcomes (Allison & Attisha, 2019). Although some authors report that being a member of a racial or ethnic minoritized group is associated with poor child health outcomes (Allison & Attisha, 2019), structural racist policies and practices contribute to these outcomes. Students living in poverty are more likely than students from higher-income families to be chronically absent from school. These students are more likely to have poorer overall health, unstable housing conditions, transportation difficulties, and exposure to violence.

Those who change schools within the school year are also more likely to experience absenteeism. Low-income families more often have youth who may be needed to care for sick family members or to stay home with younger siblings when a parent or primary caregiver is sick or cannot take time off work. In addition, students from racial and ethnic minoritized populations or who do not speak English as their primary language are more likely to be chronically absent than students who are not in these groups (Allison & Attisha, 2019).

Maltreated children or those exposed to major trauma, such as witnessing domestic violence or experiencing a natural disaster, are more likely than those without these exposures to experience absenteeism, truancy, school suspension, and increased school dropout rates. They may also have poor mental and behavioral health, poverty, homelessness, and frequent school changes. Children living in foster care are more likely to transfer schools within a year compared with the general school population, which is usually decreased in children with more stable (three months or longer) foster care placements. Immigrant and refugee children are likely to have one or more risk factors for poor school outcomes, including poverty and having exposure to major trauma (Allison & Attisha, 2019).

Poor school performance is associated with poor adult health outcomes. Adults with low educational attainment are more likely to be unemployed or work at a part-time or lower-paying jobs; are less likely to report having a fulfilling job; and are less likely to report feeling that they have control over their lives or that they have high levels of social support. The latter is associated with difficulty adhering to healthy behaviors, depression, increased inflammation, and reduced immune system function. Adults with lower educational attainment are also more likely to smoke and less likely to exercise. Not earning a high school diploma is associated with increased mortality risk or lower life expectancy. Conversely, obtaining advanced degrees and additional years of education are associated with a reduced mortality risk. Over the past 20 years, disparities in mortality rates based on educational attainment worsen for preventable causes of death (Allison & Attisha, 2019).

Chronic absenteeism is associated with engaging in unhealthy and risky behaviors, such as smoking cigarettes or marijuana, alcohol, other drug use, and risky sexual behavior, including having four or more sexual partners. These students may experience teenage pregnancy, violence, unintentional injury, and suicide attempts. Approximately 30% to 40% of female teenage dropouts are mothers, and teenage pregnancy is the most common cause of female students dropping out of school. Poor school attendance is associated with juvenile delinquency. In a study of Mississippi youth from 2003 to 2013, the authors found that those with chronic absenteeism had 3.5-times higher odds of being arrested or referred to the juvenile justice system (Allison & Attisha, 2019).

It is challenging to determine the health conditions that are more likely to be associated with chronic absenteeism, but such common health problems include influenza infection, group A streptococcal pharyngitis, gastroenteritis, fractures, poorly controlled asthma, type 1 diabetes mellitus, chronic fatigue, chronic pain (including headaches and abdominal pain), seizures, poor oral health, dental pain, and obesity. Behavioral and mental health conditions (oppositional defiant disorder, conduct disorder, depression, and tobacco, alcohol, and marijuana abuse) may further compound physical conditions that may lead to chronic absenteeism (Allison & Attisha, 2019).

Children with disabilities and those with special needs are more likely to experience chronic absenteeism. In addition, those with moderate to severe autism spectrum disorder or who have disruptive behaviors that affect their or other children's learning may be more likely to be excluded or absent from school.

Strategies to combat absenteeism include universal school-based programs for strengthening youth skills, connecting youth to caring adults and activities through mentoring and after-school programs, and creating protective community environments and a positive school climate. Strong parental monitoring and involvement can reduce levels of delinquency, which is associated with better school attendance (Allison & Attisha, 2019).

Impact of ACEs (Adverse Childhood Experiences) in Schools and on Health

Individual factors in children (hyperactivity, conduct problems, and poor perceived health), family factors (low maternal education and high levels of unemployment), and school factors (not feeling safe or not being treated with respect at school) can contribute to poor attendance. School health care providers should assess students for bullying, issues with gender identity and sexuality, and adverse childhood experiences (ACEs). In-person and electronic bullying have been shown to be associated with school absenteeism. Lesbian, gay, bisexual, transgender, queer, and questioning youth have been shown to be at risk for poor school connectedness, the latter of which is a risk for poor attendance. Students with higher numbers of ACEs are also more likely to have chronic absenteeism than students with fewer ACEs (Allison & Attisha, 2019).

ACEs are based on a 1998 CDC-Kaiser Permanente study of physical and mental health problems in over 17,000 adults, which showed a direct correlation between 10 adverse childhood experiences in children less than 18 years old and future health outcomes. These 10 ACEs included additional categories within the framework of abuse (physical, emotional, or sexual), neglect (physical or emotional), and household dysfunction (mental illness, mother treated violently, incarcerated relative, substance abuse, or divorce). Community and environmental ACEs, such as racism, bullying and community violence, impact future health consequences (Joining Forces for Children, n.d.).

School based health centers play a major role in students' educational success. They may improve educational outcomes, including grade point average and high school graduation. SBHCs provide health services to students, who otherwise may have been sent home or missed school because of illnesses, injuries, or attending medical appointments for the management of chronic health problems. SBHCs can reduce absenteeism. For example, African American male SBHC users were three times more likely to stay in school than their peers who did not use SBHCs. In two studies in New York, the authors reported that students enrolled in SBHCs had more time in class, better attendance, and fewer hospitalizations attributable to asthma (Allison & Attisha, 2019).

SBHCs have a 50% decrease in absenteeism and 25% decrease in tardiness for high school students, who received school-based mental health services. Mental health treatment in this setting was associated with improved overall educational outcomes for children. Cognitive behavioral therapy for students identified with "school refusing" has also been shown to improve attendance, anxiety, and depressive symptoms.

In "trauma-informed schools," adults in the school community are prepared to recognize and respond to those who have been affected by trauma. The life experiences of a student and how the experiences may affect the student's behavior and performance at school are critical to providing individual mental health interventions for students and/or link students and families to services in the community. Early research in this trauma-informed approach at schools has demonstrated reduced school suspensions and expulsions and improved attendance and school performance. However, additional research is needed on the long-term impact of this model of education in schools (Allison & Attisha, 2019).

Impact of the COVID-19 Pandemic on Child Health and Learning

The COVID-19 pandemic, which started in 2020, has had profound impacts on child health and its effects on the current generation of children will likely be studied for many years. Outside of the health concerns from COVID-19 infection, the physical isolation and disruption in family, school, and social routines have adversely affected the behavioral and emotional health of children (American Academy of Pediatrics, 2022). Worldwide, 1 in 4 youth have been reported to experience increased clinical depression symptoms and 1 in 5 reported experiencing anxiety (Racine et al., 2021).

The pandemic has exacerbated pre-existing disparities in morbidity and mortality, access to health care, quality education, digital and technology access, affordable housing, and safe environments (American Academy of Pediatrics, 2022). Children who were at critical learning stages (e.g., kindergarten and first grade) and those with learning disabilities or special needs are at higher risk of being negatively impacted by the interruption of formal in-person schooling. The introduction of remote learning was challenged by students and teachers with little experience with online instruction, and large disparities in digital access. The loss in scholarly and educational progress during these critical years is still being estimated, with reported projections that students returning to in-person schooling after remote learning would only achieve 63–68% of the learning gains in reading and 37–50% of the learning gains in mathematics compared to a normal school year (Kuhfeld et al., 2020).

After Hurricane Katrina hit New Orleans in 2005, research found that students took nearly two years to make up lost ground for the loss in instructional time due to that environmental disaster (Harris & Larsen, 2018).

Socio-economic disparities will impact the recovery of these educational losses such that low-income and underserved students will have less opportunity to catch-up compared to their better resourced peers.

Opportunities to Address Disparities in School-based Health

Telehealth

Telehealth technology improved access to health care during the COVID-19 pandemic as well as providing alternative communication modes among providers and students when in-person attendance of school was impossible (American Academy of Pediatrics, 2022). Disparities in digital access among low-income students can be a barrier and should be considered as this technology is developed and rolled-out in communities.

Promotion of Vaccination

Schools offer opportunities for vaccination compliance, particularly in areas where SBHCs are the primary source of preventive care for underserved students. School-based vaccination has historically been used in the United States primarily for three purposes: to accelerate the introduction of new vaccines; raise vaccination coverage in a population; and control school-based outbreaks (Lindley et al., 2008).

Statewide electronic vaccination registries can serve as tools for maintaining vaccination records for children regardless of where vaccines are administered, while serving as a means for school-based clinicians to confirm a student's vaccination history. The need to obtain and document parental consent for vaccination might be a barrier to in-school vaccination, depending on local laws related to the ability of minors to consent to medical care (Lindley et al., 2008).

Author Commentary

Some pediatricians report that health equity may not necessarily be able to be achieved within the current model of school-based health clinics (C. Phang, personal communication, July 6, 2021). The students (e.g., patients) usually need to choose between receiving care in the school-based health clinic or not receiving care from their primary care provider (PCP), in this case, pediatrician. In addition, the PCP is often disconnected from this model of care. On one hand, SBHCs can see a larger volume of patients, who are students, but on the other hand, patients do not have that relationship with a particular health care provider. Physicians are usually removed from the SBHC model of care.

As medicine expands its business model, hospitals, especially in New York, wish to maintain the patient volume and hence, reimbursement for care. Hospital systems that are primarily linked with SBHCs can bring more complex medical problems into hospitals. Inequities are usually further exaggerated in SBHCs. For instance, walk-ins are not able to be accommodated for care. Although access to care is not an issue, the quality and efficiency of care may be in question because it is unclear who a member of the medical care team is (C. Phang, personal communication, July 6, 2021).

ACKNOWLEDGMENTS

Dr. Christopher Phang for his expertise and insights as a health care consultant and pediatrician.

REFERENCES

Abramson, A. (2022). Children's mental health is in crisis. In American Psychological Association 2022 Trends Report (Vol. 53, Issue 1). https://doi.org/10.1177/0020731417707492.

Allison, M.A., & Attisha, E. (2019). Council on School Health. The Link Between School Attendance and Good Health. *Pediatrics*. 2019 Feb; 143(2): e20183648. doi: 10.1542/peds.2018-3648. PMID: 30835245.

Allison, M.A., Crane, L. A., Beaty, B. L., Davidson, A. J., Melinkovich, P., & Kempe, A. (2007). School-based health centers: Improving access and quality of care for low-income adolescents. Pediatrics, 120(4), e887–94. https://doi.org/10.1542/peds.2006-2314.

American Academy of Pediatrics (AAP) Council on Community Pediatrics, & Committee on Nutrition. (2015). Promoting food security for all children. *Pediatrics*, 136(5), e1431–e1438. https://doi.org/10.1542/peds.2015-3301.

American Academy of Pediatrics. (2013). Role of the School Physician. *Pediatrics* 2013; 131; 178. DOI: 10.1542/peds.2012-2995.

American Academy of Pediatrics. (2022). Interim Guidance on Supporting the Emotional and Behavioral Health Needs of Children, Adolescents, and Families During the COVID-19 Pandemic. https://www.aap.org/en/pages/2019-novel-coronavirus-covid-19-infections/clinical-guidance/interim-guidance-on-supporting-the-emotional-and-behavioral-health-needs-of-children-adolescents-and-families-during-the-covid-19-pandemic/.

American Psychological Association. (n.d.) Psychologists, School-Based Health Centers, and Medicaid. Retrieved from https://www.apa.org/advocacy/education/medicaid-schools-facts.pdf.

Arenson, M., Hudson, P. J., Lee, N. H., & Lai, B. (2019). The Evidence on School-Based Health Centers: A Review. *Global Pediatric Health*, 6, 1–10. https://doi.org/10.1177/2333794X19828745.

Centers for Disease Control and Prevention (CDC). (2020). What Works: Sexual Health Education. February 3, 2020. Retrieved from https://www.cdc.gov/healthyyouth/whatworks/what-works-sexual-health-education.htm.

Centers for Disease Control and Prevention (CDC). (2021). Whole School, Whole Community, Whole Child Healthy Schools. Division of Population Health, National Center for Chronic Disease Prevention and Health Promotion. https://www.cdc.gov/healthyschools/wscc/index.htm.

Children's Health Watch Research Brief. (n.d.). Too Hungry to Learn: Food Insecurity and School Readiness. Retrieved from https://www.childrenshealthwatch.org/wp-content/uploads/toohungrytolearn_report.pdf.

Community Preventive Services Taskforce. (n.d.). Health Equity: School-Based Health Centers. Retrieved from https://www.thecommunityguide.org/findings/promoting-health-equity-through-education-programs-and-policies-school-based-health-centers.

Ensign, J. & Santelli, J. (1998). Health Status and Service Use: Comparison of adolescents at school-based health clinic with homeless adolescents. *Archives of Pediatric & Adolescent Medicine*. 1998; 152 (1): 20–24. doi:10.1001/archpedi.152.1.20).

Gibson, E. J., Santelli, J. S., Minguez, M., Lord, A., & Schuyler, A. C. (2013). Measuring school health center impact on access to and quality of primary care. *Journal of Adolescent Health*, 53(6), 699–705. https://doi.org/10.1016/j.jadohealth.2013.06.021.

Gill, F. (2018). The Severe Health Consequences of Housing Instability. People's Policy Project. July 9, 2018. Retrieved from https://www.peoplespolicyproject.org/2018/07/09/the-severe-health-consequences-of-housing-instability/.

Griswold, C.H., Nasso, J.T., Swider, S., Ellison, B.R., Griswold, D.L., & Brooks, M. (2013). The Prenatal Care at School Program. *Journal of School Nursing*. 2013; 29(3): 196–203. doi:10.1177/1059840512466111.

Gundersen, C. & Ziliak, J.P. (2015). Food insecurity and health outcomes. *Health Affairs*, 34 (11) (2015): 1830–1839. Doi 10.1377/hlthaff.2015.0645.

Guttmacher Institute. (2021). Sex and HIV Education. June 1, 2021. Retrieved from https://www.guttmacher.org/state-policy/explore/sex-and-hiv-education.

Harris, D., & Larsen, M. (2018). The effects of the New Orleans post Katrina market-based school reforms on medium-term student outcomes. https://educationresearchalliancenola.org/files/publications/Harris-Larsen-Reform-Effects-2019-08-01.pdf.

Health Resources and Services Administration (HRSA). (2017). School Based Health Centers. May 2017. Retrieved from https://www.hrsa.gov/our-stories/school-health-centers/index.html.

Hecht, C. (2018). Safe water in schools: what do we know? What can we do? Green Schools National Network. February 13, 2018. Retrieved from https://greenschoolsnationalnetwork.org/safe-water-in-schools-what-do-we-know-what-can-we-do/.

HUD User. (n.d.) How Housing Instability Impacts Individual and Family Well-Being. Retrieved from https://www.huduser.gov/portal/pdredge/pdr-edge-featd-article-020419.html.

Jacobson, P. D., Boufides, C. H., Chrysler, D., Bernstein, J., & Citrin, T. (2020). The role of the legal system in the Flint water crisis. Milbank Quarterly. Volume 98. June 2020. Retrieved from www.milbank.org/quarterly/articles/the-role-of-the-legal-system-in-the-flint-water-crisis/?gclid=Cj0KCQjw0umSBhDrARIsAH7FCoch5oVIGpbLPTU9z5abJuGq7dpQciirgHAfSEIxvp698WmYcd5xjIgaAmoEEALw_wcB.

Joining Forces for Children. (n.d.) Adverse Childhood Experiences (ACEs). Retrieved from https://www.joiningforcesforchildren.org/what-are-aces/.

Keeton, V., Soleimanpour, S., & Brindis, C.D. (2012). School-based health centers in an era of health care reform: building on history. *Current Problems in Pediatric & Adolescent Health Care.* 2012 Jul; 42(6): 132–56; discussion 157–8. doi: 10.1016/j.cppeds.2012.03.002. PMID: 22677513; PMCID: PMC3770486.

Kjolhede, C., Lee, A. C., & Council on School Health. (2021). School-based health centers and pediatric practice. *Pediatrics*, 148(4), e2021053758. https://doi.org/10.1542/peds.2021-053758.

Knopf, J.A., Finnie, R.K., Peng, Y., Hahn, R.A., Truman, B.I., Vernon-Smiley, M., Johnson, V.C., Johnson, R.L., Fielding, J.E., Muntaner, C., Hunt, P.C., Phyllis Jones, C., & Fullilove, M.T. (2016). Community Preventive Services Task Force. School-Based Health Centers to Advance Health Equity: A Community Guide Systematic Review. *American Journal of Preventive Medicine.* 2016 Jul; 51(1):114–26. doi: 10.1016/j.amepre.2016.01.009. PMID: 27320215; PMCID: PMC5759331.

Kuhfeld, M., Soland, J., Tarasawa, B., Johnson, A., Ruzek, E., & Liu, J. (2020). Projecting the Potential Impact of COVID-19 School Closures on Academic Achievement. *Educational Researcher*, 49(8), 549–565. https://doi.org/10.3102/0013189X20965918.

Leeb, R. T., Bitsko, R. H., Radhakrishnan, L., Martinez, P., Njai, R., & Holland, K. M. (2020). Mental Health–Related Emergency Department Visits Among Children Aged <18 Years During the COVID-19 Pandemic—United States, January 1–October 17, 2020. *MMWR. Morbidity and Mortality Weekly Report*, 69(45), 1675–1680. https://doi.org/10.15585/mmwr.mm6945a3.

Lindberg, M. (2015). False sense of security. Teaching Tolerance. Spring 2015. Pp.22–25. Retrieved from https://www.learningforjustice.org/sites/default/files/general/False%20Sense%20of%20Security%20-%20TT50.pdf?fbclid=IwAR2eoWYAHKxEVlqhsJ7YuTNJFXTEiKQSAsktMuT69e7FPqfoTG4ZFgabVb4.

Lindley, M. C., Boyer-Chu, L., Fishbein, D. B., Kolasa, M., Middleman, A. B., Wilson, T., Wolicki, J. E., & Wooley, S. (2008). The role of schools in strengthening delivery of new adolescent vaccinations. *Pediatrics*, 121(SUPPL. 1), S46–S54. https://doi.org/10.1542/peds.2007-1115F.

National Association of School Nurses. (2018). The Role of the 21st Century School Nurse. June 2018. Retrieved from https://www.nasn.org/advocacy/professional-practice-documents/position-statements/ps-role.

National Association of School Psychologists. (n.d.). Student to school psychologist ratio 2020–2021. https://www.nasponline.org/about-school-psychology/state-shortages-data-dashboard.

National Association of School Psychologists. (2021). Comprehensive School-Based Mental and Behavioral Health Services and School Psychologists. 2021. Retrieved from https://www.nasponline.org/resources-and-publications/resources-and-podcasts/mental-health/school-psychology-and-mental-health/comprehensive-school-based-mental-and-behavioral-health-services-and-school-psychologists.

National Conference of State Legislators. (2021). State Policies on Sex Education in Schools. 2021. Retrieved from https://www.ncsl.org/research/health/state-policies-on-sex-education-in-schools.aspx.

New York State Department of Health. (n.d.). School based health centers fact sheet. Retrieved from https://www.health.ny.gov/statistics/school/skfacts.htm.

Office of Disease Prevention and Health Promotion. (n.d.) Access to Foods that Support Healthy Eating Patterns. Retrieved from https://www.healthypeople.gov/2020/topics-objectives/topic/social-determinants-health/interventions-resources/access-to-foods-that-support-healthy-eating-patterns.

Primary Care Collaborative. (n.d.) Defining the medical home. Retrieved from https://www.pcpcc.org/about/medical-home.

Podgurski, M.J. (1993). School-based adolescent pregnancy classes. AWHONNS *Clinical Issues in Perinatal Womens' Health Nursing*. 1993; 4(1):80–94. PMID: 8472053.

Racine, N., McArthur, B. A., Cooke, J. E., Eirich, R., Zhu, J., & Madigan, S. (2021). Global Prevalence of Depressive and Anxiety Symptoms in Children and Adolescents during COVID-19: A Meta-analysis. *JAMA Pediatrics*, 175(11), 1142–1150. https://doi.org/10.1001/jamapediatrics.2021.2482.

Rural Health Information Hub. School based health centers. (n.d.) Retrieved from https://www.ruralhealthinfo.org/toolkits/sdoh/2/healthcare-settings/school-based-health-centers.

School Based Health Alliance. (2016). Trauma and homeless youth. March 10, 2016. Retrieved from https://www.sbh4all.org/events/trauma-and-homeless-youth/.

United States Department of Agriculture Food and Nutrition Services (USDA). (n.d.) Eligibility Manual for School Meals. Retrieved from https://www.fns.usda.gov/cn/eligibility-manual-school-meals.

Chapter 11

Consumer Education for Attaining Life Goals

Luke Greeley

In 2013, a *TIME* magazine article cited a national public opinion poll indicating that 99 percent of American adults believe schools should teach personal finance yet lamented that only 13 states offer some form of personal finance course (Kadlec, 2013). The article provides several reasons why schools do not teach personal finance, which incidentally are supported by the research literature: teachers feel unqualified to teach such a course (Way & Holden, 2009), personal finance does not appear in standardized tests (Thieman & Carano, 2013), discrepancies in state mandates and suggested curriculum, and disagreement among educators about what type of personal finance instruction works (Brown et al., 2014). The result across the nation is a hodgepodge of public and private extracurricular efforts to provide consumers the resources and skills they need to manage their money that lack a systematic oversight, evaluation, or grounding in educational theory (Fox et al., 2005).

Simultaneously, an ever-growing advertising industry seeks to influence or undermine consumers' interests with an information overload of its own. In the United States, companies spend over $200 billion annually on advertising (eMarketer, 2017), and it is estimated that children view an average of 25,600 ads a year (Moses, 2014), all of it designed to increase consumer demand. Despite the existence of consumer education and financial literacy programs offered by some corporations and non-profit organizations, which rely on the personal motivation of consumers to participate, the *only* systematic consumer education the average consumer receives is in the form of advertising.

Following the global economic crisis of 2008, the nation's attention focused on the glaring lack of consumer education when it became apparent that producers and consumers alike acted irrationally in the marketplace (Ariely, 2009). Policy makers from disparate sectors cited nationwide studies showing most college students got a "D" or "F" on a financial literacy test (Inceptia, 2013), and that of youth 15–18 years old, just 4.7% scored 90% or higher on their financial knowledge test, and 62% scored below 69.9% on the test (National Financial Educators Council, 2014). Calls to improve financial education in schools have increased as a result. Yet, in all the discussion, there seems to be no historical context and financial literacy as presented bears no connection with a broader consumer consciousness or educational philosophy.

HISTORICAL BACKGROUND OF CONSUMER EDUCATION

It is hardly the first time in American history that people have demanded financial literacy or consumer education. Public schools seem like a natural place to help systematically develop the capacities necessary for citizens to successfully participate in a capitalist economy, yet consumer education and financial literacy have had only a minor, and sometimes non-existent, place in the curriculum. The author's use of multiple terms, consumer education *and* financial literacy, is not intended to be redundant.

One of the main signifiers that schools have failed to prepare educated consumers cohesively and systematically is the lack of a straightforward nomenclature and common approach. Hira (2009), in a brief history of the academic study of personal finance writes,

> Long before any specialty, emphasis, or a degree program in personal finance was formally offered across the nation, concepts closely related to personal finance were taught, and continue to be taught, under names such as family economics, consumer economics, consumption economics, family economics and resource management, household finances, family finances, and family financial management. (pp. 5–6)

At the primary and secondary school levels, it has been even more difficult to distinguish where and how topics of personal budgeting, personal finance, and consumer education have been taught because, if covered at all, it has been under the umbrella of other defined subjects such as social studies, health, or math and not as an independent unit of study.

Historically, the most common place in public schools to receive some form of consumer education was in home economics courses and programs. These programs assumed that men worked outside of the home as producers and women inside the home as consumers (Martin, 1994). As such, females had the responsibility of spending their husband's money wisely.

Following the women's liberation movement of the 1960s and 1970s, home economics changed its emphasis from preparing homemakers to preparing all types of students to face the challenges of living and working in a consumer society (Kennedy, 1976). This shift was reflected in the 1994 name change of the American Home Economics Association (AHEA) to the American Association of Family & Consumer Sciences (AAFCS). Even with the inclusion of both genders, however, the subject matter was still grounded in a type of consumer education related to the home, and not placed in the context of other microeconomics.

For example, the personal finance skills taught in home economics remained focused on budgeting and shopping and generally ignored consumer education related to financial products and services (e.g., credit cards) or the effects of consumer choices on a larger economic, political, and ecological environment. Even these limited consumer education efforts offered through family and consumer sciences were narrowed and minimized in the 1980s and 1990s as the school accountability movement pushed for increased emphasis on reading, writing, math, and science to prepare students for a "competitive" college and career environment (Gardner, 1983).

Despite calls for improved financial literacy and consumer education focused on healthy decision making in American schools, research in and exposure to, consumer education has become nearly moribund. Membership in American Home Economics Association/American Association of Family & Consumer Sciences, the primary organization that promotes research and teacher training in consumer education, declined from a peak of 50,000 members in the mid-1960s, to about 25,000 in the mid-1990s, and down to approximately 5,000 in 2012 (Slavin, 1995).

The number of students enrolled in family and consumer science (FCS) courses declined from 5.5 million students in 2002–2003 to 3.5 million students in 2011–12—a 38% reduction in less than 10 years. And among the 3.5 million students receiving some form of FCS coursework, there is still strong gender differentiation with a 35% to 65% male to female ratio (Werhan, 2013). Considering there were 54.8 million students enrolled in U.S. K-12 schools in 2011, the 3.5 million students enrolled in FCS represent just 6% of the total population.

In the 2000s, and especially following the financial crisis of 2008, many states created personal finance mandates, which can require schools to test students on personal finance, offer a course in personal finance, or set standards for the teaching of personal finance (Peng, 2008). Many of the mandates have limited impact, however, as only 19 states require at least a half-year course specifically in personal finance (Bartholomae & Fox, 2016).

Even within the group of states requiring a personal finance course there is great variation on what that means.

In New Jersey, for example, schools can meet the half year minimum course requirement by paying a private educational company (Educere) to administer an online personal finance course to their students. Additionally, the half year mandate allows schools to fit in the curriculum at any point in high school so that exposure to financial learning might come too early, before many students have had their first experience with a job or bank account, or too late, when some may have already made injurious financial decisions.

Often schools staff personal finance courses with teachers who have little or no training in personal finance or economics. As a result, many schools turn to global financial companies to train their teachers or provide class content to students. Wells Fargo has developed the Hands on Banking series, which they describe as "a free, non-commercial program that teaches people in various stages of life about the basics of responsible money management" and through the program offers pre-packaged curricular materials to be used by teachers (Wells Fargo, 2021).

Bank of America runs the Better Money Habits education series in partnership with Khan Academy, a self-directed video learning platform popular with young students, so that individuals can self-educate on topics such as credit, retirement, saving, and taxes. Whether these programs have educational efficacy or are more of a public relations effort is unclear. Given that the banking industry earned over $17 billion in revenue a year from overdraft and non-sufficient fund fees in 2015 (Pisani, 2017), or that Wells Fargo ran its Responsible Money Management program at the same time it fraudulently opened excess bank accounts in its customers' names (Kelly, 2020), suggests the public relations function is the true purpose.

IDENTIFYING THE NEED FOR CONSUMER EDUCATION

Consumer education in the United States needs attention, to bring clarity to its scope and to articulate the normative grounds for why it is important. As Émile Durkheim (1922) and John Dewey (1916) noted, education is a process of both intentional and unintentional reproduction where the young are socialized to adapt the physical, intellectual, and moral dispositions required to participate in the larger society. The common school was developed in the United States to achieve many of these goals, not the least of which, was market participation as both a future worker and future consumer (Bowles & Gintis, 1976). As such, intentional development of curricula that included consumer education components sheds light onto its perceived importance by the larger society. Contemporarily, as consumer education wanes in public school curricula, there is a need to assess what its function might be and more importantly *why* it is needed in the 21st century.

The neglect of consumer education in contemporary American public school curricula comes at a tremendous personal cost to students, as well as their current and future families. Consumer education has the potential to improve one's personal finances, health, and wellbeing. The skills it promotes such as research, discernment, and buyer savvy can help protect individuals from unscrupulous businesses and dangerous products while providing a sense of empowerment.

There is a political cost to poor consumer education. Without a familiarity with the policies or agencies that govern the economic marketplace and the mechanisms for influencing such policies, consumers are left to believe there is no recourse for influencing the business world. Historically, improvements to the quality of consumer products, the working conditions for those who make consumer products, and reduction in negative environmental impacts have often resulted from organized consumer movements.

Among the most pressing economic, social, and environmental issues of the 21st century in relation to consumer education are the disparities between wealthy and marginalized individuals and communities. These disparities include the frequency of fraud victimization, access to vital resources like nutrition, banking, and healthcare, as well as the high costs of poverty built into pricing mechanisms from housing to consumer goods. To address these issues, the author will answer the question of what form consumer education should take to properly prepare individuals to make informed and reflective consumer choices, which will affect themselves and their communities. The author concludes by arguing that consumer education is an essential need for 21st century society and can be an important mechanism for help students achieve life goals while simultaneously addressing some significant issues of public concern.

CONSUMER EDUCATION TO ADDRESS RESOURCE DISPARITIES

One of the most immediate benefits of consumer education is that it can help protect vulnerable populations, such as those with limited financial resources or in precarious financial situations, from becoming victims of frauds and scams. In the United States, consumers reported losses due to fraud or scams of $1.9 billion in 2020, more than doubling from the $906 million reported in 2018 (FTC, 2020). Though researchers estimate that true fraud losses are between $40 and $50 billion annually (Deevy & Beals, 2013) because many people fail to report being victims of fraud and scams, possibly out of embarrassment or out of ignorance that the fraud had taken place.

A recent 2021 study of 1,175 American and Canadian consumers who had reported a scam to the Better Business Bureau, provides useful data on the nature of common scams and variables which contribute to the likelihood that a person becomes a victim (DeLiema, Li, and Mottola, 2021). The authors describe three main categories of fraud:

1. Opportunity-based scams, where the victim is promised a positive or rewarding outcome such a great investing opportunity or the chance to win a prize;
2. Threat-based scams, where the victim is told that if they do not pay money something negative will happen and frequently the scammer misrepresents themselves to be a government agent or tech support specialist;
3. Consumer purchase scams, where the victims are sold products or services that are misrepresented or that do not actually exist.

Of the fraud victims surveyed in the study (300), they reported an average loss of $7,158.50, an amount which would be a staggering blow representing over 55% of an individual's income who was making wages at the federal poverty line, or over 27% of a family of four's income who was at the federal poverty level.

In the above referenced study (DeLiema, Li, & Mottola, 2021), and relevant to the discussion of consumer education and resource inequity, it was discovered that several factors were correlated with the likelihood of becoming a victim of consumer fraud. One factor was poor financial literacy, where respondents' relative financial literacy was determined by their correct or incorrect responses to six questions on topics like interest rates, loans, and investing. The authors summarized, "Those who understand financial concepts such as inflation and investing may be more skeptical of 'get rich quick' opportunities." (p. 24) Another factor was financial fragility, where respondents were asked how confident they were that they could come up with $2,000 if an unexpected need arose within the next month.

Even when controlling for income, financially fragile survey respondents were twice as likely to lose money compared to those who had access to $2,000 in emergency funds. The last risk factor relevant to consumer education, was whether the individual had heard about the scam before they were targeted. Individuals with knowledge of a specific scam were 75% less likely to lose money. Based on these findings the authors suggest that consumer education should target populations most vulnerable to specific scams, where they are taught how scams work and on the methods of persuasion that are typically used by scammers. If individuals are provided with basic financial literacy knowledge, are able to manage their finances in a way that avoids financial fragility, and are taught to interrogate marketing claims and offers, they will be better defended against fraud.

The other significant way consumer education can help to address financial inequities is in relation to the many high costs associated with *being poor* in the United States. To give a sense of scope of poverty, the Census Bureau (2019) reports that 34 million Americans live in poverty, representing 10.5% of the total population. For Black Americans, the Bureau reports 18.8% of the community is living in poverty, and 15.7% of the Hispanic community.

The number of financially vulnerable individuals is much higher than the official poverty statistics indicate, as nearly 4 in 10 Americans report that if they missed one paycheck they would not be able to cover their living expenses. These financially vulnerable Americans pay significantly more for costs of living, interest rates, and basic needs such as food. With scarce supplies of affordable housing in most metropolitan areas, the poor are often subjected to significant rent increases from year to year and have no choice but to pay because other options are not available (Rampell, 2021). This often leads to evictions for individuals and families when financial emergencies or job loss occur, who become marred by bad credit and then are faced with the impossible decision to over-pay for substandard housing or become homeless (Desmond & Kimbro, 2015).

America's poor pay higher rates for auto and home insurance, as they are more likely to own older vehicles or homes, which do not have the safety features which attract insurance discounts and because they are more likely to live in areas with higher crime rates (Angwin et al., 2020). Lacking wealth or savings to draw on in times of financial emergency, the poor often have to borrow money to cover financial emergencies, but because of lack of credit or access to community banks, they must resort to high interest rate borrowing in the form of credit cards, pay day loans, and other products with steep rates and harsh penalties.

Consumer education alone cannot address the structural economic and social issues that contribute to the high costs of being poor. However, consumer education can help to equip vulnerable populations with the skills to navigate common financial traps as well as to provide knowledge about alternative financial resources or living arrangements that could improve quality of life and financial wellbeing. For example, with the knowledge and skill to create a household budget, individuals can put away money each month or paycheck into an emergency fund. For unexpected bills more than what has been saved in one's emergency fund, individuals can learn to pursue alternatives to high-interest lending such as participating in informal or formal community savings and lending networks, or to seek out non-profit credit unions rather than credit cards or payday lending businesses.

In the same way individuals who had received information about common financial scams were more likely to avoid them, education about the various types of loans that exist, especially different types of predatory loans, can help individuals to avoid high-interest traps. Consumer education could additionally teach individuals about governmental and non-profit agency programs, which can help them in several important areas such as applying for government subsidized housing options, receiving free assistance on income tax filing, applying for subsidies on utility bills such as heating, or reporting unfair or exploitative treatment by businesses or landlords. Such initiatives are not solutions to poverty, but strategic education in areas of consumer interest can help improve financial security and wellbeing.

EDUCATIONAL AND ETHICAL HEURISTICS FOR CONSUMER EDUCATION

The discussion to this point has focused on the questions of *why* students should be educated in matters related to their existence as consumers. Arriving at the conclusion that yes, indeed, consumer education is necessary along a variety of dimensions, begs the question of *how* to educate consumers and *what* will that education look like specifically.

Based on economic, social, and environmental considerations, as well as relevant consumer education research, outlined below are a few educational and ethical heuristics that can prompt the kind of investigative and reflective dispositions necessary for the modern consumer citizen. Specifically, they consider the vast amount of information and disinformation modern consumers must navigate, as well as the application of value judgements in a complex digital landscape.

The first suggested heuristic draws from the burgeoning framework of Critical Media Literacy that concerns itself with educating amid the rapidly changing communication and information ecosystem engendered by new technologies and digital platforms. Specifically, the work of Funk, Kellner, and Share (2016) provides extremely practical insight into how media are being consumed and integrated into people's every experience through videos, tweets, memes, instant messages, and a host of other digital media. They write that these media are "challenging old ideas of audience, media, and relationships between senders and receivers" (p. 6).

In these new mediums, the notions of who are the producers and consumers of media are blurred, and lines between user-generated and company-generated content are made purposefully ambiguous as a mechanism for subtle marketing opportunities. Further complicating such ambiguities are the ways in which use and consumption in these digital channels drastically impact identity formation and in particular expose children to "global flows of consumption, identity, and information in ways unheard of in earlier generations" (Carrington, 2005; as cited in Funk, Kellner, & Share, 2016, p. 6). Educators seeking to ensure students have a 21st century literacy must expand their conception of reading and writing into these new modalities and equip students with a framework that helps them critically analyze and interpret the troves of messages to which they are exposed.

The framework developed by Funk, Kellner, and Share promotes six questions to guide media education specifically, but below are modifications of these guiding questions so that they apply to a broader consumer education framework where the gathering and interpreting of information to make civic, economic, and environmental judgements and decisions is vital. The guiding questions are

1. What are all the resources that were used to create this product and who were the people involved in procuring and modifying those resources?
2. How was this product created, marketed, delivered, and accessed?
3. How could this product have been created, marketed, delivered, and accessed differently?
4. What values, points of view, and ideologies are represented or missing in the creation and marketing of this product?
5. How is this product being used and how is it being disposed of or recycled at the end of its lifecycle?
6. What people and ecological systems are being advantaged or disadvantaged by this product?

Each question is specifically designed to evoke notions of social construction, positionality, politics, and representation in a classroom setting and evoke an investigative and reflective stance from students. Further, acknowledging that products, and the associated information and marketing provided by a company about them, constitute forms of media, the questions, or ones like them, can be used as a consumer heuristic. Such "critical consumer literacy" questions pose significant and intriguing prompts for analysis and exploration, which could use knowledge and application from diverse academic disciplines like social studies, the natural sciences, language arts, and mathematics to answer them.

In helping students progress from understanding to application, the second proposed heuristic is drawn from the area of applied ethics and provides some suggestions for decision making in a complicated consumer landscape. Generally, in applied ethics a primary goal is the reduction or minimization of harm and suffering. In recent decades, scholars like Peter Singer (2011) have helped to popularize ethical considerations of non-human beings as well as the importance of aiming for effectiveness in weighing possible actions.

In this vein, there is a nascent literature on consumer responsibilities and ethics that aims to articulate the challenges and tools that can be used to help consumers act ethically in the marketplace. Importantly, Peacock (2015) notes, the inability to research every product does not reduce the consumer's moral culpability:

> The impossibility of informing herself fully about every commodity does not mean that it is impossible (or even terribly difficult) for her to inform herself to some degree about some commodities. The question then becomes "About which, among the sea of commodities available, should a consumer inform herself so as to avoid the state of being culpably ignorant?" (p. 9)

Peacock's formulation, which is focused on the individual consumer, also begs the question as to what extent a company has a moral responsibility to make their business processes relatively transparent and information on their products relatively easy to find and access. In addition to these individual obligations to educate oneself, what obligations are there of public institutions, like public schools and universities, to help individuals inform themselves?

Peacock (2015), acknowledging the dearth of quality consumer data, advises that consumers prioritize research on goods or services along the following parameters:

1. Inform yourself first about products that are most likely to give rise to a moral wrong. This precept implies that consumers ought to develop a general awareness of common moral wrongs associated with modern goods and services. Even if the consumer lacks specific information about, for instance, the labor practices of a particular garment producer or the living conditions of chickens on a poultry farm, knowledge of the well-documented moral hazards of these industries should lead the consumer to be cautious and seek further information on a given product before proceeding.
2. Focus attention on purchases that cause higher degrees of negative consequences. This precept emphasizes the scale of impact. For instance, given consumer's limited time and energy constraints, decisions about what type of home or vehicle to purchase, given the level of resources and labor needed to create and maintain them, should be given greater weight and attention than what type of pencil to buy. Scale could also be measured by frequency, where the consumer ought to spend more time

researching products or services, which they regularly purchase or consume than those which they do not.

While the first and second of Peacock's precepts focus on which consumer decisions one should focus one's time and attention, his third and fourth emphasize the extent to which one should expend effort. They are:

3. pursue information that is relatively easy to research.
4. gather information only to the point that it does not place an undue burden upon you. For these precepts, Peacock applies Singer's (1972) criterion, "If it is in our power to prevent something bad from happening, without thereby sacrificing anything of comparable moral importance, we ought, morally, to do it." (p. 242)

In the context of a consumer education curriculum, educators can help students apply these precepts by equipping them with the skills to research information quickly and easily on the companies, manufacturing processes, and supply chains that produce products and services, as well as the positive and negative utility of the good or service itself. Educational institutions themselves can contribute to the data and efficacy of consumer facing research portals, with the goal of making ease of research into areas of social and environmental responsibility as simple as it currently is to access a product's customer satisfaction reviews.

Importantly, the author would add to these suggestions, which are individualistic in nature, a collective imperative that consumers undertake their obligatory research efforts in conjunction with others so that they can act on the consumer information that will make the most meaningful difference. Such precepts, akin to the critical consumer literacy prompting questions above, which ask the individual to consider other points of view and larger impact, could read:

5. investigate how others are understanding the potential moral hazards of a given industry, product, or service.
6. upon finding unresolved or unaddressed ethical concerns, take steps to reduce harm through your individual choices as well as through coordinated methods such as political advocacy, collective protest, or boycott.

Applying these guiding heuristics with modern tools of communication and investigation, creates tremendous potential for consumers to *crowd source* useful information and generate aggregate impact. Of course, digital platforms and communication run risks of supplying misinformation, and in overwhelming the individual in the sheer abundance of information and sources available. But if our society can create networks of scientific research and dissemination through healthy and engaged institutions, and supply individuals with capacities for interpretation and application, the information ecosystem within which we make consumer decisions can be dramatically improved. Our ability to collectively discern and operate within a technologically rich and complicated context is more important than the intelligence of any one person.

The modern global marketplace is confusing and overwhelming to an individual. But those armed with good heuristics for assessing quality and value, budgeting skills, and decision making skills will fare better than those who are not. And further, at the aggregate level, consumers opting for preferences such as lower cost or responsibly made products could push the market in positive (e.g., consumer-centric) directions. The consumer education suggestions and heuristics proposed above, while dependent on an appeal to an individual's ethical valuations, which will always have a personal dimension, will be successful if they are socially and culturally situated and connect students to collective resources.

CONSUMER EDUCATION IS ESSENTIAL FOR THE 21ST CENTURY

All consumer decisions, whether they are guided by economic or ethical valuations, will have a socially constituted element. As such, educational institutions and educators must help students to investigate and understand how economic and ecological processes are embedded in their daily lives and what ecological and social consequences may arise from productive and consumptive economic decisions. Further, consumer education can help to protect the most financially vulnerable students from exploitation and outright fraud.

For educators seeking to apply this broadly envisioned consumer education in the curriculum, a century's old question arises as to whether consumer education should exist as a stand-alone course of study or discipline, or should it be incorporated into prevalent and existing subject areas. To this, our nation must respond, "both and more." When society thinks about the most pressing questions of public concern like "Can democracy function if the public is consuming incomplete, biased, or false information?," "Can our economy function if consumers cannot find quality information on goods and services, and use their resources for rational and self-beneficial purposes?," or "Can our society continue if our ecosystems are polluted or damaged beyond the point of habitability?"; there is a moral imperative to enhance the quality and availability of consumer education. If our educational system does not, then our nation will continue down a path of ignorant consumerism at great peril, as well as the peril for future generations.

REFERENCES

AAFCS. (2012). *AAFCS Membership Stats*. http://us1.campaign-archive2.com/?u=bee11993ef54296c205934b97&id=d267c11ab2#member.

Angwin, J., Larson, J., Kirchner, L., & Surya, M. (2017, April 5). Minority neighborhoods pay higher car insurance premiums than white areas with the same risk. *ProPublica*. https://www.propublica.org/article/minority-neighborhoods-higher-car-insurance-premiums-white-areas-same-risk.

Ariely, D. (2009). The end of rational economics. *Harvard Business Review, 87*(7–8), 78–84.

Bartholomae, S., & Fox, J.J. (2016). Advancing financial literacy education using a framework for evaluation. *Handbook of consumer finance research*, pp. 45–59.

Bowles, S., & Gintis, H. (1976). *Schooling in capitalist America*. Basic Books.

Brown, A., Collins, J. M., Schmeiser, M. D., & Urban, C. (2014). State mandated financial education and the credit behavior of young adults. *Divisions of Research & Statistics and Monetary Affairs Federal Reserve Board, Washington, DC, Finance and Economics Discussion Series*, 2014–68.

Carrington, V. (2005). New textual landscapes, information and early literacy. In J. Marsh (Ed.), *Popular culture, new media and digital literacy in early childhood* (pp. 13–17). Routledge Falmer.

Census Bureau. (2019). *Income and poverty in the United States: 2019*. https://www.census.gov/library/publications/2020/demo/p60-270.html.

Deevy, M., & Beals, M. (2013). *The scope of the problem*. Financial Fraud Research Center. https://longevity.stanford.edu/wp-content/uploads/2016/07/Scope-of-the-Problem-FINAL_corrected2.pdf.

DeLiema, M., Li, Y., & Mottola, G. R. (2021). Correlates of compliance: Examining consumer fraud risk factors by scam type. *Available at SSRN 3793757*.

Desmond, M., & Kimbro, R. T. (2015). Eviction's fallout: housing, hardship, and health. *Social Forces, 94*(1), 295–324.

Dewey, J. (1916). *Democracy and education*. Macmillan.

Durkheim, É. (1922). *Education and sociology*. Free Press.

eMarketer. (2004) *Total US ad spending to see largest increase since 2004*. https://www.emarketer.com/Article/Total-US-Ad-Spending-See-Largest-Increase-Since-2004/1010982.

Federal Trade Commission. (2020, February 4). *New data shows FTC received 2.2 million fraud reports from consumers in 2020*. https://www.ftc.gov/news-events/press-releases/2021/02/new-data-shows-ftc-received-2-2-million-fraud-reports-consumers.

Fox, J., Bartholomae, S., & Lee, J. (2005). Building the case for financial education. *Journal of Consumer Affairs, 39*(1), 195–214.

Funk, S., Kellner, D., & Share, J. (2016). Critical media literacy as transformative pedagogy. In Yildiz, M. & Keengew, J., (Eds). *Handbook of research on media literacy in the digital age.* IGI Global.

Gardner, D.P. (1983). *A nation at risk.* The National Commission on Excellence in Education, US Department of Education.

Hira, T.K. (2009). Personal finance: past, present, and future. *Networks Financial Institute Policy Brief.*

Inceptia. (2013). *First-year college students score poorly in basic financial literacy, Inceptia survey reports.* https://www.inceptia.org/about/news/ jan-22–2013/.

Kadlec, D. (2013, October 10). *Why we want-but can't have-personal finance in school.* TIME. http://business.time.com/2013/10/10/why-we-want-but-cant-have-personal-finance-in-schools/.

Kelly, J. (2020, February 4). Wells Fargo forced to pay $3 billion for the bank's fake account scandal. *Forbes.* https://www.forbes.com/sites/jackkelly/2020/02/24/wells-fargo-forced-to-pay-3-billion-for-the-banks-fake-account-scandal/?sh=4168cbf942d2.

Martin, J. R. (1994). *Changing the educational landscape: Philosophy, women, and curriculum.* Routledge.

Moses, L. (2014, March 11). *A look at kids' exposure to ads.* ADWEEK. http://www.adweek.com/digital/look-kids-exposure-ads-156191/.

National Financial Educators Council. (2014). *National financial literacy test results.* http://www.financialeducatorscouncil.org/financial-literacy-research.

Peacock, M. (2015). Market processes and the ethics of consumption. *SAGE Open, 5*(2), 2158244015585998.

Peng, T. C. M. (2008). *Evaluating mandated personal finance education in high schools* (Doctoral dissertation, The Ohio State University).

Pisani, B. (2017, July 12). Bank fees have been growing like crazy. *CNBC.* https://www.cnbc.com/2017/07/21/the-crazy-growth-of-bank-fees.html.

Rampell, C. (2021, March 22). Rents for the rich are plummeting. Rents for the poor are rising. Why? *The Washington Post.* https://www.washingtonpost.com/opinions/2021/03/22/rents-rich-are-plummeting-rents-poor-are-rising-why/.

Singer, P. (1972). Famine, affluence, and morality. *Philosophy & Public Affairs,* 229–243.

Singer, P. (2011). *Practical ethics.* Cambridge University Press.

Slavin, S. (1995). *U.S. women's interest groups: Institutional profiles.* Greenwood Publishing Group.

Thieman, G. Y., & Carano, K. T. (2013). From the field: How Oregon social studies teachers are preparing students for the 21st century. *Oregon Journal of the Social Studies.*

Way, W.L, & Holden, K.C. (2009). Teachers' background and capacity to teach personal finance: Results of a national study." *Journal of Financial Counseling & Planning* 20(2).

Wells Fargo. (2021). *Hands on banking.* https://www.wellsfargo.com/about/corporate-responsibility/hands-on-banking/.

Werhan, C. R. (2013). Family and consumer sciences secondary school programs: National survey shows continued demand for FCS teachers. *Journal of Family & Consumer Sciences, 105*(4), 41–45.

PART V

Innovation

Chapter 12

Combatting Diseconomies of Scale

Stephen V. Coffin

The local school district is the form of governance that is closest to the students, parents, teachers, administrators, and taxpayers as well as other stakeholders. Local school districts have the expertise to most effectively decide how to provide a quality education while generating the necessary support among district taxpayers for the public funding of public education. However, to earn local taxpayers' support for their public funding of public education, the district must be sized properly to enable sound public management and oversight by a board of education that is accountable to the taxpayers.

A school district's size impacts school and student performance. If a district's enrollment is too large parental engagement decreases, which harms student achievement because parental involvement is integral to student performance. Typically, districts with disproportionately large enrollments are not only extremely difficult to manage effectively but also tend to exceed the span of control of even the most experienced leaders (Andrews et al., 2002; Coffin, 2021a; Duncombe & Yinger, 2007; Vollmer; 2010).

Antonucci (1999, p. 1) reports that,

> The larger a school district gets, the more resources it devotes to secondary or even non-essential activities. In sum, large school districts engage in "mission creep," building activities which rapidly lose any connection to the original goal of educating children.

Antonucci (1999) argues that large school districts are too large to function effectively as well as to improve school and student performance. Antonucci posits that the typical "American public school system suffers from penalties of scale" (p. 2).

Advocates for county-run school districts, such as county freeholders, argue that the larger is a school district the more economies of scale it realizes (Coffin, 2021a). However, these arguments are based on presumed and unsubstantiated economies of scale that do not account for the true nature of school systems, efficiency, economics, and span of control (Andrews et al., 2002; Antonucci, 1999; Coffin, 2021a; Duncombe & Yinger, 2007; Kenny, 1982; Kenny & Schmidt, 1994). Typically, politicians who promote county-run schools and ending local control, are motivated more by their desire to expand political power and patronage rather than trying to improve accountability and education (Coffin, 2021a; Coffin & Cooper, 2018; Fischel, 2009; Vollmer, 2010).

Large rather than right-sized traditional public school districts (i.e., T.P.S.D.s) share similar management challenges, inefficiencies, and mission creep with other overly large organizations because while scale differs, the effects of scale and scale economies are the same. Like many older, less efficient, larger, declining industries, utilities, or utility-like firms (e.g., railroads), large T.P.S.D.s (e.g., Los Angeles, New York City, Chicago, Detroit, Miami, Dallas, St. Louis, Newark, Philadelphia, and Boston) operate with diseconomies of scale because their average costs increase as educational outputs increase.

In addition, large school districts' economies resemble utility-like firms because their long run average cost exceeds their marginal cost, and these districts operate with enrollment levels that are beyond an optimal level of approximately 3,500 students (Andrews et al., 2002; Antonucci, 1999; Coffin, 2021a; Duncombe & Yinger, 2007; Kenny, 1982). Thus, most large T.P.S.D.s as well as utility-like firms require public subsidies to survive.

Like most right-sized businesses right-sized T.P.S.D.s show constant returns to scale in which their average costs do not vary as their educational outputs increase. However, like businesses of all sizes school districts should aim for economies of scale in which their average costs decrease while their educational outputs increase. Using the author's new ways of doing the business of education and raising alternative revenues while implementing the author's recommended best practices will enable districts to right-size and achieve economies of scale (Coffin, 2021a; Coffin, 2021b; Coffin, 2021c; Coffin, 2021d).

The misconception concerning T.P.S.D.s that they differ from utility-like firms but should be run as if they were autonomous private sector businesses is the root cause of many of the challenges facing our public schools. Larry Cuban explodes this conventional wisdom in *The Blackboard and the Bottom Line*. In his book, Cuban (2004, pp. 3–4) quotes Jamie Vollmer's, a former business executive who became an education reform advocate, Blueberry Epiphany, "Our schools are not factories" (2004, pp. 3–4). Cuban (2004) concludes that no business could survive if they had not only to abide by the same rules and regulations but also to operate according to the same economic and governmental constraints as those that apply to our public schools.

Large T.P.S.D.s' size influences the extent to which any form of governance or structural control can improve the school system. Large T.P.S.D.s cannot improve school and student performance because they are constrained by penalties of scale. Large school districts must be right-sized or disaggregated into several smaller sub-districts with each not exceeding approximately 3,500 students (Andrews et al., 2002; Coffin, 2021a; Coffin, 2021d). This would enable the school system to improve education and accountability while lowering costs and removing penalties of scale. The solution is to disaggregate districts with more than 3,500 students into several smaller more manageable but empowered local school sub-districts under the control of a locally elected (i.e., sub-district-based) board of education (See Chapter 17).

Los Angeles Unified School District

The Los Angeles Unified School District (L.A.U.S.D.) is the nation's second largest school district with 666,774 students, over 1,100 schools, and a $8.55 billion operating budget in the 2020–2021 academic year. The L.A.U.S.D. covers 710 square miles. The district consists of Los Angeles and portions or all of 31 other municipalities. The L.A.U.S.D. suffers from the penalties of scale that afflict large districts especially mega-T.P.S.D.s. Its extremely large size and scope as well as its politically fragmented 32 municipalities are disproportionately difficult to manage effectively and exceed the span of control of its board of education, which results in diseconomies of scale (See Chapters 14 and 15).

The L.A.U.S.D. could readily benefit from disaggregating into several smaller local sub-districts of no more than 3,500 students while providing an effective control structure under locally elected boards of education within each sub-district (See Chapter 15). Each sub-district would be empowered to allocate its financial, material, and human resources according to sub-district needs and priorities. Implementing this solution would empower each sub-district to levy their own local property taxes to fund their schools according to their needs and priorities (See Chapters 14 and 15). In addition, this would require repealing California's Proposition 13's ban that prevents local districts from levying their own local property taxes.

CONCLUSION

Once each disaggregated sub-district becomes free of the penalties of scale stemming from its former fragmented unmanageably large school district apparatus, unified under the control of a sub-district elected board of education, and regains the ability to levy property taxes, each sub-district will be equipped to generate the necessary public support for the public funding of its local public schools. Thus, the disaggregation process not only could be applied successfully to school districts nationwide with enrollments exceeding approximately 3,500 but also would greatly improve accountability and enable the disaggregated sub-districts to realize the benefits of economies of scale.

REFERENCES

Andrews, M., Duncombe, W. D., & Yinger, J. (2002). Revisiting economies of size in American education: Are we any closer to a consensus? *Economics of Education Review*, *21*, 245–262.

Antonucci, M. (1999). Mission creep: How large school districts lose sight of the objective—student learning (AdTI Issue Brief Number 176). Retrieved from http://www.adti.net/education/antonucci.mission.creep.html.

Coffin, S.V. (2021a). *Achieving economies of scale and fiscal capacity in large school districts*. [Manuscript submitted for publication]. *Education and Urban Society*.

Coffin, S. V. (2021b). *Creating a model state school finance formula to achieve equal educational opportunity and school finance equity* [Manuscript in preparation]. Rowman & Littlefield.

Coffin, S. V. (Ed.) (2021c). *Higher education's looming collapse: Using new ways of doing business and social justice to avoid bankruptcy*. Rowman & Littlefield.

Coffin, S. V. (2021d). *Strategic school finance for leading-edge equitable public education*. [Manuscript in preparation]. Rowman & Littlefield.

Coffin, S. V., & Cooper, B. S. (Eds.) (2017). *Sound school finance for educational excellence*. Rowman & Littlefield.

Coffin, S. V., & Cooper, B. S. (Eds.) (2018). *District financial leadership today: Educational excellence tomorrow*. Rowman & Littlefield.

Cuban, L. (2004). *The blackboard and the bottom line: Why schools can't be businesses*. Harvard University Press.

Duncombe, W. D., & Yinger, J. (2007). Does school district consolidation cut costs? *Education Finance and Policy*, *2*, 341–375.

Fischel, W. A. (2009). *Making the grade: The economic evolution of American school districts*. University of Chicago Press.

Kenny, L. W. (1982). Economies of scale in schooling. *Economics of Education Review*, (2) 1–24.

Kenny, L. W., & Schmidt, A. B. (1994). The decline in the number of school districts in the United States 1950 – 1980. *Public Choice*, (79) 1–18.

Vollmer, J. (2010). *Schools cannot do it alone: Building public support for America's public schools*. Enlightenment Press.

Chapter 13

Gaining Public Support for Public Funding of Public Education

Stephen V. Coffin

The United States Constitution grants the states rather than the federal government the authority to govern education. Therefore, in the American governmental system all the powers of local governments including municipalities, county governments, and school districts are derived from the state. Accordingly, whatever authority the state grants to local governments and school districts, the state also can withdraw or modify.

The tradition of local control is rooted in our democratic principles. It symbolizes our democracy in action. Local control enables a local school system to be accountable to its stakeholders rather than being controlled remotely by a governmental entity that imposes its political agenda. Typically, this agenda is incongruent with local priorities and needs. Remote governing bodies, such as county or state governments, are not as accountable to the standards necessary to provide quality education as are local schools. In addition, remote governing bodies, such as state and county governments, lack the understanding of local needs and priorities.

The locus of school district control has shifted gradually from a tradition of home rule or local control to state control during the past 50 years. Decision making and control over funding, budgeting, human resources, standards, capital projects, operations, curricula, and assessment that were once the sole province of local boards of education has been superseded increasingly by state and county governments. Increased state control has reversed the traditional operating philosophy and organizing principles for school systems that were based on limiting the power that a remote governmental entity could exert over local school districts.

Historically, Americans wanted educational decision making to be as close as possible to the students, parents, and citizen stakeholders or *homevoters* (Fischel, 2001), who were most affected. School district residents realized that by controlling what and how their children were taught as well as how and who administered and governed their schools plus how their property taxes were used that they were able to enjoy the maximum of democratic accountability. In addition, *homevoters* (Fischel, 2001) understood that local control improves and sustains property values while state or county-run schools lower property values.

A top-down, state dominated educational system is contrary to our democratic principles and traditions especially when it comes to governing our schools. Increased control by the state through state politically appointed county superintendents or departments of education, as well as consolidated countywide districts, such as in Florida, Maryland, North Carolina, West Virginia, Nevada, Utah, Louisiana, California, and New Jersey, means less local control because control is a zero-sum game (Coffin, 2021a; Coffin, 2021b; Coffin, 2021d). Thus, every increase in or recapture of state or county power results only from a corresponding loss at the local level.

Special attention is given to California and New Jersey because these states embody the problems associated with state domination of local school systems executed through county governments. During recent decades, the home rule tradition of school governance that undergirded the provision of quality education in California and New Jersey was eroded to the point where local control of education has been increasingly superseded by not only the state but also county government.

The increasing power of California and New Jersey and their county governments stems from the states' increasing domination of school finance; therefore, policy making because the states attached policy strings to funding (Fusarelli & Cooper, 2009). Legal challenges to funding inequities and disparities led to court decisions, such as *Serrano v. Priest* in California and *Abbott v. Burke* in New Jersey, establishing financial neutrality as the basis for school funding. The states tried to remedy the disparities among districts with the infusion of incremental state funds, administrative codes, and regulation.

Subsequent rulings focused on adequacy and required state governments to provide incremental resources to disadvantaged districts to enable the states' educational system to adequately meet constitutional requirements. The California Supreme Court's rulings in its three *Serrano v. Priest* (i.e., *Serrano* I, 1971; *Serrano* II, 1976; *Serrano* III, 1977) decisions effectively ended home rule or local control over school systems. New Jersey's state constitution's "T&E" clause sought to guarantee a thorough and efficient education for all students, which permeated and manifested in the *Abbott v. Burke* court decisions.

The No Child Left Behind Act of 2001 (NCLB) accelerated the trend toward adequacy through national educational standards. Under NCLB, the federal government held states and school districts accountable for improving performance. Districts that failed to improve student and school performance and achievement were penalized. Standardized test scores served as the barometer. As a result, states were forced to define an adequate level of student and school performance and achievement as well as the level of financial resources that would be constitutionally adequate in providing education. NCLB initiated a paradigm shift to a policy model within which states increasingly influenced traditional public school districts' (T.P.S.D.) financial, material, and human resources decision making according to federal guidelines with a commensurate loss of local control in the zero-sum game.

Legal challenges to subsequent state funding formulas such as lawsuits to address financial inequities and tax base disparities caused states to greatly increase taxes to generate the necessary funds with which to offset resource inequalities and student test score performance deficiencies. California and New Jersey exemplify this trend.

States increased taxes and spending that led to corresponding increases in state regulation of local school districts to enable states to better control the use of state educational aid. This led to exponential increases in state mandates for administrative regulation, program requirements, standards, and budgetary controls (Coffin, 2021a; Coffin, 2021b; Coffin, 2021d). Naturally, as state mandates and control over local schools increased, the size of state and especially county bureaucracies increased with corresponding increases in state income taxes and county property taxes as well as in the costs that were passed down to T.P.S.D.s.

County government is the entity through which states have traditionally executed their authority (Coffin, 2021a; Coffin, 2021b; Coffin, 2021c; Coffin, 2021d; Coffin & Cooper, 2017; Coffin & Cooper, 2018; Fischel, 2009). But county government, as the state's implementation arm, is too distant from the provision of education as well as the educational needs and priorities of local communities to hold local schools accountable, improve educational quality, and fulfill local *homevoters'* needs and priorities.

Increasing state control over public K to 12 education finance not only helped to centralize educational finance but also greatly expanded county governments' control and influence of local schools. This caused a corresponding loss of control by taxpayers over local educational policy, programs, and services. More importantly, increased county governmental power not only caused a commensurate degradation of educational quality but also disincentivized *homevoters* from supporting the necessary public funding for K to 12 public education.

History

The organizing principle for school districts relies on two major entities that use traditional political boundaries: counties and municipalities or townships. Every state except Hawaii employs one of these models or a combination as the basis for organizing its schools. Hawaii is the only statewide school district in the nation and its public schools are 100% financed by the state.

New England's colonial settlers established the township as the political unit within which school districts were organized with many districts coterminous with their host municipality (Fischel, 2009). Typically, the Mid-Atlantic and Southern states use the county as the organizing structure for local schools. Schools in states such as Maryland, Florida, West Virginia, North Carolina, Nevada, Utah, and Louisiana are organized into consolidated countywide districts without individual autonomous school districts and local control (Coffin, 2021a; Coffin, 2021b; Coffin, 2021c; Coffin & Cooper, 2017; Coffin & Cooper, 2018; Kenney & Schmidt, 1994, cited in Fischel, 2009). Fischel demonstrates the vagaries and inequalities of county-run schools, "the city of Baltimore is considered a county district in Maryland and is distinct from adjacent, suburban 'Baltimore County'; each is a separate (county) school district" (2009, pp. 165–166).

CALIFORNIA

California's Department of Education has overall responsibility to administer education, which it exercises through California's 58 counties. Each county department of education oversees the school districts within its boundaries. While the counties collect property taxes on behalf of the state and the mill rate is established in the state constitution, it is the state that determines the funding amount including revenue from property taxes that each district receives and how those funds are allocated.

Prior to the rise of county government, California enjoyed a tradition of local control of school district budgets, capital projects, human resources as well as the provision of educational programs and services according to local needs and priorities. The role of county governments in governing and funding local school districts was severely limited. While the state provided a minimal funding level, local school districts levied property taxes to generate most of their revenues. Taxpayers' votes determined district budgets as well as the members of their local boards of education. A district's financial and human resources allocations were based on the district's educational plan as approved by the elected local board of education.

California ended this tradition by eroding local control through strings attached to the funding it provided and the policies it mandated for local school districts. Gaining extensive control over school finance enabled the state to control educational policy in its nearly 1,000 school districts.

Today, local school districts depend almost entirely on the state for their revenues and largely lack the authority to raise revenues that only they can control. Because state funds come with powerful strings attached, the state leverages its funding to determine how a district allocates its budget and human resources. Districts have almost no discretion over their use of most of their state funds (Coffin, 2021a; Coffin, 2021b; Coffin, 2021d).

Centralized Control

The strings attached to California's state aid restrict local districts' use of most of their funds to ways prescribed by the state's mandates. Most of the unrestricted state funding finances the salaries and benefits for a district's employees. A district's financial and human resources allocation is primarily determined by the state according to its one size fits all approach, which does not account for differences in local educational needs, priorities, and costs. By controlling school finance and making policy decisions that once were the province of local school districts, California consolidated and centralized the control of education at the state level and exerted its power through county government.

Economic downturns, especially COVID-19's adverse impact caused California to reduce state aid to school districts despite promises, legislative guarantees, and the state's school funding formula. Legislation making districts disproportionately dependent on state aid rather than local property taxes worsened districts' budgetary exigency. However, local property taxes are the most sustainable and reliable revenue source for districts.

California's fiscal chaos and its concomitant adverse impact on districts' budgets began well before COVID-19. The state's fiscal chaos stems from decades of unrealistic and unsustainable state budgets even during periods of economic growth while simultaneously forcing school districts to become overwhelmingly dependent on unreliable state aid rather than local property taxes. In addition, a major state Supreme Court ruling, state constitutional amendments, and voter passed initiatives exacerbated districts' fiscal crises.

Serrano v. Priest

Districts' compulsory dependence on state aid rather than local property taxes began with the 1971 California Supreme Court's *Serrano v. Priest* ruling. In their *Serrano v. Priest* decision, California's Supreme Court declared the system of funding local school districts based primarily on local property taxes unconstitutional if differences in ratables "led to disparities in educational opportunities, which the court apparently took to mean spending per pupil" (Fischel, 2001, p. 99). The *Serrano v. Priest* decision not only ended the tradition of local control over district budgets including property tax levies as well as local public school district governance but also helped to centralize the control over district finance at the state level.

Centralizing district finance at the state level lowered the quality of education generally throughout California because it separated local taxpayers from their connection, vested interest, and stake in their local public schools. Local taxpayers' stake stems from their paying local property taxes for their local public schools. Fischel's (2001) *homevoter* hypothesis explains this phenomenon because the benefits local taxpayers derived from the quality of the education provided by their local public schools funded by their local property taxes were no longer capitalized in their property values. Fischel concludes that "voters are aware of this connection, and that statewide funding especially alienates the majority of the population who have no children in the public school system" (2001, p. 129).

According to Fischel (2001), the *Serrano v. Priest* decision led to the passage of a state constitutional amendment called Proposition 13 in 1978. Proposition 13 severely cut the amount of local property tax revenue available to local school districts as well as the amount under local control. The legislation enabled the state to collect and redistribute local property tax revenues based on the state's funding formula rather than allowing public school districts to budget according to local needs and priorities.

Proposition 13 foreshadowed the passage of Proposition 98 in 1988. Proposition 98 mandated that the state of California guarantee a minimal level or foundational amount of funding for all local school districts throughout the state. Proposition 98 cemented the separation of local taxpayers' public support from their public funding of public schools.

Prior to the *Serrano v. Priest* ruling, local school districts controlled their budgets including the levying of property taxes. Following the *Serrano v. Priest* decision, California imposed revenue limits on school districts while capping the wealthier districts' spending and providing larger subsidies to low-income districts. The affluent districts' cap combined with increased revenue for low-income districts helped the state to achieve *Serrano v. Priest's* equalization standard (Perry, 2004; Perry & Edwards, 2009).

Propositions 13, 98, and 111

Proposition 13 exceeded the *Serrano v. Priest* ruling in terms of transforming the state's school district finance role. Proposition 13 severely limited a district's ability to levy and benefit directly from local property taxes. Proposition 13 amended the California State Constitution with its core organizing principle:

> No property should be taxed at more than one percent of 1975 fair market value; municipalities may impose "special taxes" by a two-thirds vote of the electors; assessments may not grow more than two percent annually from 1975–76 levels, to which they were rolled back, except for property sold after 1975–76; and no increase in state taxes may be enacted without a two-thirds vote of each legislature. (Yudof et al., 2002, p. 798)

Proposition 13 empowered the state to establish a statewide mill rate, limit millage increases, and, more importantly, prevent local school districts from levying, collecting, and benefiting directly from local property taxes. This overturned the Separation of Sources Act (Barbour, 2007 as cited in Perry & Edwards, 2009), which had granted exclusive control over assessing, levying, and collecting property taxes to local governmental entities including school districts in 1910.

Ironically, Proposition 13 drastically reduced school districts' control over, receipt, and use of local property tax revenues, which forced the state to "bail them out by using $2.2 billion of the $3.0 billion state surplus to make up the difference" (Yudof et al., 2002, p. 798). Although the state gained control over the allocation of locally levied property taxes, funding and resource inequities among school districts became a function of the inequities in the state's school funding formula rather than ones caused by disparities in local property values, mix of ratables, and tax bases.

Proposition 98 required the state to guarantee that at least 40% of its general fund resources will be dedicated to funding public education. This guaranteed funding floor is a formulaic calculation based on the amount a district received in the preceding fiscal year for enrollment, attendance, and income levels (Edwards & Leichty, 2010).

In 1990, Proposition 111 modified Proposition 98 to the extent that if the state's General Fund revenues decline, then the growth rate of the guaranteed funding level will be lowered correspondingly. As a constitutional amendment, Proposition 111 enables the state to make "fair share" reductions to the guaranteed funding level during economic downturns (Edwards & Leichty, 2010, p. 5).

Proposition 111 forced school districts to rely upon risky state aid. Cuban (2004) explains the risk in the *Blueberry Epiphany*, in which he portrays former CEO and public school system critic, Jamie Vollmer's transformation to public school advocate.

> And so began my long transformation. Since then, I have learned that a school is not a business. Schools are unable to control the quality of their raw material, they are dependent upon the vagaries of politics for a reliable revenue stream, and they are constantly mauled by a howling horde of disparate, competing customer groups that would send the best CEO screaming into the night. (Cuban, 2004, p. 4)

State aid depends on state income and sale tax revenues that not only fluctuate with the economy but also collapse with economic downturns. Economic downturns are the time when districts especially low-income districts need state aid most! Thus, Proposition 111 forced districts to rely on risky and unreliable state aid rather than local property tax revenues that are the most sustainable and reliable revenue source.

The risk to local school district budgets of depending on unreliable state aid materialized in major ways during the economic crisis following Governor Schwarzenneger's election. To alleviate the state's budget deficit, Governor Schwarzenneger negotiated a one-year suspension of Proposition 98 (Picus as cited in Fusarelli & Cooper, 2009). Although the governor guaranteed that the funds would be repaid, he "did not include them in his annual budget" for the following fiscal year (Picus as cited in Fusarelli & Cooper, 2009, p. 14).

Nationwide the soaring cost of underfunded state mandates and regulation has forced school districts to raise property taxes or cut non-mandate protected regular education programs and services resulting in a leveling down of educational quality. California is a prime example as Greenhut (2005) reports that according to Proposition 4, which was approved in 1979, the state is required "to reimburse local school districts for the mandates it imposes on them. California owes districts more than $3.6 billion" (p. 1). These deferred payments have caused school districts severe cash flow problems.

As the state's fiscal crisis worsened while Proposition 98's guaranteed educational funding deficit skyrocketed, the state slashed educational funding (Edwards & Leichty, 2010). In this way the state not only reduced spending in the current fiscal year but also minimized its obligations going forward (Edwards & Leichty, 2010). These funding reductions not only forced districts to cut non-mandate protected regular education programs and services but also exacerbated cash flow problems.

Proposition 111's amendments compel the state to accrue a maintenance factor for any amount owed districts resulting from a suspension or changes in the minimum funding guaranteed by Proposition 98. The maintenance factor is the "difference between the actual spending level and what would have been spent under normal growth" (Edwards & Leichty, 2010, p. 5). California's cumulative maintenance factor obligation reached $11.2 billion by the second quarter of 2009, which exacerbated funding shortfalls for school districts.

The *Serrano v. Priest* ruling combined with Propositions 13 and 98 empowered the state to control funding, governance, and policy for its nearly 1,000 school districts. Thus, the state determines how educational resources are allocated among districts and largely how they will be used. The state establishes revenue limits for each district. In addition, the state rather than the school district can adjust a district's revenue limit but only through the passage of legislation. However, when the local property taxes controlled by the state increase, the majority of schools do not benefit because any incremental property tax revenue is applied to the limit and the state's component is lowered proportionately.

NEW JERSEY

Court decisions such as *Robinson v. Cahill* and *Abbott v. Burke*, as well as recreating the office of the Executive County Superintendent of Schools and the passage of S1701 into law, transformed the state's role in education in New Jersey. Although using property taxes as the primary basis for funding local school districts is inextricably linked to home rule and property values, these actions transcended local taxpayers' rights to determine the financial and human resources allocations as well as governance of their local schools.

CORE Act

When New Jersey Governor Corzine signed the CORE Act, CommUNITY Against Regionalization Efforts (2009) (i.e., a combination of Assembly Bill A4 and Senate Bill S19), into law, he transformed the role of county superintendents of education from mere disseminators of state educational policies into powerful Executive County Superintendents of Schools. The CORE Act gave the county superintendents of education the primary approval authority of district operating and capital budgets (Coffin, 2021a; Coffin, 2021b; Coffin, 2021d).

New Jersey Senate Bill S450

In passing the CORE Act, the governor empowered Executive County Superintendents to consolidate schools into K to 12 districts and ultimately to consolidate all schools within one countywide organization while the passage of S450 would have initiated the consolidation of local districts into countywide county-run districts. If New Jersey Senate bill (New Jersey

Department of Education 2010) S450 had been signed into law, it would have eliminated all local school districts and combined local districts into one countywide district in each county. In addition, it would have eliminated all administrators over the level of principal while establishing the Executive County Superintendent as the official who would govern and operate all public schools within the consolidated countywide district.

Office of the Executive County Superintendent

The Executive County Superintendent is a political appointee whose contract calls for him/her to focus on reducing expenses in all schools within the county rather than on improving student and school achievement. These political appointees are empowered to veto some or all of a school district's budget despite their previous approval by their duly elected local board of education as well as any contracts for vendors or school personnel not covered by a collective bargaining agreement. In addition, they have unilateral authority to scale down, postpone, or eliminate any non-mandate protected program or service.

New Jersey gave the Executive County Superintendent unprecedented powers over local school districts through the office of Executive County Superintendent of Schools. The county superintendents have the authority to have New Jersey duplicate Maryland's centralization of power over local school districts at the county level. Indeed, the Executive County Superintendents have the authority to consolidate all of New Jersey's 600 plus school districts serving more than 1.3 million students statewide within one of 21 countywide districts.

Maryland

By creating the office of Executive County Superintendent of Schools, New Jersey took the first steps toward replicating Maryland's county school system model. First, the state of Maryland eliminated all local school officials beyond the level of principal. It then consolidated all its schools serving less than one million students statewide within one of the 24 countywide districts in each county under an Executive County Superintendent.

Although Maryland abolished all administrators above the level of principal from the local schools in the name of saving money, cutting administrative expenses, and cutting property taxes, these small one-time savings were overwhelmed by the costs of the office of Executive County Superintendent of Schools with its ever-increasing bureaucracy. For example, in Maryland, the Montgomery County Department of Education alone has an annual operating budget of approximately $2 billion with nearly 22,000 employees despite having a total student enrollment of less than 138,000 (Coffin, 2021a; Coffin, 2021b; Coffin, 2021d; Coffin & Cooper, 2017; Coffin & Cooper, 2018). The office of Executive County Superintendent of Schools for Montgomery County, therefore, employs roughly one administrator for every six of its students.

New Jersey Executive County Superintendent

The Executive County Superintendent, who is appointed by the governor, supervises, directs, and manages the functions of the County Office of Education as a representative and subordinate of the New Jersey State Commissioner of Education. The Executive County Superintendent oversees all public school districts within his/her county. To accomplish these goals, each county superintendent is given a staff and a budget that are not subject to taxpayer input, approval, or elections (Coffin, 2021a; Coffin, 2021b; Coffin, 2021d).

Contrary to core principles of democracy, the Executive County Superintendent has the authority to override a school district's budget despite its prior approval by its duly elected board of education. He/she can do so without any prior consultation or notification of the elected board of education or the local district's superintendent or business administrator. The Executive County Superintendent's exercise of a line-item veto over costs in a local school district's budget is contrary to the will of the locally elected board of education that represents the local taxpayers as demonstrated by their previous vote of approval for vetoed line-items.

In addition, a board of education is prohibited from transferring funds into any line-item that was vetoed by the Executive County Superintendent. The County Superintendent's line-item veto authority covers all non-instructional line items including administrative expenses. The appointed Executive County Superintendent, therefore, could eliminate administrative positions deemed necessary by the elected local board of education, who would then lack sufficient recourse.

The Executive County Superintendent is empowered to review all district budgets within the county. He/she has the authority to veto a portion of the district's budget and the district will have to deduct this portion prior to the budget's posting on the ballot for the public vote in April. The district is prohibited from transferring any funds into those line items or spending any funds toward the vetoed items for the fiscal year.

The Executive County Superintendent is responsible for ensuring that each school district budget includes sufficient funds to meet the requirements of the state's Core Curriculum Content Standards (CCCS). The district's administrative and support services per pupil costs are compared to the state median. The Executive County Superintendent can administer reductions in these areas if the district's costs exceed the state guidelines.

The Executive County Superintendent is required to review, evaluate, and approve all employment contracts for administrators not covered by a collective bargaining agreement including but not limited to superintendents, assistant superintendents, and business administrators. He/she must also enforce the state mandated caps on accumulated unused vacation and sick days.

According to the School Funding Reform Act (2008) (New Jersey Department of Education, 2008), the Executive County Superintendent can withhold or recapture state aid if he/she discovers excessive spending, inefficiencies, or that the district has violated any state law or regulation. Another condition for receiving state aid stipulates that every district must refinance all outstanding debt for which a three percent net present value could be realized.

The Executive County Superintendent enforces the state mandated two percentage point cap on a local school district's annual property tax levy. The tax levy is also reduced if the district's budget is found to exceed the state's calculated adequacy level for that district and if the district receives an increase in state aid exceeding the greater of two percent or the Consumer Price Index (CPI).

The implication behind the creation of the office of Executive County Superintendent of Schools was that it would somehow save the taxpayers' money and enable the state to have lower property taxes. The experience of such a control model in the state of Maryland contradicts such assumptions as does New Jersey's county governmental control model. New Jersey's 21 counties combine to spend over $8.0 billion annually in property taxes. County government places a tremendous burden on New Jersey's taxpayers especially as compared to those in Connecticut where county government was eliminated in 1960 when Connecticut had no state income or sales tax.

Diseconomies of Scale

Diseconomies of scale apply to the private and public sectors. Typically, in the education industry, it takes a defined number of personnel per pupil to provide a defined level of service. However, larger school systems such as regional or consolidated countywide school districts are more expensive to operate than smaller, local school districts because of their diseconomies or penalties of scale (Coffin, 2021a; Coffin, 2021b; Coffin, 2021d; Coffin & Cooper, 2017; Coffin & Cooper, 2018).

Decentralization rather than centralization brings decision makers closer to the taxpayers and local priorities. Taxpayers have more of a stake in the success of their local school rather than county districts. Separating the taxpayer from his/her ability to control and influence the operating budget and educational plan of his/her local school district cuts neither costs nor property taxes. Preventing the taxpayer from having a voice and vote in controlling local property taxes for local public schools lessens public support for the public funding of public schools.

S1701

When New Jersey Governor James McGreevey signed S1701 into law on July 1, 2004, as Chapter 73, Public Laws of New Jersey 2004 (New Jersey Department of Education, 2005), the state further eroded local control over school districts especially in terms of a district's budget flexibility, administrative spending limits, and spending growth limitation adjustments. While this legislation accelerated the loss of local autonomy for school districts the state did not apply it to county and municipal governments even though these levels of government are also funded primarily by local property taxes.

S1701 reduced the maximum allowable district surplus to no more than three percent in the 2004–05 fiscal year and two percent in the 2005–06 fiscal year and beyond. Prior to the passage of S1701, the state prohibited non-Abbott districts from having a surplus of less than six percent. Because a district's surplus serves as insurance against unforeseen expenses, S1701 forces a district to either cut non-mandate protected educational programs and services such as regular education or increase property taxes.

S1701 required that any surplus more than the percentage limitations must be used for property tax relief. But the property tax relief would be implemented by limiting the amount of property taxes a district could levy in the upcoming fiscal year rather than as a direct refund to taxpayers, furthering constraining local autonomy (Coffin, 2021a; Coffin, 2021b; Coffin, 2021d).

S1701 (New Jersey Department of Education, 2005) limited a district's budgetary flexibility by restricting the growth in the base budget to the higher of two and half percent or the Consumer Price Index (CPI). In addition, it limited Spending Growth Limitation Adjustments (SGLA) that enable districts to meet unbudgeted increases in expenses for such items as hazardous route transportation, courtesy busing, insurance, utilities, or legal services. Once routine budgetary transfers such as line-item transfers exceeding ten percent as well as transfers of surplus and unbudgeted revenue now require county approval.

According to the New Jersey School Boards Association (2004), S1701 further eroded local taxpayer control by limiting a district's use of second ballot questions, which are referred to as second questions. By casting votes on second questions, citizens exert control over the authorization of funds for specific educational programs and services that are in addition to the base operating budget. Through the exercise of second questions (New Jersey School Boards Association, 2004, p. 3), "the community determines if it is willing and able to raise the money to fund the expenditure over cap for programs ranging from full-day Kindergarten and after-school enrichment programs to extra-curricular activities."

S1701 further eroded the ability of local school districts to develop, approve, and implement their operating budgets. Decision making authority over many budgetary items such as the acquisition and allocation of a school district's financial and human resources were largely transferred to the county level of government as the state's execution arm. S1701 "lessened a community's ability to determine school finance matters and related educational policy" (New Jersey School Boards Association, 2004, p. 2).

Upon taking office in January 2010, New Jersey Governor Christie announced he would withhold $475 million in promised state aid to school districts statewide as part of his effort to close the state fiscal year budget deficit of approximately $2 billion. What made the governor's plan even more burdensome is that he required districts to make up for cuts in state aid by using their surplus and reserve account funds.

New Jersey Governor Christie's plan required districts to use all their excess surplus plus 25% of the reserve accounts for capital, maintenance, emergencies, and excess. This means that most non-Abbott districts lost most if not all their state aid for the balance of the fiscal year that ends on June 30. Because the state already required districts to roll over any surplus exceeding the two percent level as property tax relief according to S1701, this reduction in surplus caused deeper cuts to non-mandate protected educational programs and property tax increases in districts statewide.

SCHOOL DISTRICT FUNDING POLICY IMPLICATIONS

Unlike state aid, local property taxes are a district's most sustainable revenue source. Local property taxes are levied on the district's tax base, which is the total assessed value of all taxable properties. Taxable properties are often called *ratables*. Property taxes can be levied only on commercial or residential properties but not public properties (e.g., government buildings, houses of worship, parks, or schools). However, the amount of non-taxable public properties shifts the tax burden to residential and commercial properties.

Land is a finite asset making it continually valuable. In addition, because some entity or someone owns all taxable land, some entity or someone can be billed for taxable land's property taxes. Thus, property taxes are the most reliable and sustainable revenue source while state aid varies, can be cut with little or no notice, and is subject to the vagaries of partisan politics as well as changing gubernatorial administrations.

However, state sales and income taxes, which are the sources for state aid, vary with the economy and collapse during difficult economic times making state aid unreliable and relatively unpredictable. During economic downturns or recessions as well as COVID-19, states have income and sales tax shortfalls because businesses and institutions close and lay off employees. State income and sales tax collections drop proportionate to the statewide decline in income and taxable sales activity.

Local property taxes meet the benefit and ability standards to a much greater extent than other forms of taxation. Most importantly, the quality of local public schools is capitalized in local property values. In addition, local property taxes reflect the costs and benefits of local public goods and services especially local K to 12 public education.

> Any benefit or burden of ownership that affects the price of property has been capitalized or reflected in the value of the capital asset. To the extent the tax has been capitalized, a new owner who has paid a lower price as a result does not bear that part of its economic burden.
>
> The tax on land is also one of the few available means of raising public revenue that does not impede economic efficiency, because the fixed supply of land cannot be altered in response to the tax. (Youngman, 2016, p. 3)

Thus, property tax revenues are the most reliable and sustainable source of revenue for schools and districts because land is a finite and property taxes must be paid regardless of the owners' income or job status.

ACCOUNTABILITY

California, Maryland, and New Jersey demonstrate the problems stemming from state domination of local school systems as executed through county government. State and county control as well as centralized funding leads to a one-size-fits-all approach for education but one that fits no district.

The specific needs of individual school districts vary to such a large degree that they render uniform state funding and policy formulas inadequate. Instead, public school districts need a mass customization of educational funding, control, and policy that can only derive from local control. Oates (1972) supports the notion that public education should be provided at the lowest level while Kenny (1982) argues for the provision of public education by local school districts.

Baker, Green, and Richards (2008, p. 66) explain how "the local property tax empowers local voters to express what they want for their local public schools." According to Baker, Green, and Richards (2008, p. 66) the consequence is that "when property taxes become statewide taxes, the political advantages of empowering local citizens and promoting competition and sorting among jurisdictions is lost." This mass standardization of school finance and policy leads to state funding guidelines that are incongruous with the needs and priorities of local school districts.

Typically, state or county-run school systems are not accountable to the taxpayer or local stakeholder. California demonstrates its lack of accountability by withholding or deferring funds that it is legally obligated to send to local school districts. As a result, California has "fallen from its position as a leader in per-student spending in the 1970's to now spending well below the national average" (Jacobson, 2007, p. 2). As Jacobson (2007, p. 3) explains, because the state has centralized control over local school finance and policy, the state's "financial resources are distributed in such an irrational way that schools serving similar student populations in similar locations receive different funding."

California regularly withholds funds that it is required to provide its public schools but uses these funds to help offset state budget deficits. California has withheld nearly $15 billion of aid for its schools. California owes local school districts more than $3.6 billion in reimbursement for underfunded state mandates in violation of Proposition 4 requirements. In addition, the state owes local school districts $11.2 billion in Proposition 111 maintenance factor obligations.

New Jersey is expanding state control and authority through its county governments at the expense of local control, autonomy, and accountability. The state increased its bureaucracy and administrative expenses through the greatly expanded Office of the Executive County Superintendent. Typically, these appointed officials override decisions made by duly elected boards of education by exercising line-item vetoes.

The authority of the Executive County Superintendent supersedes that of locally elected boards of education effectively rendering local boards of education as no longer the trustees of a district's financial and human resources whom the taxpayer can hold accountable. Taxpayers have great difficulty holding the state accountable. Examples of this include the state's recapturing surplus and reserve funds governed by S1701, the failure of the School Construction Corporation, and the growing educational resource equity gap among districts.

Any reduction in local school district control over the levying property taxes and allocating of property tax revenues decreases accountability and adversely affects public school quality. Taxpayers are more involved in, have a much greater stake in their local school districts, and act to hold these school districts accountable when they pay local property taxes directly to their local school districts rather than have their local property taxes controlled by the state and redistributed as if they were statewide revenues according to a state funding formula.

Fischel (2001, p. 152) explains the consequences of statewide property tax redistribution using voters without children in the public schools:

> At the local level, they are willing to support, or at least not oppose, high levels of spending because better schools add to the value of their homes. At the state level, voters without children do not perceive such an offsetting benefit to their taxes.

Having a lowered sense of ownership in their schools, taxpayers become more complacent as the proportion of state funding increases. This causes a corresponding reduction in the level of accountability required by the stakeholders and the quality of their public schools' education declines as a result.

State control over schools interrupts the connection taxpayers make between their property values and property taxes. As Sonstelie, Brunner, and Ardon explain (Sonstelie et al., 2000, p. 102 as cited in Fischel, 2001, p. 136) the "reason that local control produces better schools is that the local property tax system channels the revenues of nonresidential property into public education." The greater is the proportion of non-residential properties in a district's mix of ratables, the lower is the tax burden on residential properties. This lowers their "tax price" (Fischel, 2001, p. 136) making their local schools relatively less expensive and as a result, taxpayers are "induced to spend more on education."

Typical taxpayers resemble investors because they want their major asset, their home, to appreciate. As Fischel (2001, p. 136) explains, "voters tolerate property taxes only when the public services financed by them are capitalized in home values." Homeowners have a vested interest in the success of their local schools because the credit rating of a school district's host municipality is largely dependent on the financial soundness and credit worthiness of its schools. The higher a municipality's or a school district's credit rating, the lower its debt service expense.

The greater is the quality of the local school district, the greater is the taxpayer's property value because the demand for quality education leads to a higher market price. As a result, taxpayers strive to protect and improve their property values. They evaluate the quality of their school district to maximize their property values. But if their school district's quality deteriorates or is expected to decline, typical Tieboutian taxpayers will vote with their feet.

By voting with their feet, taxpayers choose the local school district that best meets their needs and one that will contribute to their property values (Tiebout, 1956). But taxpayers vote not only with their feet but also on school district operating budgets, capital projects, and board of education members. Through the exercise of these votes, taxpayers control the quality of education provided by their local schools as well as the level of property taxes levied. Their collective decisions lead to an efficient allocation of local public education. In this context, Baker, Green, and Richards (2008, p. 21) state that the "Tiebout model represents the most basic form of school choice."

Tiebout (1956) argues that because crowding and congestion affect the provision of public goods and services, it is inefficient to provide public education at a centralized level. Public education is more efficiently provided at the local level. Fischel (2001) supports this conclusion with his assessment of California's centralized school finance system in which taxpayers lost control over local schools and property taxes, which led to reduced levels of taxpayer involvement and support for public education.

Fischel (2001, p. 161) concludes "the apparent quality of public education has declined nationwide as the states' share of funding for it has risen." It is essential that taxpayers rather than states or counties have control over their local schools so they will be motivated to properly fund, support, and improve public education.

CONCLUSION

The consequences of centralizing control of a school district's financial, material, and human resources at the state level causes unintended obstacles to improving accountability. Chief among them is the contradictory challenge of trying to hold local school districts accountable to standards, which are made remotely at the state level, that conflict with local educational requirements, needs, and priorities. As a result, when states impose a one-size-fits-all approach to local school district resource allocation, state funds are used inefficiently. School systems are more accountable if decision making over financial, material, and human resources is made at the local district level.

A local school district can improve student and school performance best when the district is empowered to allocate its financial, material, and human resources according to its educational plan rather than having to follow one-size-fits-all state directives. The local school district would have all the tools it would need to hold schools and students accountable because it could make real time decisions based on specific measurable performance goals for each school and student.

The school district is the most qualified to continually calibrate local performance goals because only the local school district can combine a keen understanding of local educational necessities with the timely and specific assessment of individual school and student achievement. State control is too remote, which causes not only inappropriate delays but also decisions that are inconsistent with the district's educational plan.

State control over a district's financial, material, and human resources creates barriers for achieving accountability. When a local school district is limited by the state's one-size-fits-all approach, it is prevented from developing more innovative approaches to accountability. For local school districts to innovate, they must be empowered to use the most effective approaches for increasing accountability that are best suited to local needs. Improving accountability, therefore, requires the adaptation of new models for the control structure of local public schools that are free of state and county control.

In response to the shortcomings of state dominated local school systems, communities need greater local control over their schools so that they can benefit from increased accountability. A school district's control structure affects how all the school system's stakeholders combine to produce a quality education.

School districts nationwide are searching for the most appropriate local control structure that will maximize accountability. As a result, school districts are increasingly adapting a local control structure that provides the maximum accountability possible according to their unique characteristics, needs, priorities, and preferences. What matters most is that a school district employs the control structure that fosters the greatest public support for the maximum public funding of its public schools.

REFERENCES

Baker, B. D., Green, P., & Richards, C. E. (2008). *Financing education systems*. Pearson Education, Inc.

Coffin, S.V. (2021a). *Achieving economies of scale and fiscal capacity in large school districts*. [Manuscript submitted for publication]. *Education and Urban Society*.

Coffin, S. V. (2021b). *Creating a model state school finance formula to achieve equal educational opportunity and school finance equity* [Manuscript in preparation]. Rowman & Littlefield.

Coffin, S. V. (Ed.) (2021c). *Higher education's looming collapse: Using new ways of doing business and social justice to avoid bankruptcy*. Rowman & Littlefield.

Coffin, S. V. (2021d). *Strategic school finance for leading-edge equitable public education*. [Manuscript in preparation]. Rowman & Littlefield.

Coffin, S. V., & Cooper, B. S. (Eds.) (2017). *Sound school finance for educational excellence*. Rowman & Littlefield.

Coffin, S. V., & Cooper, B. S. (Eds.) (2018). *District financial leadership today: Educational excellence tomorrow.* Rowman & Littlefield.

CommUNITY Against Regionalization Efforts (2009). *Core Act, C.A.R.E.* Retrieved from http://www.saveoursmallschools.com/legislation.

Cuban, L. (2004). *The blackboard and the bottom line: Why schools can't be businesses.* Harvard University Press.

Edwards, B., M., & Leichty, J. (2010). *School finance 2009–10: Budget cataclysm and its aftermath.* EdSource.

Fischel, W. A. (2001). *The homevoter hypothesis: How home values influence local government taxation, school finance, and land-use policies.* Harvard University Press.

Fischel, W. A. (2009). *Making the grade: The economic evolution of American school districts.* University of Chicago Press.

Fusarelli, B. C., & Cooper, B. S., (Eds.). (2009). *The rising state: How state power is transforming our nation's schools.* SUNY Press.

Greenhut, S. (2005). State meddling hamstrings schools. *The Orange County Register.* Retrieved from http://www.ocregister.com.

Jacobson, L. (2007). California's schooling is "broken": Studies call for overhaul of finance, governance. *Education Week,* 26(28). Retrieved from http://www.edweek.org/ew/toc/2007/03/21/index.html.

Kenny, L. W. (1982). Economies of scale in schooling. *Economics of Education Review,* (2) 1–24.

Kenny, L. W., & Schmidt, A. B. (1994). The decline in the number of school districts in the United States 1950 – 1980. *Public Choice,* (79) 1–18.

New Jersey Department of Education (2005). *S1701 regulations.* Retrieved from http://www.state.nj.us/education/finance.

New Jersey Department of Education (2008). *School Funding Reform Act.* Retrieved from http://www.state.nj.us/education.

New Jersey Department of Education (2010). *S450.* Retrieved from http://www.state.nj.us/education.

New Jersey School Boards Association (2004). *S1701 Signed into law.* Retrieved from http://www.njsba.org/S1701-Update.

Oates, W. E. (1972). *Fiscal federalism.* Harcourt Brace Jovanovich.

Perry, M. (2004). *Rethinking how California funds its schools.* EdSource.

Perry, M., & Edwards, B. (2009). *Local revenues for schools: Limits and options in California.* EdSource.

Picus, L. O., (2009). California. In Fusarelli, B. C., & Cooper, B. S., (Editors), *The rising state: How state power is transforming our nation's schools,* (pp. 9–26). SUNY Press.

Sonstelie, J., Brunner, E., & Ardon, K. (2000). *For better or for worse? School finance reform in California.* Public Policy Institute of California.

Tiebout, C. M., (1956). A pure theory of local expenditures. *Journal of Political Economy,* 64, 416-424.

Youngman, J. (2016). *A good tax: Legal and policy issues for the property tax in the United States*. Lincoln Institute of Land Policy.

Yudof, M. G., Kirp, D. L., Levin, B., & Moran, R. F. (2002). *Educational policy and the law*. Wadsworth Group/Thomson Learning.

Chapter 14

Achieving Economies of Scale and Building Fiscal Capacity in Large School Districts

Stephen V. Coffin

Bigger-is-better advocates have often sought ways to provide quality education with presumed ever-increasing economies-of-scale. Consolidating local school districts into large, regional, or countywide districts are the preferred means.

The bigger-is-better belief, based on presumed ever-increasing economies of scale that would lower per unit output costs, is flawed. Economies of scale do not increase infinitely; on the contrary, economies of scale are limited. Right-sized districts with between 2,000 to 4,000 students operate in the flat or constant returns to scale portion of the long run average cost curve. Districts with larger enrollments operate beyond the pivot point on the long run average cost (LAC) curve at which their LAC exceeds their long run marginal cost (LMC), resulting in increasing per unit costs.

LARGE REGIONAL DISTRICTS

Like our nation's largest public school systems (e.g., New York City, Los Angeles, Boston, Detroit, Newark, and Chicago), large regional and county-run school districts have higher costs resulting from diseconomies of scale. Large school districts with enrollments beyond 4,000 students have long run average costs exceeding marginal costs. At this pivot point, input costs exceed the benefits of educational outputs reflecting the economic concepts of congestion and crowding.

When large regional or traditional school districts' LAC exceeds their marginal cost (MC), it often requires public subsidies to cover funding shortfalls (e.g., New York City Public Schools, Los Angeles United School District, Chicago Public Schools, New Jersey's *Abbott* districts, e.g., special needs districts) because these districts lack the tax base with which to raise the revenues necessary to provide top quality education commensurate with affluent districts without substantial state aid.

Large regional or countywide school district advocates argue that public school systems should be run as if they were large manufacturing businesses that only need to extend their *educational* assembly lines. Advocates assert that increasing assembly lines to the greatest extent possible would increase production with increased economies of scale. This thinking underlies many of the funding challenges facing public schools as Cuban (2004) highlights in the *Blueberry Epiphany*: "Our schools are not factories" (pp. 3–4). Most businesses would fail if they had to operate with the same economic constraints as those governing our public schools (Vollmer, 2010).

DISECONOMIES OF SCALE

Advocates of large regional or countywide school districts argue that economies of scale increase with enrollment size. This argument is based on unsubstantiated economies of scale that do not reflect school systems' reality (Andrews et al., 2002; Antonucci, 1999; Berry, 2004; Coffin, 2021a; Coffin, 2021b; Coffin, 2021d; Duncombe & Yinger, 2007; Kenny, 1982; Kenny & Schmidt, 1994).

However, an approximate 3,500 pupil district size is consistent with the findings of studies of the economies of scale and optimal district size (Andrews et al., 2002; Antonucci, 1999; Berry, 2004; Coffin, 2021a; Coffin, 2021b; Coffin, 2021d; Duncombe & Yinger, 2007; Kenny, 1982). Antonucci (1999) found that large school districts are too large to function effectively as well as to improve school and student performance.

> The larger a school district gets, the more resources it devotes to secondary or even non-essential activities. In sum, large school districts engage in "mission creep," building activities which rapidly lose any connection to the original goal of educating children. (p. 1)

Thus, a regional, countywide, or large traditional "American public school system suffers from penalties of scale" (Antonucci, 1999, p. 2).

Vermont

In testimony to the Vermont Senate Education Committee, Ms. Rebeca Holcombe, Vermont Secretary of Education, cited Andrews, Duncombe, and Yinger's (2002) research on the economies of scale in education in determining that an optimal district size ranges from about 2,000 to 4,000 students. Secretary Holcombe explained:

> The best of the cost function studies suggest that sizeable potential cost savings in instructional and administrative costs may exist by moving from a very small district (500 or fewer pupils) to a district with ca 2,000–4,000 pupils. The findings from production function studies of schools are less consistent, but there is some evidence that moderately sized elementary schools (300–500 students) and high schools (600–900 students) may optimally balance economies of size with the potential negative effects of large schools. (Vermont, Agency of Education, 2015, p.1)

Operating costs tend to increase once enrollment exceeds about 4,000 students.

Regional or county-run districts stemming from S2727 legislation would level-down education to the lowest common denominator and cause a commensurate reduction in property values (Coffin, 2021a; Fischel, 1998, Fischel, 2001; Fischel, 2009). However, quality school systems undergird district property values. Take away local control and locally-controlled school districts, level down the quality of education provided locally and property values, then the more affluent and mobile parents most likely will vote with their feet and enroll their children in traditional public school districts (T.P.S.D.s) that meet their preferences or charter—or private—schools (Coffin, 2020; Fischel, 2002; Fischel, 2005; Levin & Belfield 2003; Russo & Coffin, 2021).

New Jersey

Two New Jersey Senate bills exemplify the bigger-is-better belief with presumed ever increasing economies of scale: S2727 in 2015 and S450 in 2010. New Jersey bill S2727 proposes studying how to build large regional districts. New Jersey bill S450 proposed establishing countywide school districts by eliminating all local school districts and requiring the remaining local public schools to report directly to their respective Executive County Superintendent. In addition, since 2018, New Jersey State Senate President Stephen Sweeney proposed legislation to eliminate local school districts and amalgamate local schools into county-run districts, which would result in extreme diseconomies of scale (Andrews et al., 2002; Antonucci, 1999; Coffin, 2021a; Duncombe & Yinger, 2007; Kenny, 1982; Kenny & Schmidt, 1994).

Maryland

As a first step to regionalizing school districts, S2727 is a thinly veiled attempt to force countywide county-run districts as S450 proposed. S450 would have had New Jersey replicate Maryland's consolidated countywide school system model. Maryland eliminated all local school officials and their staffs beyond the level of principal and consolidated all local schools within countywide school districts under an Executive County Superintendent (Coffin, 2021a). However, Maryland's total statewide costs, especially administrative expenses, increased following the implementation of the consolidated countywide school districts (Coffin, 2021a). Maryland's countywide school districts were not accountable to the voters enabling spending to increase without taxpayer control.

Supporters of S450 insisted it would save New Jersey taxpayers' money and lower property taxes by eliminating administrators along with their staffs over the level of principal in existing T.P.S.D.s. S450 advocates suggested the bill would save approximately $553 million (Coffin, 2021a). However, Maryland's total statewide educational costs, especially administrative costs, increased following the implementation of its consolidated countywide school districts (Coffin, 2021a; Coffin, 2021b; Coffin, 2021d). In contrast, eliminating New Jersey's county governments would save approximately $8 billion annually that could be repurposed to fully fund K-16 education, infrastructure, community economic development, and pensions while providing desperately needed property tax relief.

Zero in the Zero-Sum Game

Consolidating local school districts into countywide or large regional districts removes decision-making authority from those levels most affected by educational policy decisions: the student, parent, teacher, school, and district. It concentrates policy formulation and decision-making at levels where often special interests have greater leverage on policy makers and greater control of policy outcomes. Consolidation of local school districts into countywide or regional districts, while fewer in number, results in higher state-wide total administrative costs due to the lack of accountability, excessive political patronage hiring, and reduced local voter control (Abbott et al., 2002; Andrews et al., 2002; Antonucci, 1999; Berry, 2004; Coffin, 2021a; Fischel, 1998; Vollmer, 2010).

Accountability declines with countywide or large regional districts that are too distant from where education takes place and are more easily influenced by special interest groups. Accountability declines at the levels where it is needed most. Decentralization brings decision makers closer to the taxpayers and local priorities. Taxpayers have more at stake in the success of their local school district rather than countywide or large regional districts. Separating the taxpayer from his/her ability to control and influence the operating and capital budgets as well as the educational plan of his/her local school district cuts neither costs nor property taxes while leveling down educational quality.

The size of countywide or large regional districts influences the extent to which any form of structural control can improve a school system. Countywide or large regional districts are not been accountable for improving school and student performance (Abbott et al., 2002; Antonucci, 1999; Berry, 2004; Coffin, 2021a; Coffin & Cooper, 2017; Coffin & Cooper, 2018). They have been constrained by their exceedingly large size with its concomitant penalties of scale.

The typical large school district must be disaggregated into several smaller districts with each having approximately 3,500 students. This will create the control structure necessary for the school system to improve accountability, lower costs, and avoid penalties of scale. In addition, smaller or sub-districts will facilitate a more efficient allocation and use of resources.

The solution is to disaggregate large districts especially those with enrollment exceeding 10,000. Smaller districts or sub-districts of approximately 3,500 students will not only facilitate manageability but also improve accountability to stakeholders especially parents and taxpayers. Local right-sized school districts under the control of a locally elected board of education will provide the proper span of control for avoiding diseconomies of scale.

The larger the countywide or large regional district is the greater are its diseconomies of scale. Diseconomies of scale increase costs. Any assumed savings from countywide or large regional districts would be more than offset by higher operating costs. Thus, large regional or countywide districts are equivalent to the *zero* in the zero-sum educational funding *game* that they would impose. Large regional or countywide districts increase operating costs, lower property values, and level down the quality of education to the lowest common denominator.

Solution: Shift the School Finance Paradigm

The school finance paradigm must shift to small right-sized districts and away from consolidating local school districts into countywide or large regional districts. Shifting the school finance paradigm will create a system that closes the equity gaps in school funding and the unequal distribution of educational resources among schools. Small right-sized districts are essential for achieving educational equity and equal opportunity.

Closing the educational equity gap requires distributing financial, material, and human resources so that all schools have the fiscal capacity to improve student achievement especially for disadvantaged students. Large concentrations of high-need high-cost-to-educate students exacerbate the educational equity gap.

The lack of a tax base to generate the revenues necessary to provide a quality education is the major roadblock to closing equity funding gaps. The lack of proper fiscal capacity results in poorly resourced school districts that lack the ability to raise property tax revenues commensurate with affluent districts. Often these communities are large urban districts having high levels of high-need students living in poverty who are more challenging and expensive to educate.

To fund K–12 public education properly and equitably, the states must eliminate the duplicative and unnecessary layer of county government and repurpose those tax dollars (Coffin, 2021a; Coffin, 2021c). County governments' diseconomies of scale increase costs and allocative inefficiency. In addition, county government duplicates local and state public goods and services.

> For example, ending New Jersey's unnecessary layer of county government would save about $8 billion annually in duplicative county property taxes. Repurposing the $8 billion annually would not only properly fund statewide K–16 education, infrastructure, community economic development, housing, employment opportunities, and tax relief, but also provide financial sustainability and operational survivability. In addition, disaggregating such overly large districts as Newark's approximately 35,000 students into 10 roughly similar-sized autonomous subdistricts would cut costs by eliminating diseconomies of scale. (Coffin, 2021c, p. 226)

This solution revolutionizes K–12 public education funding while freeing T.P.S.D.s from depending on unreliable and unpredictable state aid.

In addition, the author's solution "disaggregates large districts into more manageable subdistricts, centralizes common services in the former large-district apparatus, builds fiscal capacity through community economic development, and funds its implementation with the subdistricts' share of the $8 billion" (Coffin, 2021c, p. 226). Thus, the author provides the way for all T.P.S.D.s to have the tax base with which to levy the property taxes necessary to fully fund their school systems at a quality level commensurate with the most affluent and top-performing districts. In addition, and most importantly, this revenue stream is district-controlled and sustainable unlike state aid.

ACTION PLAN FOR CREATING A NEW *NEW-ARK*

Rekindle the *New-Ark* Spirit

Bigger is not necessarily better. Consolidating local school districts into countywide or large regional districts increases diseconomies of scale making fewer resources available for instruction and learning. Disaggregating large school districts will shift the school finance paradigm to a system that closes the equity gaps in school funding and the unequal distribution of educational resources among schools.

Newark, with its approximate 35,000 students, exemplifies a large district that is suffering diseconomies of scale and would benefit from disaggregating. Disaggregating into smaller sub-districts will achieve educational equity and equal opportunity. Implementing this solution requires rekindling the spirit of Newark's founders to create a new *New-ark* redesigned school district. In May 1666, Puritans, who were seeking land on which to build with access to major waterways, purchased land along the Passaic River from the Hackensack Indians and founded their "New-Ark," "New Ark of the Covenant," or "Our Town on Passaick River" (History of Newark, 2010).

Creating Smaller Sub-Districts

To achieve equal educational opportunity and resource equity, Newark should disaggregate its approximate 35,000 students into 10 roughly similar-sized autonomous independent parent-centric sub-districts to create a new *New-ark*. Each sub-district would be right sized to about 3,500 pupils. The current large district apparatus would no longer control the 10 sub-districts but would be responsible for such centralized services as purchasing, maintenance, janitorial, food services, security, transportation, and other services common to all 10 sub-districts.

Being closer to the students, parents, teachers, and taxpayers, each sub-district would be more likely to equitably decide how to provide a quality education for all students. In addition, sub-districts would be more likely to generate the necessary support among local taxpayers for the proper public funding of public education because they are closer to stakeholders.

However, the size of the school district impacts school and student performance. Like Newark, if a school district gets too large and unwieldy then parental engagement decreases, harming student achievement because parental involvement undergirds student performance (Abbott et al., 2002; Antonucci, 1999; Berry, 2004; Coffin, 2021a; Russo & Coffin, 2021; Vollmer, 2010).

Give Authority to Sub-Districts

Each sub-district would manage and direct all schools within its boundaries. Sub-districts would control decision-making for personnel (including hiring, tenure, assessment, classroom assignments, and compensation), budgets, operations, communications, facilities, curriculum, and other functions. Sub-districts lacking a middle or high school, or sufficient elementary schools would negotiate sending students to other sub-districts that have available classroom capacity (i.e., negotiating a contractual sending-receiving relationship as do many districts nationwide).

Decentralize Funding and Management

Each sub-district would develop and manage its own operating and capital budgets. Voters within the sub-district would determine whether to approve the operating and capital budgets once those budgets were approved by its elected board of education. Returning control over local schools to the people especially parents of school children and taking control away from the politicians will build sub-district social capital and give the people an ownership stake.

The sub-district's voters would elect its board of education whose members must reside within the sub-district's boundaries. The sub-district would inform the City of Newark's tax collector of the amount of property taxes to collect to fund its budget. State and federal aid would be allocated to each sub-district based on the total cost-to-educate of each student in the student's sub-district (e.g., weighted student funding).

The New *New-Ark*

Disaggregating Newark into 10 similar-sized sub-districts would cut costs by eliminating the diseconomies of scale inherent in the current over-sized district. In studying student achievement, family poverty level, and school and district enrollment size, Abbott, Joireman, and Stroh (2002) concluded: "... large district size is detrimental to achievement in Washington 4th and 7th grades in that it strengthens the negative relationship between school poverty and student achievement." Further, they state, "the negative relationship between school poverty and achievement is stronger in larger districts," and "small schools appear to have the greatest equity effects." In other words, when school poverty is high, children perform better in small districts, and the effect of school level poverty on achievement is smallest when both the district and school are small (pp. i-ii).

Having small, more manageable sub-districts enables parents to be more involved and participate more with their children's schools as well as with the administration of each stakeholder-centered sub-district. The new *New-Ark* approach gives parents and community members a voice for a change and helps them become real stakeholders.

Eliminate County Government

To fund and implement the new *New-ark* solution in large districts as well as to fund comprehensive community economic development in disadvantaged areas statewide, New Jersey must eliminate county government. New Jersey's 21 county governments collectively cost taxpayers about $8 billion annually, almost all of which comes from property taxes (Coffin, 2021a; Coffin, 2021c). County government and its property taxes are duplicative and unnecessary. By eliminating county government in 1960, Connecticut proved that county government duplicated state and local government because every public good or service that was provided by county government was already provided at either the state or municipal level (Coffin, 2021a; Coffin, 2021c).

Community Economic Development

Eliminating New Jersey's county governmental layer would generate about $8 billion annually that can be repurposed to fund community economic development statewide (Coffin, 2021a; Coffin, 2021c). Well-funded community economic development would provide sustainable improvements in housing, transportation, infrastructure, education, employment, and governmental services especially for large urban districts.

Properly funded community economic development with consequences and enforcement-teeth for those firms and entities that are incented to join but fail to deliver, would help to alleviate poverty, avoid systemic disinvestment, and build a sustainable tax base while helping to reverse many of the problems stemming from redlining's legacy. Urban areas especially those with high concentrations of poverty would have the fiscal capacity to generate revenues necessary to close the equity gaps in educational funding with affluent districts.

SOLUTION

Recapturing the spirit that created *New-ark* in 1666 while disaggregating Newark's approximate 35,000 students into 10 roughly similar-sized autonomous independent parent-centered sub-districts would create a new *New-ark* of education for all students, parents, and schools. Building a new *New-ark* of education requires the following steps.

1. Provide wider local and state commitment to right-sizing New Jersey's large districts from unresponsive units, to smaller, more active, responsive, customer-centric community-based school systems.
2. Make funding more flexible, local, and responsive to individual, familial, and communal needs.
3. Improve sensitivity by local school leaders and teachers to the needs of individual students and their families, regardless of the race, ethnicity, religion, income, or ability of children they teach or supervise.
4. Build and support talented leaders in the sub-districts and their schools where they will be held more accountable.

The Wallace Foundation consultants (2013) highlighted the issue when they advised the finding, promoting, and supporting of skilled school leaders. They advised schools to find and build a large corps of well-qualified candidates for the principalship. Indeed, the *smaller is better* concept, as reflected by the rationale supporting smaller schools, has many advocates.

The idea behind smaller schools is simple: having fewer students in each school should create a more nurturing environment where all kids can receive the attention they need—and none fall through the cracks that may develop at a larger school. Among its followers, the small-schools movement includes some of the heaviest hitters in the education world, such as the Bill and Melinda Gates Foundation, the Annenberg Foundation, and the New York City school system. For several years, reformers in New York City have been carving large comprehensive high schools into several smaller "learning academies" or "schools within a school" housed within the same building. (Berry, 2004, p. 1)

The *New-Ark* redesigned school district demonstrates that *smaller is better* for all stakeholders.

Wealth Neutrality

The new *New-Ark* design disaggregates larger districts into smaller, more manageable sub-districts, centralizes common services in the former large district apparatus, builds fiscal capacity through community economic development, and funds the solution with the sub-districts' share of the $8 billion made available annually by eliminating New Jersey's county governments. Implementing the aforementioned four steps would eliminate inequities resulting from fiscal capacity disparities among affluent and poor schools and districts.

The new *New-Ark* design is equivalent to applying Coons, Clune, and Sugarman's (1970) wealth neutrality concept to education funding. Wealth neutrality neutralizes affluent districts' property tax revenue advantage that enables affluent districts to spend disproportionately more than poor districts and have much better resourced schools. Disparities in resources cause disparities in the quality of education.

Educational equity requires the fair distribution of financial, material, and human resources among schools and districts based on student need. Educational services and facilities must be equitably available, accessible, and affordable for all students. No student's access to education should be denied or minimized, based on his or her cost to educate, race, ethnicity, gender, or socioeconomic class.

Achieving educational equity requires avoiding a one-size-fits-all approach that levels up or down to the mean without accounting for differences in property wealth, educational resources, accessibility, and individual student needs as well as the per-pupil cost to educate. To neutralize affluent districts' fiscal capacity advantage and close the resultant per-pupil educational opportunity funding gap, per-pupil resources must be equitably distributed among schools and districts based on student needs.

POLICY IMPLICATIONS

Equity in Resource Distribution

Money matters. Resources matter. The degree to which a sub-district has the financial, material, and human resources necessary to meet students' needs is the degree to which its schools can provide quality education for all students. Once a school is properly resourced, the school will have the ability to provide an equal educational opportunity for all students. A properly resourced school is much more likely to sustain equal opportunity. Achieving an equitable distribution of educational financial, material, and human resources is essential for achieving equal educational opportunities.

To achieve an equitable distribution of educational resources among schools and districts statewide, students' ability to receive a quality education comparable to that which the more affluent students receive should not be limited by the student's district's property wealth. Affluent districts can leverage their tax base to provide disproportionately higher quality resources including teachers, administrators, facilities, laboratories, technology, curricula, small class sizes, extracurricula activities, Advanced Placement, and honors courses.

Higher quality and levels of resources translate into higher educational outcomes for students of affluent districts such as test scores, graduation rates, rates of college admission, and rates of admission to more selective universities as well as lower grade retention, truancy, and dropout rates (Coffin, 2020; Coffin, 2021c; Cooper et al., 2009). Without resource equalization among schools and districts, poor districts lack the necessary resources to provide an education comparable to affluent districts, disenfranchising their students.

Inequalities in educational outcomes stem from inequities in educational resource allocation among schools and districts. Inequities in educational resource allocation stem primarily from overreliance on insufficient tax bases to fund public education especially in poor districts.

Districts lacking the tax base from which to levy the property tax revenues commensurate with affluent districts are unable to provide an educational quality commensurate with that provided by affluent districts. High property wealth tax bases advantage students attending affluent districts while low property wealth tax bases disadvantage students in high poverty districts. Thus, affluent districts can afford higher property taxes to fund a higher quality education.

Education Debt Concept

Poor districts cannot afford the same property tax burden as affluent districts. Therefore, poor districts are less able to provide an education commensurate with affluent districts. This educational inequality is reflected in Ladson-Billings' (2006) education debt concept.

Ladson-Billings (2006) posits that the annual educational deficit is equivalent to the annual fiscal operating budget deficit while the education debt is equivalent to the cumulative legacy costs of educational inequality.

> The education debt is the foregone schooling resources that we could have (should have) been investing in (primarily) low-income kids, which deficit leads to a variety of social problems (e.g., crime, low productivity, low wages, low labor force participation) that require on-going public investment. This required investment sucks away resources that could go to reducing the achievement gap. (p. 5)

Educational inequities stem from inequalities in resource allocation among schools and districts.

Students attending schools in poor districts lack access to the same quality and level of resources as their affluent counterparts. Therefore, students attending under-resourced schools lack the educational opportunity equal to their affluent counterparts. However, federal and state school funding formulas fail to provide sufficient funds for the resources to meet all students' needs properly and equitably regardless of where they attend school. The new *New-Ark-type* district is designed to succeed where state and federal school funding formulas fail.

Local Control

The governance structure essential to creating a new New-Ark is local control that generates and maintains community specific social capital and the public support necessary for the public funding of public education (Fischel 1998; Fischel 2001; Fischel 2002; Fischel, 2009). Fischel (2005) posits local public education creates a bond among parents increasing their belief in the value of locally provided public education that facilitates and galvanizes local support for locally provided public education.

> Having children in local schools increases parents' "community-specific social capital." Through local connections, parents get to know other adults in their community better, which in turn reduces the transaction costs of citizen provision of local public goods. (Fischel, 2005, p. 1)

> . . . community contacts obtained through public schools have a multiplier effect.. . . . Positive experiences from such activities create mutual bonds that increase people's sense of trust in others. (Fischel, 2005, pp. 14–15)

Thus, "community-specific social capital facilitates collective action" that undergirds, mobilizes, and sustains public support for local public schools (Fischel, 2005, p. 6). The absence of local control or having students attend schools in other districts provides no community-specific social capital and undermines public support for public education.

Taxpayers resemble investors because they want their major asset, their home, to appreciate. The greater the quality of the local school district's education, the greater the taxpayer's property value because demand for quality education leads to a higher market price. As a result, taxpayers strive to protect their property values by overseeing the quality of education provided by their local district to maximize property values.

Thus, most taxpayers, who at any one point in time, do not have children or do not have children attending local public schools, support their local public schools. Homeowners have a vested interest in the success of their local schools causing them to strive to offset risks. The greatest risk to homeowners' property values and the quality of education that is capitalized in their property values are those posed by countywide or large regional school districts, which cannot be easily diversified.

Under local control, each sub-district determines its own operating and capital budgets, which are the financial representation of its educational plan (Coffin & Cooper, 2017; Coffin & Cooper, 2018). Each sub-district can collect increasing amounts of local property taxes as its tax base is enhanced annually through community economic development. The sub-district's community economic development is funded by the sub-district's share of the $8 billion in annual savings realized by eliminating New Jersey's county government. Thus, the new New-Ark solution helps to ensure equal educational opportunity and equitable educational revenues to fully fund the cost-to-educate of every student regardless of where s/he attends school.

Fischel (1998) suggests that court decisions such as Serrano v. Priest that eroded local control and ended local property tax funding of local schools have "undermined political support for education by divorcing voters' property-tax payments from the quality of their local schools" (p. 1). Fischel (1998) explains that locally provided and property tax funded public education undergirds local property values and promotes public support for local public education.

In addition, Fischel (1998) suggests that maintaining local control and funding achieves positive capitalization more than other funding approaches.

> *Most of the court decisions that have overturned property tax financing of education have helped divorce the value of one's home from the quality of schools. (Capitalization occurs much less at the state level because potential residents cannot shop around for states the way they can shop around for communities.) This divorce has most probably contributed to the declining quality of public education and, at least in some states, to a reduction in public support for education as a whole. (p. 42)*

Thus, locally provided, and local property tax funded public education with tax bases augmented by community economic development funded by each sub-district's share of the $8 billion in annual savings realized by eliminating New Jersey's county government can provide an optimal approach for providing a quality education for all students regardless of need, cost-to-educate, residence, or school location.

The new *New-Ark* solution provides the funding necessary to enable all sub-districts and right-sized districts to fund their public schools at levels commensurate with the more affluent districts. The optimal mix of traditional public schools would be determined by the district's *homevoters* once this equitable solution is implemented (Fischel, 2001; Fischel 2002). Funding equal to that of affluent districts enables residents of all sub-districts and right-sized districts to focus more on developing the community-specific social capital necessary for fostering and sustaining local public support for local public schools.

REFERENCES

Abbott, M. L., Joireman, J., & Stroh, H. R. (2002). *The influence of district size, school size and socioeconomic status on student achievement in Washington: A replication study using hierarchical linear modeling* (Technical Report No. 3). Washington School Research Center.

Andrews, M., Duncombe, W. D., & Yinger, J. (2002). Revisiting economies of size in American education: Are we any closer to a consensus? *Economics of Education Review, 21*, 245–262.

Antonucci, M. (1999). *Mission creep: How large school districts lose sight of the objective—Student Learning (AdTI Issue Brief Number 176)*. Retrieved from http://www.adti.net/education/antonucci.mission.creep.html.

Berry, C. (2004). School inflation: Did the 20th-century growth in school size improve education? *EducationNext. 4*(4), 56–62.

Coffin, S. V. (2020). *State policy determinants of charter school market share* (Doctoral dissertation). Rutgers University, Graduate School of Education.

Coffin, S.V. (2021a). *Achieving economies of scale and fiscal capacity in large school districts*. [Manuscript submitted for publication]. *Education and Urban Society*.

Coffin, S. V. (2021b). *Creating a model state school finance formula to achieve equal educational opportunity and school finance equity* [Manuscript in preparation]. Rowman & Littlefield.

Coffin, S. V. (Ed.) (2021c). *Higher education's looming collapse: Using new ways of doing business and social justice to avoid bankruptcy*. Rowman & Littlefield.

Coffin, S. V. (2021d). *Strategic school finance for leading-edge equitable public education*. [Manuscript in preparation]. Rowman & Littlefield.

Coffin, S. V., & Cooper, B. S. (Eds.) (2017). *Sound school finance for educational excellence*. Rowman & Littlefield.

Coffin, S. V., & Cooper, B. S. (Eds.) (2018). *District financial leadership today: Educational excellence tomorrow*. Rowman & Littlefield.

Coons, J. E., Sugarman, S. D., & Clune, W. H. (1970). *Private wealth and public education*. Belknap Press of Harvard University Press.

Cooper, B. S., Spielhagen, F. R., & Coffin, S. (2009). Fighting truancy with consumer choice in education. In M. P. Conolly & D. O'Keeffe (Eds.), *Don't fence me in: Essays on the rational truant.* (pp. 47–67). University of Buckingham Press.

Cuban, L. (2004). *The blackboard and the bottom line: Why schools can't be businesses*. Harvard University Press.

Duncombe, W. D., & Yinger, J. (2007). Does school district consolidation cut costs? *Education Finance and Policy, 2*, 341–375.

Fischel, W. A. (1998). *School finance litigation and property tax revolts: How undermining local control turns voters away from public education.* Lincoln Institute of Land Policy Working Paper: Cambridge, MA.

Fischel, W. A. (2001). *The homevoter hypothesis: How home values influence local government taxation, school finance, and land-use policies.* Cambridge, MA: Harvard University Press.

Fischel, W. A. (2002). *An economic case against vouchers: Why local public schools are a local public good.* Dartmouth Economics Department Working Paper: Dartmouth College, Hanover, NH.

Fischel, W. A. (2005). *Why voters veto vouchers: Public schools and community-specific social capital.* Dartmouth Economics Department Working Paper: Dartmouth College, Hanover, NH.

Fischel, W. A. (2009). *Making the grade: The economic evolution of American school districts.* University of Chicago Press.

History of Newark. (2010, October 31). In Wikipedia. http://www.en.wikipedia.org/wiki/HistoryOfNewark,NewJersey.

Kenny, L. W. (1982). Economies of scale in schooling. *Economics of Education Review*, (2) 1–24.

Kenny, L. W., & Schmidt, A. B. (1994). The decline in the number of school districts in the United States 1950 – 1980. *Public Choice*, (79) 1–18.

Ladson-Billings, G. (2006). From the achievement gap to the education debt: Understanding achievement in U.S. schools. *Educational Researcher,* 35(7), 3–12.

Levin, H. M., & Belfield, C. R. (2003). The marketplace in education. *Review of Research in Education,* 27, 183–219.

Russo, C. J., & Coffin, S. V. (2021). The USA. In P. T. Clarke, K. Walker, & C. J. Russo (Eds.), *Student safety in changing times and places: Dealing with religious and cultural differences in schools.* [Manuscript in preparation]. Rowman & Littlefield.

Vermont, Agency of Education, Rebeca Holcombe, Secretary. (2015). *Research brief on optimal school district sizes.* Retrieved from http://www.education.vermont.gov.

Vollmer, J., (2010). *Schools cannot do it alone: Building public support for America's public schools.* Enlightenment Press.

Wallace Foundation, (2013). *New Report Profiles School Districts' Early Efforts to Develop Effective Principals.* Retrieved from http.www.wallacefoundation.org.

Chapter 15

K-12 N.A.P.R. Holistic Budgeting Model

Stephen V. Coffin

America's traditional public schools (Tpss) and districts (Tpsds) need a new, holistic budgeting model to improve financial, material, and human resource allocation and decision-making to close the educational resource equity gap. The Needs-Assumptions-Priorities-Rationale (N.A.P.R.) holistic budgeting model provides the solution with a custom designed budgeting approach that builds operating and capital budgets based core needs, assumptions, priorities, and rationales (Coffin, 2021).

The author's innovation is distilling the challenges stemming the nation's K-12 educational resource equity gap in a new way and assessing the need for financial sustainability, operational success, educational quality, equal opportunity, and resource equity in the context of this more complete and holistic budgeting model.

The N.A.P.R. budget model provides Tpss and Tpsds with ways to improve budgeting and resource management. The needs, cost structures, and revenue mixes of Tpss and Tpsds are as diverse as their mission statements, value propositions, faculty, administrators, curricula, and enrollment. America's Tpss and Tpsds have different assumptions undergirding their needs as well as the rationales that support their resource equity and allocative efficiency. The N.A.P.R. budget model adds a holistic conceptual framework to the traditional budgeting process.

First, the N.A.P.R. process identifies and defines needs. Second, N.A.P.R. specifies assumptions (e.g., educational, pedagogical, operational, financial, legal, or cultural) that undergird the needs that are represented as line items. This includes its specific expenditures and revenues. Third, needs, which are represented as line items, are prioritized in descending order (Coffin, 2021; Coffin & Cooper, 2017).

The prioritization can use as few as three (e.g., high, medium, low) or multiple gradations. Fourth, the stakeholders for the budgetary process, provide rationales consistent with the educational plan, value proposition, mission statement, and sound financial managerial practices (Coffin, 2021; Coffin & Cooper, 2017). The rationales must support the priority level assigned to each line item.

The rank ordering of priorities varies by school and district because needs as well as costs and revenues vary by school and district. In addition, the magnitude of various needs varies by TPS and TPSD. School and district budgets vary along a continuum of budgetary line items, which result in differing levels of budgetary expenditures paired with correspondingly different revenue mixes (Coffin, 2021; Coffin & Cooper, 2017). The N.A.P.R. budget model helps TPSs and TPSDs to understand and demonstrate how well educational, operational, and strategic plans are represented in their budgets.

Needs: First Step

First, budgetary stakeholders compile a comprehensive list of needs without a specific rank order (Coffin, 2021; Coffin & Cooper, 2017). Central to developing a consensus list of needs is making sure that all stakeholders are involved. TPSs and TPSDs are increasingly involving faculty, administrators, staff, student representatives, educational and credit rating agencies as well as key alumni or community members to identify needs. The budget office translates these needs into quantifiable line items (Coffin, 2021; Coffin & Cooper, 2017).

Assumptions: Second Step

Each stakeholder involved in identifying needs develops an assumption for the line items associated with those needs, which is essential for sound budgeting. Assumptions answer the "why is this needed?" question and help in decision-making (Coffin, 2021; Coffin & Cooper, 2017). Stakeholders must keep in mind that those who will use their input to make final budgetary decisions may not fully understand their goals or the core budgetary process. However, the extent to which assumptions are well defined, they will reflect the degree of support for the level of need and communicate its relative importance (Coffin, 2021; Coffin & Cooper, 2017).

Priorities: Third Step

Needs (i.e., line items) are prioritized based on their assumptions and importance. Stakeholders must prioritize their needs before submitting them to their supervisors, department heads, or assistant principals who in turn add their needs, assumptions, prioritization, and rationales before submitting them to the principal. In turn, the principal adds his/her needs, assumptions, prioritization, and rationales to the budgetary document including her/his overview of her/his department's educational, operational, and strategic plan. A consensus report is sent to the district school business administrator or senior finance officer if the entity is a school.

Rationale: Fourth Step

During the budgetary process stakeholders provide a rationale for the priority level assigned to each line item. The rationales justify the relative importance of line items in the budget (Coffin, 2021; Coffin & Cooper, 2017).

K-12 N.A.P.R. Model

Once the N-A-P-R process is complete, the TPS' or TPSD's budget can be compared to prior year's budgets as well as to the operating and capital budgets of comparable or competitor schools and districts. Important lessons can be learned through these comparisons. All stakeholders should remain available in the process, should the TPS or TPSD experience unexpected revenue shortfalls or unforeseen expenses such as those caused by the epic COVID pandemic (Coffin, 2021; Coffin & Cooper, 2017).

To help to close educational resource equity gaps, Tpss and Tpsds must identify ways of raising alternative revenues and developing new ways of doing business that generate savings (Coffin, 2021; Coffin & Cooper, 2017). This foreshadows Chapter 16, the Rescue Plan.

REFERENCES

Coffin, S. V. (Ed.) (2021). *Higher education's looming collapse: Using new ways of doing business and social justice to avoid bankruptcy.* Rowman & Littlefield.

Coffin, S. V., & Cooper, B. S. (Eds.) (2017). *Sound school finance for educational excellence.* Rowman & Littlefield.

PART VI
Conclusion

Chapter 16

Rescue Plan

Stephen V. Coffin

When the state courts rule that the state's school funding formula is unconstitutional or components violate the constitution, the courts mandate state legislatures to find ways for the formula to meet constitutional requirements. Typically, these new best practices include establishing a portfolio of necessary educational inputs (e.g., essential resources), outcomes (e.g., student performance, achievement, or level of attainment), and metrics that fulfill the courts' constitutional requirements.

Despite decades of increasingly rigorous court decrees, state remedies for state school funding formulae shortcomings vary widely while states struggle to provide the educational inputs necessary to achieve targeted outcomes. In addition, states struggle to develop reliable measures to ascertain equal educational opportunity and educational resource equity for all students and schools.

Schools must have the necessary financial, material, and human resources or inputs to meet or exceed constitutional requirements and achieve targeted academic outcomes. However, state school finance formula shortcomings exacerbate disparities in the provision of quality education among school districts and lessen equal educational opportunities.

In addition, the COVID-19 pandemic worsened state school finance formula-based inequities, funding inadequacies, educational resource allocative inefficiencies, and tax base disparities. Thus, the adverse impact of state school finance formula shortcomings and COVID-19's unforeseen expenditures drive budgetary and operational exigency amid state aid reductions and increasingly scarce quality material and human resources.

Educational resource inequities and academic outcomes as well as attainment disparities stem from the unequal distribution of resources among schools. These factors disenfranchise especially low-income or tax base-poor districts with high concentrations of high cost-to-educate pupils.

Ladson-Billings (2006) blames faulty state school funding formulae primarily for under-resourced school systems rather than schools, administrators, and teachers for test score disparities among minority and majority students. States must redesign school funding formulae to close educational resource gaps by allocating resources equitably so that schools have the necessary capacity to improve student achievement and attainment especially for disadvantaged students.

On a macro-level, the Rescue Plan is to adopt this book's best practices, strategies, and lessons learned in the context of N.A.P.R., the more complete and holistic budgeting model (Coffin & Cooper, 2017; Coffin & Cooper, 2018; Coffin 2021). In this way, schools and districts facing financial exigency or closure can adopt new ways of establishing financial sustainability and operational excellence to provide quality education.

On a micro-level, schools and districts must adjust their budgeting paradigm to adopt new ways of performing the business of education constructively and equitably with equal opportunity. These new best practices applied in the context of the more complete and holistic budgeting model center on raising alternative revenues and generating savings by using new ways of doing the business of education.

Alternative Revenues

Lease Incubators to Entrepreneurs

Typically, inventors, entrepreneurs, innovators, and start-up venture leaders possess creativity and innovative ideas for potentially groundbreaking products or services but lack proper space or facilities such as office space, access to laboratories, and research facilities with which to turn their ideas into products or services that are successful in the marketplace (Coffin, 2021). A district that leases unused or under-used facilities to entrepreneurs will simultaneously provide opportunities for student and faculty research and publications, as well as part-time jobs working alongside entrepreneurs (Coffin, 2021).

Business, financially, or budgetary trained or experienced faculty and administrators can help to develop business plans, venture capital presentations, balance sheets, cash flow, operating and capital budgets, and product development timelines for entrepreneurs (Coffin, 2021). Many inventors and entrepreneurs lack the basic business and financial skills to obtain venture capital and negotiate with venture capital firms (Coffin, 2021). Faculty can provide valuable insights in developing income statements, cash flow, balance sheets, strategic plans, and financing plans (Coffin, 2021).

On-campus incubators provide students with opportunities to earn research positions and internships. Engineering, sciences, and technology faculty can help to develop product and service value propositions and descriptions (Coffin, 2021). The district can charge entrepreneurs rent based on the size and value of the space ranging from basic rent for office space to premium rent for laboratory or special facilities, which will generate alternative revenues (Coffin, 2021).

Securing Grants, Sponsorships, and Advertising

Districts can train faculty members to apply for grants that will complement the business office's efforts (Coffin, 2021). Sponsorships such as recruiting sponsors to pay for district events and activities (e.g., graduation) and advertising will generate alternative revenues (Coffin, 2021). In terms of sponsorships, districts must perform background checks and due diligence to make sure that sponsors and advertisers have the appropriate character, reputation, and resources to support their sponsorship or advertisements (e.g., to avoid Bernie-Madoff-type pyramid schemes) (Coffin, 2021). Advertising can include ads in the yearbook or in athletic, music, theatre, or cultural events' programs or playbills (Coffin, 2021).

Renting Facilities and Selling Naming Rights

Renting unused or underused assets including vehicles, technology centers, laboratories, playing fields, and large multi-purpose rooms (e.g., gymnasiums, auditoriums, and classrooms) generates alternative revenue (Coffin, 2021). Selling the naming rights for facilities, whether individual rooms, laboratories, departments, playing fields, or even a school (e.g., John J. Smith High School), in return for large donations (i.e., named for the donor because of her/his donation) can raise large amounts of money (Coffin, 2021).

Securing Donations

Securing donations from alumni and major stakeholders generates alternative revenues (Coffin, 2021). Donations will vary by donor and year. In addition, districts must perform background checks on donors' ability to fulfill their financial commitments (Coffin, 2021). A donor database must be developed and kept up to date (Coffin, 2021).

New Ways of Doing Business

Implement Self-Insurance for Health Care

Districts can self-insure for health insurance, which if designed and managed properly, can result in major savings (Coffin, 2021).

Renegotiate Debt

Districts can negotiate lower interest rates as well as the number of years of repayment on outstanding debt (i.e., bonds) (Coffin, 2021). In addition, refinancing debt can eliminate balloon payments, which are disproportionately large lump-sum payments that are typically due at the end of the term (Coffin, 2021).

Hosting, Establishing, Sharing Programs and Services

Districts can host, establish, or share programs, services, faculty, administrators, and facilities with other schools, municipalities, and community organizations as well as colleges and universities, which include but are not limited to (Coffin, 2021):

- Enabling local high school students to attend university courses.
- Establishing or expanding adult, technical, vocational, drivers' education, or "special" (e.g., GED, ESL) tuition-based programs or training in classrooms or online.
- Establishing year-round day care for employees' children with no or minimal charge with subsidies for low-income families while charging higher fees for non-district personnel. This will help to attract and retain quality personnel while raising revenue. Creating childcare requires appropriate licenses, insurance, facilities, faculty, and staff plus supplies, materials, and security.
- Capacity-constrained districts can educate special education students in local university facilities with special education trained faculty (fee-based). However, the district and university must have the required licenses as well as the proper special education facilities, educators, staff, and transportation (contractual basis with school districts; typically, the cost of which is less than the regular cost of out-of-district special education).
- Bringing back special education students who are currently educated outside the district or bringing in regular education students (i.e., through sending-receiving contracts) from capacity constrained districts will generate savings and alternative revenues. Districts must have

proper facilities, teachers, and staff as well as transportation and insurance to bring back special education students.
- Educating students in your district from a facility or classroom (e.g., grade level) capacity constrained districts by negotiating sending-receiving agreements that earn per-pupil tuition from the sending district or districts.

Offering or Expanding Online Courses

Districts can offer a wide variety of online courses, which would cost less than in-person courses (Coffin, 2021).

Joint Purchasing Arrangements, Purchasing Upgrades, and Sharing Personnel

Districts can negotiate joint purchasing arrangements with other districts, municipalities, universities, and community organizations to share lower unit prices by group purchasing in larger quantities to realize savings (Coffin, 2021). Joint-purchasing and checking inventories on-hand will generate savings and should be performed regularly. Surprisingly, many districts do not take advantage of these easy to perform actions (Coffin, 2021).

Districts should standardize requisition processes, match requisitions with inventory, and combine requisitions centrally to avoid duplication and unnecessary purchases as well as to ensure purchasing's accuracy while obtaining the lowest per-unit prices (Coffin, 2021). In addition, districts can hire grants writers as well as demographers to improve enrollment forecasting and share the services and cost with other districts or municipalities (Coffin, 2021).

Energy Efficiencies

Districts can achieve energy efficiencies by lowering temperatures when buildings or rooms are not in use, replacing windows and doors with energy efficient ones (e.g., secure grants for new windows and doors), and replacing outdated furnaces or HVAC systems (Coffin, 2021). Energy savings depend on usage, fuel costs, building conditions, climate, HVAC efficiency, and weather conditions (Coffin, 2021).

Uniform Minimum Chart of Accounts

Districts nationwide must have a Uniform Minimum Chart of Accounts that is consistent with generally accepted accounting principles (GAAP) as well as with host state administrative codes (Coffin, 2021). A Uniform Minimum

Chart of Accounts will provide a uniform system of record keeping, accounting, financial reporting, auditing, and credit ratings (Coffin, 2021).

In addition, standardizing financial information, reporting, and auditing systems will facilitate more accurate evaluations and comparisons of districts' financial position, risk, financial well-being, credit ratings, and survivability as well as sustainability (Coffin, 2021). The standardized financial information should be provided to the National Center for Education Statistics (NCES) to facilitate research, analysis, and comparisons (Coffin, 2021).

Districts in states that lack a uniform minimum chart of accounts could be more prone to misrepresentation, mismanagement, and faulty books and records as well as more susceptible to waste, fraud, or financial wrongdoing (Coffin, 2021). Having a uniform minimum chart of accounts would provide full, accurate, and proper disclosure of financial position as well as comprehensive and consistent in-depth financial reporting. Having a uniform minimum chart of accounts would not only improve financial reporting and record keeping but also minimize risk (Coffin, 2021).

The states' uniform minimum chart of accounts must share common definitions of the major Funds especially the Governmental Funds. The overall Governmental Fund category includes the General Fund (i.e., uses fund code 10), Special Revenue Fund (i.e., uses fund code 20), Capital Fund (i.e., uses fund code 30; e.g., the Capital Budget Fund 30), and Debt Service Fund (i.e., uses fund code 40) as well as a Permanent Fund (i.e., uses fund code 50) according to some states' administrative codes (New Jersey Department of Education, 2020).

The uniform minimum chart of accounts has two additional overall Fund categories: Proprietary Funds and Fiduciary Funds. The Proprietary Fund contains legally restricted revenues and expenditures for enterprises that districts run like private sector or for-profit businesses (Finkler et al., 2020). The Fiduciary Fund contains funds that the district does not own but manages on behalf of people, groups, organizations, or other entities outside the district's control (Finkler et al., 2020).

The General Fund contains general purpose, unrestricted revenues and expenditures for daily operations (Finkler et al., 2020). Typically, the General Fund is the largest portion of the operating budget because it contains such line items as regular salaries and benefits that can account for more than 70% of a district's operating budget (Coffin & Cooper, 2017; Coffin & Cooper, 2018).

The Special Revenue Fund contains legally restricted revenues and expenditures for specific operations, programs, services, or personnel (Finkler et al., 2020; New Jersey Department of Education, 2020). Typically, the Special Revenue Fund contains government mandate-protected programs and services such as Special Education, No Child Left Behind (NCLB),

Free-and-reduced price lunches (FRPL), English Language Learners (ELL), Americans with Disabilities Act (ADA), English as a Second Language (ESL), and anti-bullying (HIB).

The Capital Fund contains revenues and expenditures for capital projects, which is the capital budget. Typically, bond revenues fund capital projects, and many states prohibit districts from using loans to finance capital projects. The Debt Service Fund is used to repay long-term debt (i.e., bonds' principal and interest) (New Jersey Department of Education, 2020).

Policies

Districts must have Board of Education approval and policies governing initiatives for raising alternative revenues and establishing new ways of doing business (Coffin, 2021; Coffin & Cooper, 2017; Coffin & Cooper, 2018). The district must perform due diligence (i.e., check the background, history, financial and legal position, as well as reputation) for all donors, sponsors, advertisers, partners, lessees, and renters to protect its reputation and help to ensure that promised funds are received in full (Coffin, 2021). Absent due diligence and proper background checks, a district could lose enrollment and donations if it accepted funds from a Bernie-Madoff-type hedge fund or entity, whose Ponzi scheme operation would ruin its reputation and financial position (Coffin, 2021).

CONCLUSION

Harambee

Although Roger Hull, former president of Beloit and Union Colleges, recommends that higher education practice *harambee*, practicing *harambee* will be equally beneficial for K to 12 education. *Harambee* means "'all pull together,'" which schools could apply as an organizing principle to their business and educational models (Coffin, 2021; Hull, 2020, para. 1).

However, applying Hull's recommendation to K to 12 education, the outcome probably would be like that for higher education because the typical response to the economic and operational devastation wreaked by COVID-19 reveals how "colleges [districts] will be hard-pressed to make that claim" (Coffin, 2021; Hull, 2020, para. 3). Contrary to "the concept of everyone working together, of *harambee*," higher education's COVID-19 response has "shattered" the possibility for a *we-are-family* practice (Coffin, 2021; Hull, 2020, para. 5).

Hull argues that furloughs and layoffs have exposed the seamy flip side or perhaps hypocrisy of the time-honored claim that colleges [districts] differed from "their for-profit counterparts" because they were "'caring communities'" or "'families'" (Coffin, 2021; Hull, 2020, para. 2). The solution is to not balance the budget "on the backs of those working at the college [district]" (Coffin, 2021; Hull, 2020, para. 10).

Quality teaching is the new differentiator that will determine the extent to which schools provide quality education as well as attract and retain enrollment, which will undergird the capitalization of the school system's perceived worth in property values. Online instruction heightens the importance of quality teaching, which K to 12 education has traditionally undervalued (Coffin, 2021). Thus, cutting faculty and essential staff, who are integral to providing quality instruction, not only will be counterproductive but also will hasten a likely degradation of property values (Coffin, 2021).

To survive the COVID-19 pandemic amid the struggle to maintain sufficient enrollment and achieve financial sustainability, K to 12 education must reexamine its decision-making process and rethink its business models (Coffin, 2020; Coffin, 2021; Coffin, 2022a; Coffin, 2022c). Thus, the extent to which K to 12 education employs *harambee* as a core organizing principle may determine the extent to which public schools and districts survive the competition for increasingly scarce quality educational resources (Coffin, 2020; Coffin, 2021; Coffin, 2022a; Coffin, 2022c).

Universal State School Finance Formula

As a graduate student at the Maxwell School of Citizenship and Public Affairs, Syracuse University, the author co-authored a United Nations report. The report entitled *A Study of the American Educational System*, which was funded by the United Nations, evaluated the American system of K-to-16 education (Coffin, 2020; Coffin, 2021; Coffin, 2022a; Honey & Coffin, 1977).

Despite decades of reform little has changed since that report and states' school funding formulae continue to cause inequities as well as financial disparities. However, when the courts have tried to dictate specific state remedies the result is often a constitutional crisis, legislative stalemate, divisiveness, and political polarization.

Our nation must adopt a universal state school funding formula model. A model formula would provide practitioners, educational leaders, and most importantly, policymakers with the guidelines necessary for providing sound educational finance that undergirds quality education for all students statewide while meeting constitutional requirements. The author provides his model universal state school funding formula in his forthcoming books and journal articles (Coffin, 2022a; Coffin, 2022b; Coffin, 2022c; Coffin, 2022d).

REFERENCES

Coffin, S. V. (2020). *State policy determinants of charter school market share* (Doctoral dissertation). Rutgers University, Graduate School of Education.
Coffin, S. V. (Ed.) (2021). *Higher education's looming collapse: Using new ways of doing business and social justice to avoid bankruptcy.* Rowman & Littlefield.
Coffin, S.V. (2022a). Achieving economies of scale and fiscal capacity in large school districts. [Manuscript submitted for publication].
Coffin, S. V. (2022b). *Creating a model state school finance formula to achieve equal educational opportunity and school finance equity.* [Manuscript in preparation]. Rowman & Littlefield.
Coffin, S. V. (2022c). *Stop blurring the lines between public education and privatization: Reinventing the business model to save public education.* [Manuscript in preparation]. Rowman & Littlefield.
Coffin, S. V. (2022d). *Strategic school finance for leading-edge equitable public education.* [Manuscript in preparation]. Rowman & Littlefield.
Coffin, S. V., & Cooper, B. S. (Eds.) (2017). *Sound school finance for educational excellence.* Rowman & Littlefield.
Coffin, S. V., & Cooper, B. S. (Eds.) (2018). *District financial leadership today: Educational excellence tomorrow.* Rowman & Littlefield.
Finkler, S. A., Smith, D. L., & Calabrese, T. D. (2020). *Financial management for public, health, and not-for-profit organizations* (Sixth Edition). Sage Publications.
Honey, J., & Coffin, S.V. (1977). *A study of the American educational system.* Report to the United Nations.
Hull, R. H. (2020, November/December). Harambee. *Association of Governing Boards, Trusteeship Magazine.*
Ladson-Billings, G. (2006). From the achievement gap to the education debt: Understanding achievement in U.S. schools. *Educational Researcher 35*(7)3–12.
New Jersey Department of Education. (2020). The uniform minimum chart of accounts for New Jersey public schools and approved private schools for students with disabilities. https://www.nj.gov/education/finance/fp/af/coa/COA2021.pdf.

Chapter 17

Redlining Education

Stephen V. Coffin

The redlining of education stems from the lack of resource equity and equal educational opportunity in state school funding formulae. Although traditional redlining employs racial, ethnic, religious, and socio-economic status discrimination to deny, limit access, or increase the cost of capital, especially mortgages, credit, and housing, the educational redlining applies the same practices to school finance but without the same overt four-color coding system. Educational redlining is the school finance exclusionary practices that result in the disinvestment primarily of traditionally underserved and under-resourced traditional public schools (TPSs) and districts (TPSDs).

State funding formulae do not provide funding in formulaic coordination with local and federal funding to enable every district to have the combined funding necessary to provide a quality education commensurate with the most affluent districts. Therefore, educational redlining manifests in state funding formulae that are not based on the actual cost to educate each student in the district that s/he attends.

Typically, state funding formulae do not fully account for the property wealth and income gaps among districts and, therefore, do not provide the funding necessary to close the fiscal capacity gaps among affluent and poor districts. Instead, state formulae typically provide minimally adequate funding levels that maintain resource inequity.

Beginning in the 1930s, traditional redlining established housing and residential patterns that undergird current residential compositions, district property values, and tax bases. Like traditional redlining, educational redlining is place-based adversely affecting many of the same communities suffering redlining's legacy.

Educationally redlined places are typically urban districts with large concentrations of poverty as well as racial, religious, and ethnic minorities. High poverty districts require more per-pupil resources than low poverty districts to provide the same quality education. Thus, educational redlining results in the disinvestment of traditionally under-resourced and underserved districts lowering the educational quality provided.

Educational redlining denies students living in redlined districts equal access to a quality education commensurate with the education provided in affluent districts. Redlined districts' lower educational quality is negatively capitalized in housing values undermining local housing markets, property values, and tax bases. This leads to a self-perpetuating adverse cycle in which redlined neighborhoods' property values do not constitute the tax base necessary to properly fund education locally increasing reliance on state and federal aid.

Typically, state and federal funding do not properly fund the full cost to educate all students because of inequitable state and federal formulae. Instead, state funding typically aims to achieve adequacy in funding levels rather than an equitable educational resource allocation among schools and districts.

School Finance Gordian Knot

State formulaic aid that underfunds redlined districts that lack the necessary fiscal capacity perpetuates the decline or stagnation of property values, tax bases, and local economies. An equitable state funding formula should account for differences in per-pupil education costs and districts' differential ability to provide and pay for a quality education. To cut the school finance Gordian knot, each district must receive combined local, state, and federal funding that are a direct function of districts' per-pupil educational costs, fiscal capacity, and cumulative educational redlining legacy.

Metzler (2003) found "no connection can be made between a state's basic approach to education finance and the equality of educational opportunity provided to students" (p. 564). Although flat grants, foundation grants, percent equalization aid, guaranteed tax base guaranteed tax yield, and incremental state funding provide some degree of wealth equalization, these funding approaches make little difference in the equity of their outcomes (Metzler, 2003).

Metzler (2003) draws this conclusion despite Coons, Clune, and Sugarman's (1970) design for the guaranteed tax base and guaranteed tax yield to achieve wealth neutrality. Metzler (2003) concludes that "almost no characteristic of a state's school finance program—not even the basic funding approach—was significantly correlated with equity measures" (p. 586). Thus, inequities result from disparities in state school finance formulae especially among affluent and economically challenged districts and schools.

Adequacy Is Inadequate

State aid formulas based on any of the approaches referenced above may generate a level of revenue that a state may deem necessary to provide an adequate education. Such approaches are inequitable because students' needs and the cost to educate each student based on his/her needs vary widely by school, district, region, and state. Adequacy approaches may fund districts based on average per-pupil costs but result in under-resourced districts especially those with disproportionately high per-pupil costs such as large urban districts.

Foundation aid formulas provide approximately the same aid per district regardless of the district's ability to raise property tax revenue, which exacerbates the inequitable resource gap among affluent and under-resourced districts. Adequacy formulas, even those with varying levels of aid based on district needs, aim to generate an adequate level of resources to meet an adequate level of state educational performance standards or outcomes.

Therefore, funding to achieve adequacy achieves adequate but inequitable educational resource allocation among schools and districts. Equity requires funding based on the cost to educate each student in the district, which s/he attends. Equitable funding must be provided to enable every district to have the combined local, state, and federal funding necessary to provide a quality education commensurate with the most affluent districts. Equity will not be achieved by providing only a minimally adequate level that maintains inequitable resource gaps.

Optimal Funding Mix

An optimal mix of funding would require each district to raise property tax revenues based on its fiscal capacity with the most affluent districts raising almost all their revenues from property taxes while high poverty districts would receive a combination of state and federal aid without raising property taxes until their fiscal capacity (i.e., tax base increased in value) enabled them to do so. The combination of state and federal aid would decline relative to a district's fiscal capacity.

High poverty districts require more per-pupil resources than low poverty districts. The amount of property taxes that districts raise would increase commensurate with its fiscal capacity with the most affluent districts funding their TPSs almost completely from property taxes while low-income districts would increase their tax bases by implementing the solution that the author provides. An equitable state funding formula should account for these differences in student education costs and the district's ability to pay for the education it provides.

Given the federal government's propensity for underfunding education mandates (e.g., special education), additional sources of state aid must be identified, which the author identifies. First, states must eliminate the layer of county government that duplicates state and local governmental programs and services. Second, states should shift the duplicative taxes, which county governments levy annually, to fully fund the states' respective K-12 education aid. Repurposing county governments' duplicative property tax levies would provide the necessary funds for statewide allocatively efficient and equitably resourced K-12 education.

For example, New Jersey and California would save over $8 billion and $100 billion annually respectively in duplicative property taxes by eliminating county government (Coffin 2021a, 2021b; Coffin, 2022). Shifting the $8 billion to fund New Jersey's public education system would more than double state K-12 aid. In addition, eliminating New Jersey's county government layer would slash property taxes statewide and sharply reduce the tax burden that would improve the public support for public funding of public education.

Wealth Neutrality

To neutralize inequities resulting from the disparities in fiscal capacity among schools and districts, Coons, Clune, and Sugarman (1970) developed the concept of wealth neutrality. Applying wealth neutrality neutralizes affluent districts' property tax revenue advantage that enables affluent districts to spend disproportionately more than poor districts and have much better resourced schools. Disparities in resources cause disparities in the quality of education.

Educational equity requires the equal distribution of financial, material, and human resources among schools and districts based on student need and cost to educate. Educational services and facilities must be equitably available, accessible, and affordable for all students. No student's access to education should be denied or minimized based on his/her cost to educate, race, ethnicity, gender, or socioeconomic class. Achieving educational resource equity requires avoiding a one-size-fits-all approach that levels down to the lowest common denominator without accounting for differences in property wealth, educational resources, accessibility, as well as individual student needs and costs to educate.

Resource Equity

Money matters. Resources matter. The degree to which a school has the financial, material, and human resources necessary to properly meet its students' needs is the degree to which the school can provide a quality education for all students. Once a school is properly resourced, the school will be able to provide an equal educational opportunity, which is much more likely to be achieved. Thus, achieving an equitable distribution of educational financial, material, and human resources is essential for achieving equal educational opportunities.

Achieving an equitable distribution of educational resources among schools and districts statewide requires that a student's ability to receive a quality education comparable to those which other students receive is not limited by his/her district's property wealth. Lacking resource equalization among schools and districts, affluent districts can leverage their tax base to provide disproportionately higher quality resources including but not limited to teachers, administrators, facilities, curricula, small class sizes, extra curricula activities, Advanced Placement, and honors courses.

Higher quality and levels of resources translate into higher educational outcomes for advantaged students (e.g., test scores, graduation rates, rates of college admission, admission to more selective universities, as well as lower grade retention, truancy, and dropout rates). Lacking resource equity, economically challenged districts lack the resources with which to provide an education comparable to affluent districts, which disenfranchises their students.

Inequalities in educational outcomes result primarily from inequities in educational resource allocation among schools and districts. Inequities in educational resource allocation stem primarily from overreliance on insufficient tax bases as well as unreliable state and federal aid to fund public education in economically challenged districts.

Districts lacking the tax base on which to levy the property tax revenues commensurate with revenues raised by affluent districts are unable to provide educational quality commensurate with that provided by affluent districts. Tax bases providing almost unlimited property tax revenue raising potential privileges students in affluent districts while the lack of which disadvantages students in high-poverty districts. Affluent districts can afford higher property taxes to fund a higher quality education because of their tax base advantage.

Education Debt Concept

Typically, property-wealth poor districts lack the tax bases enjoyed by their affluent counterparts. Therefore, economically challenged districts lack the ability to levy property taxes with which to provide an educational quality commensurate with affluent districts.

Ladson-Billings' (2006) focuses on this educational inequality in her education debt concept. Ladson-Billings (2006) posits the annual educational deficit is equivalent to the annual fiscal operating budget deficit while the education debt is equivalent to the cumulative legacy costs of educational inequality.

> The education debt is the foregone schooling resources that we could have (should have) been investing in (primarily) low-income kids, which deficit leads to a variety of social problems (e.g., crime, low productivity, low wages, low labor force participation) that require on-going public investment. This required investment sucks away resources that could go to reducing the achievement gap. (p. 5)

School funding formulas must provide the financial, material, and human resources necessary to properly meet all students' needs regardless of their need level and where they attend school.

Students attending schools in poor districts lack access to the same quality and level of resources as their affluent counterparts (Coffin 2021a, 2021b; Coffin, 2022; Coffin & Cooper, 2017, 2018). Therefore, students attending under-resourced schools lack the educational opportunity equal to their affluent counterparts. Educational inequities stem from inequalities in educational resource allocation among schools and districts.

Educational Redlining

The lack of equity and equal opportunity in state school funding formulae generate educational redlining. Although redlining is traditionally associated with denying, limiting access, or arbitrarily increasing the cost of housing and capital especially mortgages, educational redlining applies these practices to school finance without the same four-color coding scheme. Educational redlining is the school finance exclusionary practices that result in the disinvestment primarily of traditionally underserved and under-resourced traditional public schools and districts.

Educational redlining manifests in state funding formulae that are not based on the per-pupil cost to educate students in the schools that they attend. State funding formulae do not provide funding in formulaic coordination with local and federal funding to enable every district to have the resources to provide a quality education commensurate with the most affluent districts.

Typically, state funding formulae do not fully account for the property wealth and income gaps among affluent and poor districts; therefore, do not provide the funding necessary to close the fiscal capacity gap among affluent and poor districts. Instead, state formulae provide minimally adequate funding levels that maintain inequitable resource gaps.

Beginning in the 1930's, traditional redlining established housing and residential patterns that undergird current residential compositions, school catchment areas, district property values, and tax bases. Like traditional redlining, educational redlining is place-based adversely affecting the communities that are suffering redlining's legacy.

Typically, educationally redlined places are urban districts with large concentrations of poverty as well as racial and ethnic minorities. High poverty districts require more per-pupil resources than low poverty districts to provide the same quality education. Thus, educational redlining results in the disinvestment of traditionally under-resourced and underserved districts lowering the educational quality provided.

Educational redlining denies students, who live in redlined districts, access to a quality education commensurate with the education provided in affluent districts. Redlined districts' lower educational quality is negatively capitalized in housing values undermining local housing markets, property values, and tax bases. This leads to a self-perpetuating adverse cycle in which redlined neighborhoods' assessed property values do not constitute the tax base necessary to properly fund education locally, which increases reliance on the vagaries of state and federal aid.

REFERENCES

Coffin, S.V. (2021a). *Achieving economies of scale and fiscal capacity in large school districts*. [Manuscript submitted for publication]. *Education and Urban Society*.

Coffin, S. V. (Ed.) (2021b). *Higher education's looming collapse: Using new ways of doing business and social justice to avoid bankruptcy*. Rowman & Littlefield.

Coffin, S.V. (2022). Achieving school district economies of scale and allocative efficiency. [Manuscript submitted for publication]. *Education and Urban Society*.

Coffin, S. V., & Cooper, B. S. (Eds.) (2017). *Sound school finance for educational excellence*. Rowman & Littlefield.

Coffin, S. V., & Cooper, B. S. (Eds.) (2018). *District financial leadership today: Educational excellence tomorrow*. Rowman & Littlefield.

Coons, J. E., Sugarman, S. D., & Clune, W. H. (1970). *Private wealth and public education*. Belknap Press of Harvard University Press.

Ladson-Billings, G. (2006). From the achievement gap to the education debt: Understanding achievement in U.S. schools. *Educational Researcher, 35*(7), 3–12.

Metzler, J. (2003). Inequitable equilibrium: School finance in the United States. *Indiana Law Review, (36)*3, 561–608.

Chapter 18

Achieving Educational Resource Equity

Stephen V. Coffin

LOCAL CONTROL

Local control is the governance structure that facilitates full and equitable funding for K-12 public education. Local control is essential for generating and maintaining community specific social capital and the public support necessary for public funding of public education (Fischel 1998, 2001, 2002, 2005, 2009).

Fischel (2005) explains how local public education creates a bond among parents increasing their shared belief in the value of locally provided public education that facilitates and galvanizes local support for locally provided public education.

> Having children in local schools increases parents' "community-specific social capital." Through local connections, parents get to know other adults in their community better, which in turn reduces the transaction costs of citizen provision of local public goods. (p. 1)

> . . . community contacts obtained through public schools have a multiplier effect.. . . . Positive experiences from such activities create mutual bonds that increase people's sense of trust in others. (pp. 14–15)

"Community-specific social capital facilitates collective action" that undergirds, mobilizes, and sustains public support for local public schools (Fischel, 2005, p. 6). The absence of local control or having students attend schools in other districts provides no community-specific social capital thereby undermining public support for public education.

Under the local control governance structure recommended by the author, each district determines its own operating and capital budgets, which are the financial representation of its educational plan. Each district collects local property taxes at its maximum capacity adjusted for its DFG status. Repurposed county tax dollars primarily as well as state and federal aid augment local property tax revenue to ensure equal, full, and equitable funding based on the district's per-pupil cost to educate.

The cost to educate two special education students in different districts with the same IEP should not vary except for factors such as local labor market conditions, cost of living, legal, insurance, and transportation differences, which can be accounted for by adjusting the repurposed county tax dollars as well as state and federal aid. Moreover, per-pupil funding is not place or catchment area limited but travels with the student to the school he or she attends.

Fischel (1998) posits court decisions such as *Serrano v. Priest* that eroded local control, ended local property tax funding of local schools, or substituted state-funded school finance for local property tax funding augmented by state aid "undermined political support for education by divorcing voters' property-tax payments from the quality of their local schools" (p. 1). Fischel (1998) explains that the quality of locally provided and property tax funded public education undergirds local property values and promotes public support for local public education. In addition, maintaining local control and funding achieves positive capitalization in local property values and tax bases more than other funding approaches.

> Most of the court decisions that have overturned property tax financing of education have helped divorce the value of one's home from the quality of schools. (Capitalization occurs much less at the state level because potential residents cannot shop around for states the way they can shop around for communities.) This divorce has most probably contributed to the declining quality of public education and, at least in some states, to a reduction in public support for education as a whole. (p. 42)

Thus, locally provided, and local property tax funded public education augmented primarily by repurposed county tax dollars as well as state and federal aid based on district fiscal capacity adjusted by a New Jersey DFG-type ranking provides the optimal approach for providing a fully and equitably resourced quality education for all students regardless of need, cost to educate, residence, or location of school.

The author's solution provides the necessary funding that enables districts to fund their TPSs at levels commensurate with affluent districts. Funding levels equal to those of affluent districts enable residents of all districts to focus more on developing the community-specific social capital necessary for fostering and sustaining local public support for local TPSs.

INEQUITABLE EQUILIBRIUM

Why has there been so little significant lasting improvement despite the preponderance of court rulings and school finance reform? Why despite years of state school funding formulae reforms designed to improve the equitable distribution of school aid and resources has so little changed?

Metzler (2003) answers these questions using his education finance inequitable equilibrium theory. Metzler (2003) explains that different court ordered state school funding formulae result in few if any major sustained improvements in equitable resource allocation among schools and districts statewide because education finance regresses to an inequitable equilibrium over time.

> . . . while a court decision declaring the education finance system unconstitutional may force the legislature to make immediate changes in the system, subsequent amendments and formula modifications are likely to shift the allocation of resources back to the balance that existed before the court decision. (p. 594)

Metzler posits that political power reaches and maintains an education finance equilibrium within each state that sustains the allocative framework for federal and state aid as well as district resources.

Metzler (2003) frames the equilibrium as inequitable because it enables affluent districts to exploit their property tax base advantage that provides affluent districts with disproportionate revenues with which to outspend less affluent districts that lack sufficient tax bases. Thus, compared to poor districts, affluent districts can more easily afford a higher quality of education with higher quality school resources stemming from their property wealth advantage.

Although state legislative and court ordered school finance reform has made the distribution of educational resources more equitable in many states, reform is short lived and tends to regress to the inequitable equilibrium. Metzler (2003) argues that despite court rulings to equalize educational per-pupil spending or the allocation of educational resources statewide, state legislatures, or more importantly, the political forces controlling state legislators work to restore the education finance inequitable equilibrium.

Metzler (2003) found a state's school finance formula or system matters little in achieving a lasting equitable distribution of education aid because formulae are manipulated or amended to maintain the inequitable equilibrium.

> My empirical demonstration focuses on a statistical analysis of the correlation between a state's basic approach to education finance and the degree of equity in that state's allocation of education resources. This analysis, which includes all 50 states, shows that the distribution of education resources in a state does not significantly depend upon the funding approach a state adopts for allocating education resources. (p. 565)

Metzler (2003) concludes that achieving equitable educational resource distribution among schools and districts requires addressing the "political dynamics that perpetuate the inequitable equilibrium of school finance" (p. 566).

To determine the educational equal opportunity and equity generated by the author's solution, the author applies the wealth neutrality score and targeting score approach that Metzler (2003) recommended. Metzler (2003) defines the wealth neutrality score as "an ex-post measure of Coons's ideal of fiscal neutrality" (Coons et al., 1970) that reflects the extent to which per-pupil spending correlates with district property wealth (p. 571).

The author's solution achieves a wealth neutrality score that indicates a high level of equal opportunity and equity (Coffin, 2021a; Coffin, 2022). In addition, the author's solution achieves a negative targeting score because state and federal per-pupil aid is inversely related to district property wealth and proportionately allocated to poor districts (Coffin, 2021a; Coffin, 2022).

The author's solution provides per-pupil spending that is not just a function of insufficient district tax bases but allocates a high level of repurposed county tax revenues to build sustainable tax bases to fund K-12 education statewide fully and equitably. Repurposed county tax revenues and rebuilt sustainable tax bases combined with state and federal per-pupil aid proportionate to a district's economic disadvantage vis-à-vis affluent districts fully and equitably fund K-12 education.

SOLUTION

Recommendation

Typically, county governments not only acquire and allocate their resources inefficiently compared to local and state governments but also incur diseconomies of scale in producing goods and services because their average costs increase as output increases (Coffin, 2021a, 2021c; Coffin, 2022). In addition, county governments duplicate local and state public goods and services that are produced with greater economies of scale. This results in duplicative taxation by county government (Coffin, 2021a, 2021c; Coffin, 2022). For example, New Jersey's 21 county governments levy about $8 billion annually in property taxes while California's 58 counties levy about $100 billion annually in property taxes (Coffin, 2021a, 2021c; Coffin, 2022; Coffin & Cooper, 2017). The solution is to eliminate county governments with their duplicative property taxes and repurpose their tax dollars to fund K-12 public education fully and equitably.

Eliminating county governments nationwide and repurposing their property tax revenues would provide approximately $500 billion annually to fund K-12 public education fully and equitably (Coffin, 2021a; Coffin, 2021c; Coffin, 2022). In addition to eliminating county governments and repurposing their property tax revenues, disaggregating large school districts will realize savings through economies of scale.

> Disaggregating overly large districts such as Newark's approximate 35,000 students into 10 roughly similar-sized autonomous sub-districts would cut costs by eliminating diseconomies of scale. The author's groundbreaking design disaggregates large districts into more manageable sub-districts, centralizes common services in the former large district apparatus, builds fiscal capacity through community economic development, and funds its implementation with the sub-districts' share of the $8 billion. (Coffin, 2021a, p. 226)

Thus, eliminating county government nationwide, repurposing county governments' property tax revenues, and disaggregating large school districts to achieve economies of scale are the three fundamental elements for fully and equitably funding K-12 public education.

Large school districts and other overly large organizations share similar management challenges, inefficiencies, and mission creep because while scale differs, the effects of scale and scale economies are the same (Andrews et al., 2002; Antonucci, 1999; Berry, 2004; Coffin, 2020; Coffin, 2021a; Coffin & Russo, 2022; Duncombe & Yinger, 2007; Finkler et al., 2020; Hoxby, 2001; Kenny, 1982). Like many older, less efficient, larger, declining industries, utilities, or utility-like firms (e.g., railroads), large T.P.S.D.s (e.g., Los Angeles, New York City, Chicago, Detroit, Miami, Dallas, St. Louis, Newark, Philadelphia, and Boston) operate with diseconomies of scale.

Large school districts' scale economies resemble utility-like firms because their long run average cost exceeds their marginal cost, and these districts operate with enrollment levels that are beyond an optimal level of approximately 3,500 students (Andrews et al., 2002; Antonucci, 1999; Coffin, 2020; Coffin, 2021a; Duncombe & Yinger, 2007; Finkler et al., 2020; Hoxby, 2001;

Kenny, 1982). Thus, most large T.P.S.D.s as well as utility-like firms require public subsidies to survive.

Like businesses that achieve economies of scale, right-sized T.P.S.D.s show constant returns to scale in which their average costs do not vary as their educational outputs increase. However, like businesses school districts should aim for economies of scale in which their average costs decrease while their educational outputs increase. Using the author's new ways of doing the business of education and raising alternative revenues while implementing the author's solution including his best practices will enable districts to achieve economies of scale while public education is fully and equitably funded nationwide (Coffin, 2021a; Coffin, 2021b; Coffin, 2021c; Coffin, 2021d; Coffin, 2022).

Equitable Full Funding

To achieve equitable full funding, districts would raise the maximum amount of property taxes possible adjusted for comparable districts' equitable fiscal capacity within the state while repurposed county property tax dollars would make up the difference between the districts' total amount of local property taxes levied and districts' total operating budget and capital budgets' amounts. Comparable districts' equitable fiscal capacity is the capacity of the district to raise property taxes based on its tax base relative to comparably sized districts (i.e., enrollment and per-pupil cost-to-educate).

Fiscal capacity would be adjusted according to a New Jersey District Factor Group-type code (i.e., DFG) with districts having DFG code J receiving little or no repurposed county property tax dollars or state and federal aid while districts having DFG code A would receive the maximum amount of repurposed county property tax dollars as well as state and federal aid proportionate to their fiscal capacity. In addition, repurposed county property tax dollars would be invested to build sustainable tax bases equivalent to affluent districts' tax bases especially for low-property wealth (i.e., low total assessed value tax bases) districts that typically are large urban or city-situated districts (e.g., Chicago, New York City, Los Angeles, San Francisco, Boston, Detroit, Dallas, Miami, Philadelphia, Houston, and Newark) (Chyn & Katz, 2021; Coffin, 2021a, 2021c; Coffin, 2022; Coffin & Russo, 2022; Hoxby, 2001; Kenny, 1982; Levin & Belfield, 2003).

The author's solution enables all students to have an equal opportunity to receive a top-quality education in schools having educational resource equity. The solution provides equitable full funding compared to state funding formulas that match a minimum level, fund only to an adequate but not equitable level, try to guarantee a tax base or tax yield, provide only foundation aid or flat grants, or have ceilings well below the most affluent district's maximum fiscal capacity.

Typically, state and federal funding does not properly, fully, or equitably fund the full cost to educate all students because of inequitable state and federal formulae. Instead, state funding formulae typically aim to achieve adequacy in funding levels, which is inadequate especially for low property wealth districts, rather than an equitable educational resource allocation among schools and districts. However, the author's solution, which eliminates county government nationwide, repurposes county governments' property tax revenues to equitably fund schools, and disaggregates large school districts to achieve economies of scale, provides equal educational opportunity, fair full funding for K-12 public education, and resource equity among schools and districts.

REFERENCES

Andrews, M., Duncombe, W. D., & Yinger, J. (2002). Revisiting economies of size in American education: Are we any closer to a consensus? *Economics of Education Review, 21,* 245–262.

Antonucci, M. (1999). *Mission creep: How large school districts lose sight of the objective—Student Learning (AdTI Issue Brief Number 176).* Retrieved from http://www.adti.net/education/antonucci.mission.creep.html.

Berry, C. (2004). School inflation: Did the 20th-century growth in school size improve education? *EducationNext. 4*(4), 56–62.

Chyn, E., & Katz, L.F. (2021). Neighborhoods matter: Assessing the evidence for place effects. *Journal of Economic Perspectives, 35*(4), 197–222.

Coffin, S. V. (2020). *State policy determinants of charter school market share* (Doctoral dissertation). Rutgers University, Graduate School of Education.

Coffin, S.V. (2021a). *Achieving economies of scale and fiscal capacity in large school districts.* [Manuscript submitted for publication]. *Education and Urban Society.*

Coffin, S. V. (2021b). *Creating a model state school finance formula to achieve equal educational opportunity and school finance equity* [Manuscript in preparation]. Rowman & Littlefield.

Coffin, S. V. (Ed.) (2021c). *Higher education's looming collapse: Using new ways of doing business and social justice to avoid bankruptcy.* Rowman & Littlefield.

Coffin, S. V. (2021d). *Strategic school finance for leading-edge equitable public education.* [Manuscript in preparation]. Rowman & Littlefield.

Coffin, S.V. (2022). Achieving school district economies of scale and allocative efficiency. [Manuscript submitted for publication]. *Education and Urban Society.*

Coffin, S. V., & Cooper, B. S. (Eds.) (2017). *Sound school finance for educational excellence.* Rowman & Littlefield.

Coffin, S. V., & Russo, C. J. (2022). *Achieving free speech, freedom of expression, and student safety in changing times and places: Dealing with religious and cultural differences in schools*. [Manuscript in preparation]. In P. T. Clarke, K. Walker, & C. J Russo, (Eds.). Rowman & Littlefield.

Coons, J. E., Sugarman, S. D., & Clune, W. H. (1970). *Private wealth and public education*. Belknap Press of Harvard University Press.

Duncombe, W. D., & Yinger, J. (2007). Does school district consolidation cut costs? *Education Finance and Policy*, 2, 341–375.

Finkler, S. A., Smith, D. L., & Calabrese, T. D. (2020). *Financial management for public, health, and not-for-profit organizations* (Sixth Edition). Sage Publications.

Fischel, W. A. (1998). *School finance litigation and property tax revolts: How undermining local control turns voters away from public education*. Lincoln Institute of Land Policy Working Paper.

Fischel, W. A. (2001). *The homevoter hypothesis: How home values influence local government taxation, school finance, and land-use policies*. Harvard University Press.

Fischel, W. A. (2002). *An economic case against vouchers: Why local public schools are a local public good*. Dartmouth Economics Department Working Paper: Dartmouth College.

Fischel, W. A. (2005). *Why voters veto vouchers: Public schools and community-specific social capital*. Dartmouth Economics Department Working Paper: Dartmouth College.

Fischel, W. A. (2009). *Making the grade: The economic evolution of American school districts*. University of Chicago Press.

Hoxby, C. M. (2001). All school finance equalizations are not created equal. *Quarterly Journal of Economics*, *116*(4), 1189–1231.

Kenny, L. W. (1982). Economies of scale in schooling. *Economics of Education Review*, (2) 1–24.

Levin, H. M., & Belfield, C. R. (2003). The marketplace in education. *Review of Research in Education, 27*, 183–219.

Metzler, J. (2003). Inequitable equilibrium: School finance in the United States. *Indiana Law Review, (36)*3, 561–608.

Index

4201 School Association, 91–92

Abbott, Martin L., 210
Abbott districts, 32, 33–34, 36, 38, 47, 102, 193, 194, 204
Abbott v. Burke court decisions, 32, 33–34, 38, 182, 189, 204
absenteeism, 120, 131, 133, 137, 138, 147–49
achievement gap, 57, 59, 61, 86, 95, 96, 100, 102, 214, 240
adequacy approach, 13, 35, 41, 183, 192; court rulings on, 27, 32, 36–38, 182; in New York and New Jersey, 47–49; SFRA weighting and, 42–43, 47; state funding aims, 236, 237, 240
Adjusted Foundation, 43
adverse childhood experiences (ACEs), 149–50
Alabama, 115–16, 121
Alaska, 120–21
Alliance Scholarship, 104
alternative school funding resources, 226–27
American Academy of Pediatrics (AAP), 132, 141
American Association of Family & Consumer Sciences (AAFCS), 159

American Home Economics Association (AHEA), 159
American Rescue Plan Act, 139
American School for the Deaf, 89
American Sign Language (ASL), 89, 91, 93, 94, 97–98, 99, 100–101
American Sign Language Proficiency Interview (ASLPI), 91
Americans with Disabilities Act (ADA), 91, 93, 231
Andrews, Matthew, 205
anti-bullying (HIB) program, 231
Antonucci, Mike, 175, 204
Ardon, Kenneth, 197
Arizona, 113
Arkansas, 115–16
Aronica, Lou, 79
attention deficit disorder (ADD), 84
autism, 84, 93, 148
Average Daily Membership (ADM), 43

Baker, Bruce D., 40, 45, 100, 196, 198
Baldwin, Timothy T., 67, 68
Baltimore/Baltimore County, 184
Bandura, Albert, 57
Bank of America, 160
Bank Street School for Children, 83
Bilingual Education Act, 98

Blackboard and the Bottom Line (Cuban), 176–77
Bloom, Allan, 82
Blueberry Epiphany concept, 176–77, 187–88, 204
Boske, Christa, 55
Boston Public Schools, 176, 203, 247, 248
Boyer-Chu, Lynda, 82
Brion, Corrine, 69–70, 71
Broad, Mary L., 67, 69–70
broadband access, 92
Brown, Scott, 145
Brown v. Board of Education court case, 82, 96
Brunner, Eric J., 197
budgets, 8, 32, 113, 168, 177, 198, 214, 232; for 4201 schools, 91–93; adequacy budgets, 36–38, 41, 42; CA, school district budgets in, 184–86, 188, 196; for deaf education, 99–100; education debt concept, 239–40; Executive County Superintendents' power to veto, 190, 191–92; N.A.P.R. budgeting model, 219–21, 226; New Jersey, budget flexibility in, 193–94; pandemic effect on, 7, 225; PD events, school administrators budgeting for, 66, 67; personal budgeting, teaching of, 158, 159, 163; state and county control over, 4, 181, 183; *See also* capital budgets
Burgess, Dave, 85

Caffarella, Rosemary S., 69
California, 104, 121, 183, 189, 196, 198; county government in, 182, 238, 247; local control of school district budgets, 184–85; Proposition 4 reimbursement to local school districts, 188; Proposition 13 limitations on local property taxes, 177, 187; *Serrano v. Priest*, local control ended with, 182, 185–86,

187; state domination of local school systems, 182, 195
Calvin, John, 14
Campaign for Fiscal Equity (CFE), 35–36
capital budgets, 189, 207, 226, 244, 248; Capital Budget Fund, 230, 231; in N.A.P.R. budgeting model, 219, 221; sub-district management of, 210, 216
capital projects, 4, 92, 181, 184, 198, 231
Captioning by Remote Technology (CART), 90
categorical aid, 37, 38, 43
Centers for Disease Control and Prevention (CDC), 130, 136–37, 140, 149
charter schools, 28, 83–84, 205
Chicago Public Schools, 176, 203–4, 247, 248
Child and Adult Care Food Program (CACFP), 115, 140, 143
childcare, 111, 120, 123, 125, 228
Childcare and Development Fund (CCDF), 115
child study teams (CSTs), 90
Chomsky, Noah, 93
Christie, Chris, 34, 194
class size, 28, 33, 214, 239
Clerc, Laurent, 89
Closing of the American Mind (Bloom), 82
Closson, Rosemary B., 68–69
Clune, William H., 213, 236, 238
cochlear implants, 89, 91, 92, 99, 104–5
Cogswell, Mason, 89
Coke, Edward, 15–16
Colorado, 116, 141
Combined Wealth Ratio (CWR), 41, 46
Committee of Special Education (CSE), 92
common schools, 18, 19, 30, 34, 80, 160
Community Eligibility Provision, 139

Comprehensive Educational Improvement and Financing Act (CEIFA), 33, 37
Connecticut, 8, 89, 113, 115, 192, 211
Constitutional Sovereignty: historical basis, 15–16; implications of Constitutional Sovereignty, 16–17; philosophical basis, 14–15; *Rose* court case illustrating need for, 13–14, 29; Supreme Court of Kentucky as embracing, 18–20
consumer education: educational and ethical heuristics for, 164–68; as essential for 21st century, 168; historical background of, 158–60; identifying the need for, 160–61; lack of, 2008 global crisis revealing, 157–58; resource disparities, addressing, 161–64
Consumer Price Index (CPI), 39, 192, 193
Context and Environment, 69–70, 72
Continuing Professional Development (CPD), 68
Coons, John E., 213, 236, 238, 246
Cooper v. Aaron court case, 17, 23n59
CORE Act, 189
Core Curriculum Content Standards (CCCS), 33–34, 37, 41, 47, 192
Corzine, Jon, 189
county school system, 28, 176, 181, 199; in historical context, 4–5; large regional districts and, 203–4; local school districts, consolidating countywide, 182, 206–7, 209; in New Jersey, 8, 94, 189–94, 195–96, 205, 206, 208, 211–12, 216, 238, 247; repurposing county property tax revenues, 244, 246, 247, 248–49
COVID-19 pandemic, 7, 91, 126, 221; COVID-19 pandemic, 134; finance formula-based inequities worsened by, 7, 225; higher educations' response to, 231–32; impact on child health and learning, 134, 150–51; state aid shortfalls due to, 185, 195
CRT. *See* culturally responsive pedagogy
Cuban, Larry, 176–77, 187–88, 204
Culturally Proficient Professional Development (CPPD), 61, 65, 67, 74
culturally responsive pedagogy (CRP), 56, 58–61, 69, 101
culture, 61, 70, 81, 95, 138; cultural archetypes, 59–60; culturally grounded asset-based mindset, 57–58; cultural proficiency in school leaders, 71; culture and learning, 56–57; deaf culture, 94, 97; learning transfer, cultural differences and, 67–69; PD, taking culture into consideration, 72–75; role of culture in learning, 55, 65–66
Current Population Survey Food Security Supplement (CPS-FSS), 143

Daffron, Sandra R., 68
Dallas School District, 176, 247, 248
deaf education, 89, 94; communication modes in teaching deaf children, 90–91; deaf black students, 95–97; deafness, not viewing as a disability, 92–93; funding in deaf education, 101–3; deaf schools in rural areas, 97, 104; multiculturalism in deaf education, 97; state funding and, 104; technology services, 99–101
DeGrasse, 35–36
Delpit, Lisa, 60
Democracy in America (Tocqueville), 80
demonstrably effective program aid (DEPA), 33
Denver Public Schools, 142
Desimone, Laura M., 66
Detroit Public Schools Community District, 176, 203, 247, 248
developmental delays, 119, 143–44, 146
Dewey, John, 81, 83, 160
digital divide, 82

Dintersmith, Ted, 82
disabilities, 43, 90, 119, 131, 140; absenteeism in children with, 148; deafness not a disability, 92–93; laws impacting students with, 93–94; learning disabilities, 93, 133, 150; police targeting of students with, 141; preschool funding for children with, 122, 123; VR program for students with, 103–4
Disabilities Education Act (IDEA), 90, 93, 99, 103, 115, 122, 134–35
disciplinary issues, 55, 67, 141, 142
diseconomies of scale, 204; of county governments, 8, 246; large districts operating with, 176, 177, 192, 203, 207, 247; in New Jersey, 205, 209, 210;
district factor group (DFG), 32, 33, 38, 248
diversity, 55, 57, 59–61, 67, 81, 138
Division of Adolescent and School Health (DASH), 136
Division of Early Childhood Education (DECE), 123
Donnelly, Louis, 145
Douglass, Frederick, 17
Downey, Douglas B., 85
Doyne, Peter E., 34
dual language learners, 122
Duncombe, William D., 44, 205
Durkheim, Émile, 160
dyslexia, 93

Early Care and Education (ECE), 111–12, 117, 122–23, 125, 126
early childhood program aid (ECPA), 33
Early Periodic Screening Diagnostic and Treatment (EPSDT), 130
economies of scale. *See* diseconomies of scale
Educational Interpreter Performance Assessment (EIPA), 101
educational resource equity gap, 7, 8, 196, 219, 221

education clauses, 18–20, 29, 30, 31, 34
education debt concept, 30, 214, 239–40
Education Law Center (ELC), 32
Edwards, Malik, 31
Eligibility Manual for School Meals, 139–40
English as a Second Language (ESL), 84, 99, 228, 231
English Language Learners (ELLs), 43, 44, 57, 59, 84, 231
equal educational opportunities, 5, 7, 8, 28, 49, 216; county government, effect of elimination on, 249; resource equity and, 3, 213, 225, 239; in smaller sub-districts, 209; in state school funding formulae, 235;
ethnocentric monoculturalism, 56
Executive County Superintendent, office of, 189–92, 196, 205, 206
Expected Minimum Local Contribution (EMLC), 43–44
expense-based aid, 39
Extraordinary Needs (EN), 40, 44

family and consumer science (FCS), 159
federal poverty level (FPL), 119, 131, 162
financial crisis of 2008, 157, 159
First Wave funding, 27, 36
Fischel, William A., 184, 186, 197, 198, 215, 216, 243, 244
Florida, 19, 104, 120–21, 182, 184
food insecurity, 142–44
Ford, J. Kevin, 67, 68
foster care, 119, 147
Foundation Aid State Sharing Ratio, 41
foundation formulae, 37, 41–47, 47–49, 112
four-year-olds, 111, 117, 118, 119, 123
Franklin, Benjamin, 80
free-and-reduced-price-lunches (FRPLs), 7, 43, 44, 45, 119, 139–40, 231
free appropriate public education (FAPE), 90, 101

free milk program, 139–40
Freire, Paulo, 57
Funk, Steven, 164–65

Gabriel, John G., 84
Gallaudet, Edward, 97
Gallaudet, Thomas, 89
Gardner, Howard, 84
Gemeinschaft (Habermas), 80
general education, 80, 83–84, 89, 90, 93, 123–24
generally accepted accounting principles (GAAP), 229
Geographic Cost Adjustment (GCA), 37
Geographic Cost of Education Index (GCEI), 44
Georgia, 113
Goertz, Margaret E., 31
Green, Preston C., 196, 198
Greenhut, Steven, 188
Guam, 111, 116
guaranteed tax base formula (GTB), 31
Guskey, Thomas R., 73
Guttmacher Institute, 137

Habermas, Jurgen, 80
Hamilton, Alexander, 81
Hammond, Zaretta, 59
harambee, practice of, 231–32
hard-of-hearing students. *See* deaf education
Hawaii, 121, 184
Head Start, 111, 115, 119, 123, 124, 125, 140
Health Care for the Homeless (HCH), 146
Health Resources and Services Administration (HRSA), 130
Healthy, Hunger-Free Kids Act, 139
hearing aids, 89, 90, 91, 92, 97, 99, 104
Hearing Loss Association of America, 104
high-need high-cost-to-educate students, 30, 42, 49, 208
Hira, Tahira K., 158

Hirsch, Eric D., 80, 81
HIV/AIDS, 136–37
home economics, 158–59
homelessness, 84, 119, 140, 145–46, 147, 163
Holcombe, Rebeca, 205
Holton, Elwood F., III, 68
homevoters, 4, 182, 183, 186, 216
Hull, Roger, 231–32
Hurricane Katrina, 150
hyperactivity, 84, 149

Idaho, 111, 120–21
Illinois, 46, 118
implicit bias, 95–96
Income Wealth Index (IWI), 44
Indiana, 111
Individualized Education Plans (IEPs): assistive equipment eligibility for IEP students, 99; child study teams, role in, 90; cross-district costs for IEP education, 244; for deaf learners, 95, 100, 101, 103; financial support for disabilities with IEP, 104; Medicaid assistance for IEP holders, 134, 244
individualized family service plans (IFSPs), 135
Individuals with Disabilities Education Act (IDEA), 90, 93, 99, 103, 115, 122, 134
inequitable equilibrium theory, 245–46
Iowa, 115
itinerant teachers, 89, 94

Jacobson, Linda, 196
James, Henry, 81
Jensen, Eric, 85
John, King of England, 15
Joireman, Jeff, 210

K-3 teachers, 121
K-12 public education, 79, 83, 89, 159, 189, 243; funding for, 8–9, 122, 208, 219–21, 246, 249; Hull's

recommendations, applying to, 231–32; new ways of business, need for, 3–4; property taxes earmarked for, 28, 195, 238, 247; *See also* preschool
K-16 schools, 3–4, 8, 206, 208, 232
Kansas, 113
Kellner, Douglas, 164–65
Kenny, Lawrence W., 195
Kentucky, 13–14, 18–20, 28–29, 104
Khan Academy, 160
kindergarten, 43, 112, 120–21, 143, 144, 147, 150, 194
Kozol, Jonathan, 82
Kronman, Anthony, 80, 81, 82

Ladson-Billings, Gloria J., 30, 58–59, 214, 226, 239–40
large school districts: disaggregation of, 177, 178, 207, 209, 247, 249; economies of scale in, 176, 247; large regional districts, 203–4; mission creep, engaging in, 175, 176, 204, 247
learners, 55, 68, 70, 84; adult learners, increasing skills and abilities of, 67, 74; CRP as presenting information to, 58; deaf learners, laws impacting, 93–94; PD studies on, 71–72; *See also* English Language Learners
learning disabilities. *See under* disabilities
learning transfer, 61, 66, 67–68, 72. *See also* Multidimensional Model of Learning Transfer
Learning Transfer System Inventory (LTSI), 68
least restrictive environment (LRE), 93
Levittown v. Nyquist court case, 34–35
LGBTQIA+ students, 141–42, 145, 149
limited English proficiency (LEP), 37, 43, 44–45
Lindsey, Randall B., 56, 65
local autonomy, 36, 46, 112, 118, 122, 151, 175, 176, 207, 210; accountability in local school systems, 5, 195–98; in California, 177, 184–89; community social capital through local control, 243–45; consolidation of local school districts, 203, 206, 209; county efforts as duplicating local services, 8, 208, 211, 238, 246–48; county influence over local schools, 183, 184; local boards of education, 4, 181, 184, 190, 191, 196; local educational requirements, 4–5, 199; local fair share and minimum local contribution, 40, 41, 42–43, 47; local fair share funding, 27; local fiscal capacity, 39, 41; *New-Ark*, creating under local control governance, 215–17; New Jersey, local autonomy in, 182, 190, 191, 193, 205, 212; state funding not coordinating with local funding, 235, 240; state preschool, local funding for, 114, 115, 126
local educational agencies (LEAs), 139
Locke, John, 79
long run average cost (LAC), 176, 203–4, 247
long run marginal cost (LMC), 203
Los Angeles Unified School District (L.A.U.S.D.), 176, 177, 203–4, 247, 248
lottery revenues, 104, 113
Louisiana, 182, 184
Love, Bettina L., 56, 61
Lucas, Tamara, 59
Lundberg, Ian, 145

Magna Carta, 15
Maine, 114–15, 116
Mann, Horace, 80
Mansfield, Harvey C., 79
marginal cost (MC), 176, 203–4, 247
Marie Katzenbach School for the Deaf (MSKD), 104
Marshal, William, 15, 22n33
Maryland, 96, 182, 184, 190–91, 192, 195, 206

Marzano, Robert J., 84
maternity care for pregnant students, 137–38
Mayflower Compact, 16
McClelland, David C., 57
McGreevey, James, 193
medical home, 132–33
Metzler, Jeffrey, 236, 245–46
Miami Public Schools, 176, 247, 248
Michigan, 120–21, 140, 144
Minnesota, 120–21
Mississippi, 114–15, 115–16, 117, 118, 121, 148
Missouri, 13
Moll, Luis C., 57–58
Montana, 111
Moskowitz, Eva, 83, 84
Multidimensional Model of Learning Transfer (MMLT), 65, 67, 69–71, 73, 74–75
multitiered system of supports (MTSS), 138

National Association of School Psychologists (NASP), 134, 138
National Center for Education Statistics (NCES), 230
National Institute for Early Education Research (NIEER), 114, 121
National Institute of Technology (NTID), 103
National School Lunch Program (NSLP), 139–40
National Staff Development Council, 67
Nebraska, 114–15
Needs-Assumptions-Priorities-Rationale (N.A.P.R.) holistic budgeting model, 219, 226
Nevada, 182, 184
Newark City School District, 102, 176, 203, 208, 209–13, 247, 248
New Hampshire, 111, 120
New Jersey, 30, 40, 44, 104, 125, 160, 183, 191; *Abbott v. Burke*, application of, 32, 33, 182, 189, 204; Core Curriculum Content Standards, 33–34, 37, 41, 47, 192; county governmental control, 8, 192, 206, 208, 211, 212, 216, 238, 247; deaf education in, 90, 94, 99, 101, 102; DFG-type adjustments, 244, 248; ECE system, combining funding across, 112, 123; Head Start providers in, 124; kindergarten not required in, 120–21; preschool program, 117, 118; property taxes in, 8, 192, 193, 206, 238; S1701 legislation, 189, 193–94, 196; SFRA formula, applying, 41, 42–43, 48; state domination of local school systems, 182, 190, 195, 196, 205; T&E educational clause, 29, 31, 182
New Jersey Deaf Education Advisory Group (NJDEAG), 99
Newstrom, John W., 67–68, 69–70
New York, 41, 42, 49, 81, 83, 141, 248; court findings on adequate education content, 35–36, 48; deaf education in, 91–92, 94, 99, 102, 104; diseconomy of scale, NYC schools operating with, 176, 203–4, 247; Education Article, utilizing, 30, 34; kindergarten not required in, 120–21; local contribution, expected minimums for, 43–45; property taxes, effect on school funding, 39–40; school-based health care in, 130, 131, 149, 152; STAR program, state aid provided through, 45–47
New York State Education Department (NYSED), 35, 43
New York State School Tax Relief (NYSTAR) program, 39–40, 45–47
No Child Left Behind (NCLB), 183, 230
normalcy, rise of, 81
North Carolina, 113, 115, 117, 182, 184
North Dakota, 117

Oates, Wallace E., 195
Ohio, 113, 141

Oklahoma, 114–15
online instruction, 150, 160, 228, 229, 232
Oregon, 117

Peacock, Mark, 166–67
Pennsylvania, 22n46, 46, 96, 118, 121
personal finance, 157–61. *See also* consumer education
Philadelphia City School District, 176, 247, 248
Picower, Bree, 81
Plessy v. Ferguson court case, 96
Pondiscio, Robert, 83–84
post-training, 70, 71, 73, 75
Prenatal Care at School (PAS) program, 137
preschool, 95, 140, 143, 147; ECE funding and, 111–12, 122, 126; funding methods and revenue sources, 112–14; inequalities in program access, 117–21; in New Jersey, 123–25; state preschool resources, 114–17
Preschool Education Aid (PEA), 123–24, 125
pretraining, 69, 70, 71, 73, 74
primary education, rise of, 80
private schools, 28, 91, 111, 123, 125, 205
Problem Based Learning (PBL), 85
professional development (PD), 56, 61, 65, 66–67, 69, 71–75, 121
professional learning communities (PLCs), 73, 101
progressive education, 81, 83
property taxes, 38, 42, 47, 178, 183, 196, 208, 238; in California, 184–89, 198, 247; county taxes and, 244, 249; local district control and, 197, 207; in Maryland, 190, 206; in New Jersey, 8, 33, 192–94, 206, 210, 211, 247; NYSTAR program and, 39, 40, 46; in poor and affluent districts, 31, 37, 48, 208, 213, 214, 239, 245; school district funding policy implications and, 194–95; school funding based on, 28, 56, 113, 177, 237, 248
Proposition 4, 188, 196
Proposition 13, 187–89
Proposition 98, 186, 188–89
Proposition 111, 186, 187–89, 196
psychological services, 138–39
Public School Education Act of 1975 (Chapter 212), 31, 32
Pupil Need Index (PNI), 40, 43–44

Quality of Education Act (QEA), 32, 33

Rahyuda, Agoes G., 68
Ravitch, Diane, 83–84
redlining education, 3, 211, 235–36, 240–41
Regents Learning Standards, 35, 36, 47
Regional Cost Index (RCI), 40–41, 43–44
Registry of the Deaf (RID), 91
remote learning, 150
"Research Note on the Prevalence of Housing Eviction Among Children Born in American Cities" (Lundberg/Donnelly), 145
Reock, Ernest C., Jr., 33
resource allocation, 112, 219, 245, 249; adequacy *vs.* equitable allocation, 236, 237; inequalities in, 214, 239, 240; one-size-fits-all approach, state imposing, 4, 198;
Rhode Island, 117, 121
Richards, Craig E., 196, 198
right-sized school districts, 176, 177, 203, 207, 209, 216, 248
Robinson, Ken, 79
Robinson v. Cahill court case, 31, 189
Rogers, Lina, 131
Rose v. Council for Better Education court case, 13–14, 18–19, 20, 28–29
rural population, 134, 139, 144; deaf schools in rural areas, 97, 100,

Index   259

105; SBHCs, health care accessed
  through, 129, 135; well water quality
  in rural areas, 140

Safe Drinking Water Act (SDWA), 140
Samuels, Christina A., 96
Savage Inequalities (Kozol), 82
Scholarship Reconsidered (Boyer), 82
school-based health centers (SBHCs),
  129–31, 133, 134, 135, 145–46,
  149, 151–52
School Breakfast Program
  (SBP), 139–40
School Finance Reform Act (SFRA),
  34, 36–38, 39, 41, 42–43,
  47–48, 102, 192
school meals, 139–40
school nurses, 131–32, 134, 135
school physicians, 132–33
school psychologists, 133–35, 138–39
school resource officers (SROs), 141–42
school vouchers, 28, 83, 104
Schwarzenneger, Arnold, 188
Second Wave funding, 27, 36
Section 504 Rehabilitation Act, 93–94,
  99, 101, 103
segregation, 13, 55–56
Senate Bill S450, 189–90, 206
Separation of Sources Act, 187
Serrano v. Priest court case, 27, 182,
  185–86, 187, 189, 216, 244
sexual education within the school
  system, 136–37
SFRA, 47
Share, Jeff, 164–65
sign language, 89–90, 91, 92–93, 94,
  97–98, 101
Silenced Dialogue (Delpit), 60
Singer, Peter, 166, 167
Smart Snacks protections, 140
Snell, Lisa, 104
social capital, 58, 210, 215, 217,
  243–44, 245
Sonstelie, Jon, 197
South Carolina, 113

South Dakota, 111
special education, 79, 80, 100, 101,
  130, 230, 238; Black students
  placed in, 96; deaf students placed
  in, 95; digital divide and, 71, 82;
  district requirements to bring back
  students, 228–29; general education
  implications for, 83–84; IEPs and,
  90, 93, 244; in New Jersey, 32, 37,
  43, 102, 123; in New York, 43, 92;
  policy recommendations for, 85–86
special needs, 7, 40, 42, 79, 104, 150;
  in Abbott school districts, 38, 47,
  204; absenteeism in special needs
  children, 148; foundation formula
  weights for special needs students,
  112; of urban students, 33, 34
Special Needs Districts (SNDs), 33, 102
Special Supplemental Nutrition Program
  for Women, Infants, and Children
  (WIC), 143
Spending Growth Limitation
  Adjustments (SGLA), 193
standardized tests, 101, 157, 183
state operated schools (SOS), 91–92
state supported schools (SSS), 91–92
Steiner, David, 81
stereotypes, 70, 96
St. Louis Public School District,
  82, 176, 247
Strickland, Carol Ann, 84
Stroh, Heather R., 210
student-centered methods, 57
*Study of the American Educational
  System* (report), 7, 232
Success Academy, 83, 84
Sue, Derald W., 56, 60
Sugarman, Stephen D., 213, 236, 238
Summer Food Service Program
  (SFSP), 139, 140
Supplemental Nutrition Assistance
  Program (SNAP), 143
Sweeney, Stephen, 205

teacher attrition rate, 66, 83

teacher morale, 67, 121
Temporary Assistance to Needy Families (TANF), 115
Tennessee, 116
Texas, 103, 121
Third Wave funding, 13, 27, 36
thorough and efficient (T&E) clause, 29–30, 31, 32, 34, 182
three-year-olds, 111, 117, 118–19, 123
Thurber, Amie, 145
Tiebout, Charles M., 198
TIME magazine, 157
Tocqueville, Alexis de, 79, 80
Tomlinson, Carol Ann, 84
Total Aidable Foundation Pupil Units (TAFPU), 39, 43
total communication, 91, 92
Total Wealth Foundation Pupil Units (TWFPU), 43–44
traditional public school districts (TPSDs), 3, 183, 205, 208, 235; CEIFA funding and, 33, 34; centralized control, unintended consequences of, 4–5; educational redlining and, 235; funding formulae remedies for, 27–28; large TPSDs, 176–77; N.A.P.R. budgeting model, applying to, 219–20, 221; in New Jersey, 31, 32, 49, 206; in New York, 39, 43, 49
traditional public schools (TPSs), 3, 28, 235; advocating for, 83–84; in affluent districts, 237, 245; deaf programs in, 89, 90; holistic budgeting model for, 219–20, 221
trauma-informed schools, 150
tuition, 92, 103, 104, 105, 115, 119, 124, 125, 228, 229

Uniform Minimum Chart of Accounts, 229–30
United States Department of Agriculture (USDA), 142–43
U.S. Department of Education (DOE), 99, 102, 103, 141, 146
Utah, 117, 182, 184

vaccinations, 130, 135, 151
Vermont, 105, 118, 205
Villegas, Ana María, 59
Virginia, 113, 116
vocational education, 29, 37, 42, 104, 228
vocational rehabilitation (VR), 103–4
Vollmer, Jamie, 176–77, 188
Vygotsky, Lev S., 56–57

Wagner, Tony, 82–83
Washington D.C., 96, 103, 111, 116, 117, 118, 137
wealth-equalized aid, 37, 38, 39
wealth neutrality score, 246
Webster, Noah, 80–81
Wells Fargo Bank, 160
West Virginia, 117, 182, 184
"What Explains Differences in How Homelessness and Housing Interventions Affect Child Well-Being" (Brown/Thurber), 145
white flight, 81
Whole School, Whole Community, Whole Child (WSCC) model, 130
Winthrop, Delba, 79
Wyoming, 111

Yang, Baiyin, 68
Yeskel, Felice, 56
Yinger, John, 44, 205
Yosso, Tara J., 57

About the Editor and Contributors

Stephen V. Coffin, Ph.D., MBA, MPA, is an Adjunct Professor of School Finance and Higher Education Economics and Finance for Montclair State University's Graduate School of Education and an Adjunct Professor of Finance for the University of Dayton's Online Ed.D. Program.

In addition, Dr. Coffin taught School Finance as a part-time instructor for Rutgers University's Graduate School of Education and doctoral students Higher Education Finance and Economics as well as School Finance as an adjunct instructor for Fordham University's Graduate School of Education.

Dr. Coffin earned his Ph.D. in education at Rutgers University, an MBA in finance from New York University, and an MPA in public administration from the Maxwell School of Citizenship and Public Affairs, Syracuse University. Dr. Coffin's research focuses on education finance and economics; charter schools; community economic development; educational business administration; equal educational opportunity; and resource equity.

Dr. Coffin provides his proprietary N.A.P.R. Budgeting Model for K-12 schools and districts as well as higher education through teaching and consulting services.

Dr. Coffin's dissertation, *State Policy Determinants of Charter School Market Share*, identified the predictive strength of state policies as well as supply and demand influences that determine the charter school share of the public education market and the influence of charter school enrollment on overall enrollment in public education. Dr. Coffin found that parental interest in public and charter schools is heightened by their preferences for specific peer groups and lower-cost alternatives to private and religious schools.

Dr. Coffin serves on four editorial review boards, the National Education Finance Academy, the New Jersey Association of School Business Official's (NJASBO) Legislative Committee, Education Committee, and Public Relations Committee as well as NJASBO's Diversity, Equity, and Inclusion Committee.

As the Chair of the Education Law Association's (ELA) Finance Special Interest Group, Dr. Coffin reviews state and federal court cases, analyzes only those cases that advance an education finance law issue, and identifies the meaning for educators, administrators, and policymakers. He provides the education finance implications stemming from constitutional mandates as well as state and federal court decisions. Dr. Coffin publishes his assessments in the ELA's Ed Law Update.

Dr. Coffin serves on seven AERA SIG's, Fiscal Issues, Policy, and Education Finance; Charters and School Choice; Politics of Education; School Turnaround and Reform; Law and Education; Leadership for Social Justice; and Queer Studies.

He is a former school business administrator, has performed management consulting for KPMG and IBM, and has published books, journal articles, chapters, and reports as well as co-authored the United Nations Report, *A Study of the American Educational System*.

Select Rowman & Littlefield Books

Coffin, S. V. (Ed.) (2021). *Higher education's looming collapse: Using new ways of doing business and social justice to avoid bankruptcy*. Rowman & Littlefield.

Coffin, S. V., & Cooper, B. S. (Eds.) (2017). *Sound school finance for educational excellence*. Rowman & Littlefield.

Coffin, S. V., & Cooper, B. S. (Eds.) (2018). *School district financial leadership: Educational excellence tomorrow*. Rowman & Littlefield.

Cooper, B. S., McCray, C. R., & Coffin, S. V. (Eds.) (2017). *Why school leaders need vision: Managing scarcity, mandates, and conflicting goals for educational quality*. Rowman & Littlefield.

Books in Progress

Coffin, S. V. *Strategic school finance for leading-edge equitable public education*. [Manuscript in preparation]. Rowman & Littlefield.

Coffin, S. V. *Stop blurring the lines between public education and privatization: Reinventing the business model to save public education*. [Manuscript in preparation]. Rowman & Littlefield.

Coffin, S. V. *Creating a model state school finance formula to achieve equal educational opportunity and school finance equity*. [Manuscript in preparation]. Rowman & Littlefield.

Coffin, S. V. *Who should provide public education: Imperfect markets or imperfect government?* [Manuscript in preparation]. Rowman & Littlefield.

Coffin, S. V. *Ramifications of school finance allocative inefficiency and market failure*. [Manuscript in preparation]. Rowman & Littlefield.

About the Editor and Contributors

* * *

Thomas Barger, who is deaf and hard of hearing, is an itinerant teacher of the deaf at several schools in New York City. He has taught for over 25 years. He holds a Bachelor of Science degree in biology from the Rochester Institute of Technology/National Technical Institute for the Deaf in Rochester, NY. He holds a Master of Science degree in General Education from Western Maryland College and a Master of Science degree in Deaf Education from the University of Rochester.

Thomas is involved in designing a science curriculum for the deaf summer programs. He provides workshops and professional development to teachers on how to communicate using basic American Sign Language with deaf students in their mainstream classes. Thomas has taught teachers how to use the assistive technology devices to help deaf and hard of hearing students use their hearing aids and cochlear implants in the classrooms. In February 2020, he received the United Federation of Teachers award for Outstanding Career and Technical Educator. Thomas is currently attending Montclair State University to earn his Master of Science in School Administration that he will complete by the end of 2022.

Corinne Brion, Ph.D., M.Ed., is an Assistant Professor at the University of Dayton. The overall framework for her research is cultural proficiency to foster equity, diversity, and inclusion and create socially just educational systems. Dr. Brion has two main lines of inquiry. First, she seeks to understand how educational leaders support adult and student learning and development. Specifically, she examines how school leaders support refugee and immigrant students, offer culturally proficient professional learning events for teachers, provide social-emotional learning opportunities for adults and students, and lead in times of trauma and crisis. Second, Dr. Brion focuses on how culture affects women in leadership positions. She explores how cultural norms affect women leaders in PK-12 schools and higher education institutions.

Dr. Brion earned her Ph.D. at the University of San Diego, M.Ed. at Southern Oregon University, and B.A. at L' Ecole Nationale de Commerce, Paris, France. Dr. Brion has published many peer-reviewed journal articles, reports, and chapters.

Camille A. Clare, MD, MPH, CPE, FACOG, is a board-certified obstetrician and gynecologist. She received her medical degree from the Albert Einstein College of Medicine, Bronx, New York, and completed her obstetrics and gynecology residency at the State University of New York at Buffalo. She obtained a Master of Public Health in Health Policy and Management at New York Medical College. In May 2018, Dr. Clare was inducted into the Alpha Omega Alpha Honor Society, Iota Chapter, New York, New York Medical College as a Faculty member. Dr. Clare is Chair of the Department of Obstetrics and Gynecology, Downstate Health Sciences University (DHSU) and tenured Professor in the College of Medicine and Professor of Health Policy and Management in the School of Public Health, a role that she began in January 2021. She is also the Interim Fellowship Director of Gynecologic Oncology at DHSU. She previously served as the Associate Dean of Diversity and Inclusion at New York Medical College and attending physician at New York City Health + Hospitals/Metropolitan.

Dr. Clare is an active member of the National Medical Association (NMA), and has served in leadership roles on the local, regional, and national levels. Currently, she is the NMA Region 1 Trustee and the Secretary of the NMA Board of Trustees. She is also the Chair Elect of the NMA Obstetrics and Gynecology Section. Dr. Clare has received the National Medical Association Scroll of Merit award in 2016, which is the highest honor that the NMA bestows. She also received the Region 1 Service award in 2012, and the National Medical Association Obstetrics and Gynecology Section Award for Best Practices in Breastfeeding in 2017. She is an active member of the NMA Obstetrics and Gynecology Section Breastfeeding Alliance, advocating for the elimination of disparities in breastfeeding rates in African American women.

Dr. Clare is also an active member of American College of Obstetricians and Gynecologists (ACOG), serving in leadership roles on the section, district, and national levels, and previously on several national committees. She currently serves as the ACOG District 2 Chair, and ACOG Chair of the Industrial Exhibits Committee. She is a member of the Social Media workgroup for ACOG. Dr. Clare is the National Advisor for the Junior Fellow College Advisory Council for the past two years.

Keith Dewey, Ph.D., earned his doctorate from Vanderbilt University in 1998 and has worked in various fundraising and development jobs or as adjunct faculty at Rutgers University, DeVry University, Rider University, Thomas Edison State College, and The College of New Jersey, starting with Rutgers as Associate Director of Corporate and Foundation Relations in 2000. In 2010, he retooled as a K-12 teacher, earning standard certificates in special education, language arts (English), and social studies (history). He earned School Business Administrator (SBA) certification from Montclair State University in 2012. Dr. Dewey is a special education leave replacement teacher at Princeton High School.

Karin A. Garver, M.A., is an Early Childhood Education Policy Specialist at the National Institute for Early Education Research (NIEER). Her research interests are in national and state early education policy trends, preschool special education, data systems, and public program finance. Karin works on NIEER projects such as the State of Preschool Yearbook, Preschool Cost of Quality and Revenue, and several other projects related to early childhood policy and finance. Karin spent almost 16 years with the New Jersey Department of Education, where she served as Chief of Staff, Deputy Chief Academic Officer, and in several positions within the Division of Early Childhood Education. During her time at the NJ DOE, Karin worked extensively on the preschool funding rates that were integrated into New Jersey's current school finance legislation. She has a B.A. in Sociology and Anthropology from Colgate University, an M.A. in education policy from the Bloustein School at Rutgers University, and is pursuing a Ph.D. in early childhood education policy at Rutgers University.

Luke Greeley, Ph.D., is an Assistant Professor of Professional Practice at Rutgers Business School, Newark and New Brunswick and previously served as Assistant Dean. He has worked for over a decade in higher education administration, leading a diverse array of projects and initiatives to improve academic offerings and student outcomes. As a researcher, he studies the intersections of education and the economy from historical and philosophical perspectives. His dissertation defended the thesis that consumer education should be an essential component of public education based on civic, economic, and environmental ethical frameworks. His published work has examined diverse topics such as online learning platforms, representations of education in popular culture, and fundraising practices in higher education.

Recently, Luke was named as the Rutgers-Newark Scholar-In-Residence Fellow for the 2022–2023 year. The fellowship program supports scholars researching and implementing evidence-based pedagogies in the curriculum, as well as to study methods that promote equitable outcomes for students.

Tanya Orie Rogo, MD, MPH, TM, FAAP, is Associate Professor of Pediatrics at the Warren Alpert Medical School of Brown University. She is the Associate Program Director of the Fellowship in Pediatric Infectious Diseases, Global Health Educator in the Department of Pediatrics, and Medical Director of Antimicrobial Stewardship at Hasbro Children's Hospital in Providence, RI. She completed her undergraduate education at the University of North Carolina at Chapel Hill and received her medical degree and Master of Public Health and Tropical Medicine from Tulane University. Dr. Rogo completed her residency in general pediatrics at the Inova Fairfax Hospital for Children in Falls Church, VA, followed by her fellowship in Pediatric Infectious Diseases at Brown University/Hasbro Children's Hospital.

Charles J. Russo, J.D., Ed.D., M.Div., is the Joseph Panzer Chair in Education in the University of Dayton's School of Education and Health Sciences, Director of its Ph.D. Program, and Research Professor of Law in the University of Dayton's School of Law. The 1998–99 President of the Education Law Association, and 2002 recipient of its McGhehey (Achievement) Award, Dr. Russo has authored or co-authored more than 325 articles in peer-reviewed journals; authored, co-authored, edited, or co-edited 73 books, and has more than 1,100 publications focusing on issues in Education Law. He has spoken extensively on issues in Education Law in the United States and other countries. In addition, he edits two academic journals and serves on more than one dozen editorial boards.

Along with having spoken in 34 states and 31 countries outside of the U.S. on six continents, Dr. Russo has taught summer courses in England, Spain, and Thailand. He has served as a Visiting Professor at Queensland University of Technology (Brisbane) and the University of Newcastle (Australia); the University of Sarajevo (Bosnia and Herzegovina); South East European University (Macedonia); the Potchefstroom and Mafeking Campuses of Northwest University (Potchefstroom, South Africa); the University of Malaya (Kuala Lumpur, Malaysia); the University of Sao Paulo (Brazil); Yeditepe University (Istanbul, Turkey); Inner Mongolia University for the Nationalities (Tongliao, Inner Mongolia); and Peking University (Beijing, China). He is currently a Visiting Professor at Capital Normal University (Beijing) and the Faculty of Law at Notre Dame University of Australia, Sydney campus.

Before joining the University of Dayton's faculty as Professor and Chair of the Department of Educational Administration in July 1996, Dr. Russo taught at the University of Kentucky (Lexington, KY) from August 1992 to July 1996 and at Fordham University (New York City) from September 1989 to July 1992. He taught high school for eight and a half years, both prior to and after graduation from law school. He received a Bachelor of Arts degree in Classical Civilization (1972), Juris Doctor Degree (1983), and Doctor of Education degrees in Educational Administration and Supervision (1989) from St. John's University (New York City). He received a Master of Divinity degree from the Seminary of the Immaculate Conception (Huntington, New York) (1978). He received a Ph.D. Honoris Causa from Potchefstroom University, now the Potchefstroom Campus of Northwest University (Potchefstroom, South Africa) (2004) for his contributions to the field of Education Law.

William E. Thro, M.A., J.D., is the General Counsel of the University of Kentucky, former Solicitor General of Virginia, past President of the Education Law Association, and current President of the National Education

Finance Academy (2022–23). In addition to receiving Stetson University's Kaplin Award for Higher Education Law & Policy Scholarship and the Education Law Association's McGhehey Award for Education Law, he is a Fellow of the National Association of College & University Attorneys and a Distinguished Research Fellow of the National Education Finance Academy. He writes in his personal capacity and not on behalf of the University of Kentucky.

www.ingramcontent.com/pod-product-compliance
Lightning Source LLC
Chambersburg PA
CBHW032034300426
44117CB00009B/1056